Michigan Vacation Guide

Cottages, Chalets, Condos, B&B's

SEVENTH EDITION

2003-04

Editor/Writer: Kathleen R. Tedsen
Associate Editor: Clara M. Rydel
Writer/Photographer: Beverlee J. Rydel
Business Manager: Christian Tedsen

COTTAGES
CONDOS
Vacation
Guide
CHALETS
B & B'S

Cover Photographs:
Front Cover: Big Bay Lighthouse B&B, Big Bay
Back Cover: (top) East Tawas Junction B&B, East Tawas; (below) Johnson Cottage, Munising; Drummond Island Getaway, Drummond Island

For information, contact:

TR Desktop Publishing
P.O. Box 180271
Utica, MI 48318-0271
(586) 228-8780

Email: info@mivg.com

PRINTED IN THE UNITED STATES OF AMERICA

ISBN: 0-9635953-5-0

Michigan

Let me take you to the land once called "Michigania" across
flat planes to ever increasing slopes, hills and mountains;
through virginal forests and crystal lakes, dotted
by cottages resting on sugar white sand.
Where falls are painted by an artist's brush
and winters are blanketed in white.
Here are the forests and wildlife, quaint cities
and great cities, museums and shipwrecks,
and so much more.

I am your dream maker ...
the great outdoors ...
the vacation land for all seasons.

by C. Rydel

HOW TO USE THIS BOOK

Welcome to the Seventh Edition of *The Michigan Vacation Guide to Cottages, Chalets, Condos, B&B's*. This simple to use publication, arranged by region and alphabetically by city, is designed to assist you with one of your first vacation priorities...where to stay. Our intention is to offer some interesting alternatives to the usual hotels/motels. We hope our Guide helps you find your perfect vacation lodging as quickly and effortlessly as possible.

Understanding Special Notes:

Editor's Note   Our staff has not had the opportunity to visit every listed property in this book. Descriptions have been supplied by owners. When we have visited a lodging, the Editor's Note reflects our overall impression of the property. If (based on photographs supplied by owners) a newly added property looks interesting or major updates have been made at an existing property, an Editor's Note will be added to provide our readers with relevant information.

Editor's Choice Indicates places our staff have visited which, in our opinion, meet or exceed the basic requirements of comfort, cleanliness, location and value for the area.

Reviews   This edition of the MVG features all new reviews never published in previous editions of our guide. All comments are solely the opinion of our staff and do not necessarily reflect the opinions of others.

Whenever possible, prices have been included. However, prices frequently change or fluctuate with the seasons. We recommend calling to verify rates when making reservations. If the owner requires an advance deposit, verify refund policies (if any). **As a renter, be sure you understand the terms of the rental agreement.**

VISIT OUR OFFICIAL WEBSITE
www.MiVG.com
-or-
www.michiganvacationguide.com

Join Us at our NEW Website

www.MiVG.com

Also accessed via ... **www.michiganvacationguide.com**

*Join us on-line as we continue
on our journey through Michigan*

➡ Use our **Advanced Accommodations Search** to quickly find the property best suited to your interests and needs.

➡ **Join in our Interactive Forum.** It's fun and informative, so come on in! Ask a question...give an answer. Share your recent Michigan adventure or a great new restaurant... or just chat a bit.

➡ Sign-up for our **Email List** and receive late-breaking news on our MVG discoveries. Plus, **information on area events, discounts or other specials** our property owners are offering.

➡ Access our **Newsletter** and find out about our most recent discoveries and late-breaking news.

*Discover the Beauty of Michigan and
Your Home Away From Home
at the new ... www.MiVG.com!*

Michigan Area Code Changes

There's a whole lotta changing going on and that includes area codes. Michigan communities, like many others in our nation, find area code changes and overlays a continuing process.

We've attempted to update phone number area codes as accurately as possible in this publication. However, if you attempt to contact a property owner in our book and receive a response indicating *"there's no such number"*, **chances are very good the area code changed**. Below is a map outlining valid Michigan area codes at the time of this publishing.

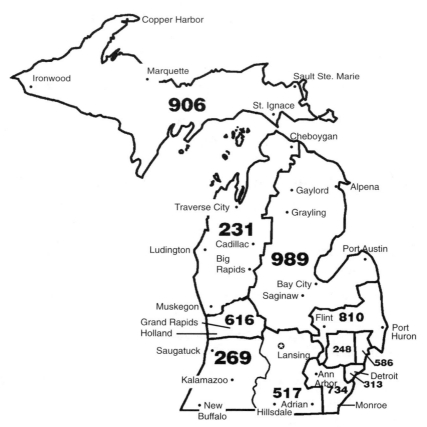

To get the latest information on area code changes in Michigan, contact:

ON-LINE: www.ameritech.com/areacode
TELEPHONE: 1-800-831-8989

Table of Contents

REGIONAL DIVISIONS

Blissfield, Irish Hills & Surrounding
Ann Arbor/Chelsea, Brigthon, Saline & Ypsilanti
Lansing & Surrounding
Port Huron & Lapeer
Lexington, Port Austin, Caseville & Surrounding
Bay City, Frankenmuth, Saginaw

Oscoda, the AuSable & Surrounding
Alpena,Thunderbay & Surrounding
Mackinaw City, Mackinac Island
Houghton Lake, Cheboygan, Bois Blanc
    Island & Surrounding

Selecting an Accommodation

Staying at a cottage, condo or bed and breakfast is truly a unique and enjoyable experience. However, it is **different** than staying at a hotel or motel. We've provided some information to help you understand and appreciate the differences.

The Basics

Don't be afraid to ask the owner questions. Ask about the *House Rules*. If staying at a cottage or condo which accommodates small groups, you may want to ask specifically how many bedrooms/bathrooms. Additional questions may be related to housekeeping policies, amenities or location which are important to your comfort and enjoyment.

Always be sure you understand the terms of the rental agreement. Determine advance deposit and cancellation/refund policies prior to booking.

Clean up after yourself. Please be courteous and leave your lodging in the same condition in which it was found.

Terminology

Fully Equipped Kitchens. Includes stove, refrigerator, pots, pans, dishes, eating utensils and sometimes (not always) microwaves, toasters, automatic coffeemakers, dishwashers.

A/C and CATV. A/C refers to air conditioning (may or may not be central air conditioning); CATV refers to color cable television.

Modern Cottage. Does not mean new. It refers to electricity and indoor plumbing (private bath, hot water, etc.). Most of today's cottages are considered modern.

On the Water. Refers to a lodging which fronts water. It does not necessarily mean the property has a swimming beach (see below) or a place to dock your boat.

Swimming Beach. A water area with gradual incline, no surprise drop offs, no strong currents. It may or may not be a smooth, sand beach.

Full Breakfast. Beverages, main course and, sometimes, dessert.

Continental Breakfast. Beverages with breads and/or pastries.

American Plan Resorts. All meals included in the price.

What Are the Differences?

While it's impossible to give a single description for each type of accommodation, there are certain traits that make each distinctively different and appealing.

RESORT COTTAGES:

Atmosphere: Most resorts were built in the 1950s-60s with some dating back even further. Resort environments are family-friendly.

While there are cottage resorts which provide luxury, most are simple. You may find a ceiling fan but only a few have air conditioning. Furniture is sometimes a collection of older, second-hand items. A fireplace in your cabin is not uncommon and wood is usually provided. Resorts generally do not provide daily maid service.

Features: Many resorts offer on-site activities for the family. For example, those by the water often have a safe swimming area with a canoe or rowboat as part of the rental price. You can usually bring your own boat (not all allow high speed motors). There may be a children's play area, badminton, basketball or tennis courts. Game rooms may include pinball, video arcades, etc. Many rent motors, paddle or pontoon boats and other watercraft. Nature/snowmobile trails, chartered fishing along with planned daily group activities, or American Plan programs may be available.

Rates/Rental Policy: Resorts often provide the most economically priced lodging, especially those not located on the water. A few begin renting as low as $450 weekly with several exceeding $2,000. During prime season, most require weekly rentals (Saturday to Saturday). Advance deposits are generally asked with refund policies varying.

What to Bring: Towels, linens, cleaning and paper products.

PRIVATE COTTAGES & CHALETS:

Atmosphere: These accommodations offer a private vacation. Whether overlooking the water, woods or ski slopes, this place will seem like your own private retreat.

Since these cottages are used by the owners, interior decor will vary greatly. Some are small and simply furnished while others are spacious, contemporary and luxurious.

Please note, privately owned cottages or homes may or may not have a "cleaning service" and many have special "house rules". Also very important, ask who your contact is should there be any problems while you're there.

Features: You usually won't have all of the outdoor amenities found at resorts, such as basketball/ tennis courts or video game rooms. However, interiors tend be more comfortable. Private cottages may have fireplaces, but you'll probably have to supply your own wood. Other extra features may include ceiling fans, air conditioning, hot tubs, stereos, TVs, VCRs and kitchens with dishwashers.

Rates/Rental Policies: Owners frequently need to be contacted during evenings or weekends when they're not working. During prime season, most will rent weekly (Saturday to Saturday) some will agree to a 2-day minimum stay. Prices may be a little higher than resorts with average rates from $800 to over $3,000. Most require up front deposits with varying refund policies.

What to Bring: See "Cottage Resorts".

CONDOMINIUMS:

Atmosphere: For those who enjoy the anonymity and comfort a hotel/motel provides but also want the added convenience of a full kitchen, living room, etc., condos are a good choice. While there are a few older condos, most were built in the last 5 to 20 years. You will generally find the interior furnishings newer with matching sofa, chairs, tables and decor.

Features: Air conditioning is often available. Rooms may have Jacuzzi tubs and wet bars. Condo "resorts" frequently feature championship golf courses, heated swimming pools, tennis and health clubs.

Rates/Rental Policies: Units are rented by private owners or associations with more flexible policies (not all require week long rentals). Weekly rentals prices are similar to private cottages from $800 to over $3,000. Advance deposits are required with varying refund policies.

What to Bring: See "Cottage Resorts".

BED & BREAKFASTS:

B&B's and inns provide a quiet, relaxing atmosphere and are equally enjoyed by business and vacation travelers alike. While some establishments welcome well behaved children, most cater to the adult traveler. A bed and breakfast is not the place for loud parties. However, with notice, many cater to small group gatherings.

Proprietors take great pride in decorating and maintaining their lodgings in a style which will welcome their guests and provide a comfortable, inviting setting. As a result, courtesy and respect of property is expected.

Features: These establishments can be very diverse in features and amenities. Some may be small homes in subdivisions with private or shared bath. Others may be large historical estates or contemporary with 10 or more guest rooms. These accommodations are frequently decorated with antiques and/or authentic reproductions. Additional features may include in-room Jacuzzi and fireplace, air conditioning.

Price/Rental Policies: Prices vary greatly with averages between $75 to $100 daily and a few luxury suites exceed $200. Most bed and breakfasts rent daily and may offer special week or weekend package rates. Advanced deposits are generally requested, refund policies vary.

What to Bring: Just your clothes and a smile.

Breakfasts: Breakfasts are part of every B&B package (those categorized as inns may not include breakfast). Breakfasts vary from continental to full. Ask the owner about serving times. Some establishments encourage guests' mingling at a common table during breakfast. Others may provide private tables or will bring breakfast directly to your room. Many innkeepers are happy to accommodate special dietary needs but will need to be told in advance.

Just remember, if you're not sure about something ...
ASK THE OWNER.

We wish you a safe and most enjoyable Michigan vacation!

Featured Property Reviews

COTTAGES, CONDOS, RESORTS

Beechwood Resort
Houghton Lake

Drummond Island Getaway
Drummond Island

Drummond Island Resort
Drummond Island

House on the Hill
Harbor Springs

The Lake House
Mears

Mason House
Saugatuck

R&H Chalet
Boyne Falls

Rainbow Lodge
Newberry

Rosewood Retreat
Saugatuck

Sunset Cabins
Grand Marias

Timberlane Resort
East Tawas

Up North Getaway
Welston (Manistee)

Woodland Acres Lake Home
Manistee

BED & BREAKFASTS

Big Bay Point Lighthouse
Big Bay

Candlewyck House
Pentwater

Captain's Inn B&B
Port Austin

Deer Lake B&B
Boyne

Dutch Colonial
Holland

East Tawas Junction B&B
East Tawas

Parish House
Ypsilanti

Raymond House
Lexington

Rummel's Tree Haven
Sebewaing

Schoenberger House
Ludington

The Captain's Inn

Port Austin, Michigan
Telephone: 888-277-6631
989-738-8321

Located
in
Region 1

Innkeepers:	David and Debbie Ramey
Accommodations:	Bed and breakfast, 5 rooms (3 private/2 shared baths)
Extras:	Continental plus breakfast. Queen beds. CATV, ceiling fans. BBQ grill. Kitchen available. Coffee, tea, hot chocolate always available.
Rates/Payment:	Nightly $64-$125. Check.
Miscellaneous:	No pets/smoking. Caters to adult travelers.
Open:	Year around

Perhaps the brightest new star on Michigan's eastern coast is the very impressive Captain's Inn. From its newly painted exterior to its tastefully appointed interior, the inn stands as an excellent example of the beauty that can be restored through careful renovation.

Built between 1858-1861, this pre-Civil War colonnade home was the former residence of wealthy lumber baron, Frederick Ayres. During the Civil War,

Impressively renovated with inviting decor, Captain's B&B is one of Port Austin's shining new stars.

Mr. Ayres' son, Eben, served as a captain for the Union Army and frequently recruited troops in the Port Austin area. The home has been named to honor Eben's rank and his contributions during the Civil War.

Spacious, antique filled gathering room is ideal for mingling.

David and Debbie officially opened their bed and breakfast in January 2000. Since that time, they have blended antiques, reproductions and country decor into rooms that wrap visitors in a welcoming embrace.

The antique filled gathering room and dining area are open and

The library is a great spot for reading or watching TV.

invite guests to mingle. Off to the side is the library, where dark wood paneling, cozy furnishings and warm colors combine to create a perfect spot to catch up on reading or quietly chat with friends or family. Perhaps you'd like to join with a friend in a challenging game of chess using their unique *condiment* chessmen (a variety of salt and pepper shakers make the complete set).

The five guest rooms continue the inn's relaxed, thoughtful styling. Lace or light floral prints trim windows. Colorful quilts and chenille spreads cover beds with antiques and wall accents adding to each room's theme. Three of the five guest rooms have private baths and the remaining two share a bath. *Jennifer Lyn* is their most spacious room. Surrounded by six windows, it's bright and airy with a delightful view of the grounds and historic Lake Street.

Guest rooms vary in size and amenities, with private or shared baths.

The queen size, open-canopied bed along with a chair for two make a very nice choice for those seeking a special getaway. We found the unique collection of antique hats and hat boxes in the *Melissa Lyn* room particularly fun and interesting.

In the morning guests are treated to a continental plus breakfast, served in the lovely dining room or patio (weather permitting). Along with coffee, tea, juice, and fresh fruits or fruit salad, Debbie serves up some of her mouth-watering coffee cakes and muffins. The kitchen is available to guests for

Breakfasts are served in the dining room or, during nicer days, on the patio.

storing their favorite beverage and snacks. Guests may also take advantage of the outdoor barbecue grill. For those late-nighters, coffee, tea and hot chocolate are always available.

Located on Lake Street, Captain's is close to area shops and restaurants. Bird Creek's 800 ft. beach is just a few blocks away. Enjoy nature hikes, scenic bicycle trips and other outdoor adventures at nearby Port Crescent State Park or the Wilderness Arboretum. If you're interested, Dave and Debbie will be happy to assist you with golf or charter fishing excursions.

The Captain's Inn is truly a distinctive bed and breakfast in the friendly, laid back community of Port Austin. Come on over, Dave and Debbie will take good care of you.

Parish House Inn

Ypsilanti, Michigan
Telephone: 734-480-4800
800-480-4866

Located in Region 1

Innkeeper:	Chris & Lance Mason
Accommodations:	Bed and breakfast, 9 rooms with private baths
Extras:	Full breakfasts. A/C, ceiling fans. In-room telephones, data ports, voice mail, CATV. Some with VCR, fireplace, Jacuzzi. Limited handicap access.
Rates/Payment:	Nightly $89-$150. Major credit cards, check.
Miscellaneous:	Listed on the National Register of Historic Places. No pets/smoking. Corporate rates.
Open:	Year around

In a quiet neighborhood, just a block from Huron Street shops and restaurants, is the charming Parish House Inn. Built in 1893, this Queen Anne styled home originally served as the parsonage for the First Congregational Church. In 1987 the home was moved to its current setting with full restoration completed in 1993. Since then, the home's interior has been carefully maintained with a

Well-styled and impressively maintained, the Parish House is close to Hope College and many Ypsilanti attractions.

distinct Victorian ambiance. Period furnishings, original wood floors with wood trimmed archways and windows increase its nostalgic appeal. Of course, Chris has added her own special touches, which include her little Victorian Christmas corner and original, hand-painted wall art.

Beautifully landscaped backyard has hosted private weddings, including the Masons' own nuptials.

Parish House is a truly special place for its current innkeepers, Chris and Lance Mason. The couple married in the home's lovely backyard overlooking a meandering section of the Huron River. Today, while both enjoy interacting with guests, Lance is frequently occupied with other business leaving the daily operations to Chris. This works out just fine since her education and interests focus on culinary arts and hospitality.

There are nine guest rooms of varying sizes. Patchwork quilts, lace-trimmed windows, period wallpaper and floral prints add to the 1800's theme. Unique split baths, which separate sinks from shower and toilet, are distinctive and very reminiscent of an earlier time. Sterno-burning fireplaces are found in several rooms. Room 9 is their special Jacuzzi room, which features lovely hand-painted wall murals. Of course, modern conveniences are included in each room, such as cable TV (7 rooms with VCR's), telephones, voice mail and data ports.

Part of the home's charm lies in the culinary treats Chris skillfully prepares each morning. A main dish, created from Michigan products, follows fresh juice, muffins and scones. Chris is particularly proud of her Michigan Baked

Each of the Inn's 9 guest rooms maintain a distinct Victorian ambiance.

Oatmeal that combines cereal with cherries, almonds, milk and a touch of brown sugar blended into a flavorful baked casserole.

For those seeking an escape to this area of Michigan, The Parish House is well located. Visitors will find it close to Eastern Michigan University as well as Ypsilanti's many seasonal jazz and art festivals. It's also located in the town's Historic District. This historic area is part of the Sauk Trail, used by early-American Indians, trappers and traders almost 200 years ago. Ask Chris for a copy of the walking tour to enjoy a leisurely stroll along this historic path.

Whether for business or pleasure, Parish House will serve as a comfortable retreat while exploring Ypsilanti and the surrounding communities.

Raymond House Inn

Port Sanilac, Michigan
Telephone: 800-622-7229
810-622-8800

Located
in
Region 1

Innkeepers:	Gary and Cristy Bobofchak
Accommodations:	Bed & breakfast, 7 rooms (5 private/ 2 shared baths)
Extras:	Full breakfast. A/C. In-room CATV-VCR, phones. Video library. Art gallery and gift shop.
Rates/Payment:	Nightly $65-$115. Major credit cards, check.
Miscellaneous:	Listed on the National Register of Historical Sites. Mystery weekends. Special holiday packages. Caters to adult travelers. No pets/smoking.
Open:	Year around

Built in 1872, the Raymond House represents a Victorian time capsule of the 1800's with dark woods, lace-trim, period furnishings ... and, just maybe, a ghost. The home was owned by one of the town's original founding families, the Raymonds, and is on Michigan's Register of Historical Sites. This old beauty went through major renovations in 1983 appealing to our contemporary needs.

Set back from Lake Street, the turreted roof and brilliant white trim is a clear representation of America's historical restoration period. The home is situated on one-acre and is surrounded by an immaculately maintained lawn and grounds.

Victorian-styled Raymond House sits on one-acre of land.

ALL RATES SUBJECT TO CHANGE

The cozy gathering room retains its 1800's ambiance.

The 1800's parlor looks like it came straight from the pages of a history book. The focal point is a fireplace draped with a white-fringed mantel cover and accented by a gilded mirror. Period wall hangings and Tiffany lamps grace the dramatically wallpapered room. Sit in a Victorian chair and look in the mirror. Picture yourself sipping sherry with friends, discussing the up-

Bright and appealing rooms invite relaxation.

coming presidential elections. Would Ulysses S. Grant win a second term with his conservative *Old Guard* or lose to the liberal *Narrow-Headed Men*?

After a full evening of political reform talk, yesterday's or today's, you'll be exhausted...time to head up to bed. Rooms can be found on the first, second and third floors of the home. Guest quarters are styled with a brightened Victorian theme. Most have private baths with several featuring sitting areas. All contain TV/VCR, A/C and phone. The third floor rooms share a bath and are ideal for two couples.

Creatively tucked along hallways you'll find intimate sitting areas. They're perfect for conversation, cards or quiet time with your favorite books, like Charles Dickens' *David Copperfield* (somehow works by Steven King or Patricia Cornwall don't seem right in this 1800's home ... but go ahead if you must).

After a wonderful night's rest, the aroma from breakfast finds its way upstairs to awaken your senses to what awaits downstairs. Cristy assured us the morning meal is plentiful and diverse. The formal dining room walls are graced with curio cabinets and candelabra. Pulling the room together, a formal, darkwood table is accented by white lace tablecloth, English bone china and leaded crystal to make you feel truly special. Breakfast is staggered from 8:30 a.m. to 10:00 a.m. for early and late risers and starts with fresh fruits, juices, biscotti, muffins and granola. Cristy has a large variety of main course selections that will fill you for the day. If requested, she will gladly meet any special requests. Naturally, coffee and their large assortment of special teas are available beginning at 7:00 a.m.

You'll want to take some time to browse the B&B's interesting gift shop, which contains the work of many local artisans and Gary's beautiful photographs. As a professional photographer, his works are unique portrayals of the United States landscape.

Full breakfasts are served in the elegant dining room.

The gift shop is filled with the work of area artisans, including Gary's beautiful photographs.

If you have a group of friends on your trip, Cristy will design and host a mystery weekend for you. The Raymond House also offers special New Year's Eve packages. In addition, Cristy is working on developing juried art and craft events.

Something a little more fitting for the 130-year-old home is the ghost. Cristy has never seen signs from the beyond, but guests and her daughter disagree. There have been reported footsteps, moans, crying and doors closing ... normal ghost stuff. Nothing too scary, rather the perfect finishing touch for a century old house.

What can vacationers find to do in the area? Plenty. Water sports, parks, golf, shops and antique shopping are favorites for people in the thumb of our state. The Barn Theater Community Playhouse and Huron City historic village are a nice change of pace. Frankenmuth is a perfect day trip, only an hour away, it's a must for travelers.

This area is a great choice for people who enjoy vacationing in Michigan but don't want to spend hours driving. The Raymond House is a good value, historic yet contemporary, and a very enjoyable place to stay.

Rummel's Tree Haven
Bed & Breakfast

Sebewaing, Michigan
Telephone: 989-883-2450

Located in Region 1

Innkeepers:	Carl and Erma Rummel, Jr.
Accommodations:	Bed & breakfast, 2 rooms with private baths
Extras:	Continental to full breakfast. A/C. In-room CATV. Use of re-frigerator, microwave. Morning newspaper.
Rates/Payment:	Nightly $40-$55. Check.
Miscellaneous:	Pets allowed in garage
Open:	Year around

Up to your ears in computers, PDA's, pagers, cell phones and day planners? Had enough? Regain your sanity and actually relax for a few days at Rummel's Tree Haven. The B&B looks like a little doll house sheltered under the protective limbs of the 120-year-old maple that sits before it. The home and tree have been partners in more than a century of growth, bending and blending in harmony. They were started sometime around the 1870's and have been lovingly cared for by Carl and Erma Rummel for the last 35 years.

Erma is the first to say the home is not large and assuming. Indeed, its charm is in its homey, small town Michigan ambiance. The couple have taken their

You'll enjoy the simple charms of Rummel's Tree Haven.

truly unique, friendly personalities and blended them into every corner of their bed and breakfast.

The common/living room gives you the first look into your hosts' passion for nature. Carl's duck decoy collection is impressive. Comfortable chairs, fireplace and family photos add to the homey air that continues into the den. Here a natural stone wall displays an assortment of decoys and the large Franklin stove adds to the cozy, woodsy atmosphere. The room is often filled with music from Erma's collection. This is a favorite spot for early morning risers. Often guests will sit in the den or at the kitchen table and chat with Erma while she prepares breakfast. Do you remember kitchen tables and talk? It used to be a wonderful part of daily life before on-the-go meals, video games and cable TV.

The homey breakfast room is the ideal spot to enjoy a tasty breakfast that frequently includes delicious homemade maple syrup.

The breakfast menu varies, from continental to full, depending on the season and what guests want. We strongly recommend the mouthwatering rhubarb muffins or pancakes. Top your pancakes off with their homemade maple syrup taken right from 'grandpa' maple tree. Their maple syrup is not what you find in a market. No-siree! Carl and Erma make just about the finest we have ever tasted.

Over your last cup of coffee, enjoy the view from their windows. The 1-1/2 acres of natural grounds are teeming with wildlife. Rummel's Tree Haven is also a nature haven with rabbits, hedgehogs, raccoon, opossum, squirrel and a vast variety of birds. Carl feeds the birds year around and there is quite a diverse collection always perched around the feeders.

The two guest rooms include double beds with sitting areas. Simply and comfortably decorated, they fit well with the rest of the home. Some guests plan extended stays for a week or more. To accommodate, the rooms include a coffeemaker and microwave (one room with a small refrigerator), for that evening snack. Both have private baths, cable TV and air conditioning. A gas BBQ grill is available to guests in the summer.

Guest rooms have twin or full beds.

Sitting areas with coffee-maker, micro-wave and CATV are also included in rooms.

Carl and Erma are native to the area and will gladly help you plan your visit, offering suggestions on things to do and places to go. The Rummels have a fishing dock available for guests just a mile down the road. Fishing is popular in Bay Port and Sebewaing while Caseville draws swimming and water sport enthusiasts. The entire area boasts good shops, historic sites, golf and more. In under an hour you can be in Saginaw or Bay City for the nightlife or head up to Pinconning and sample some of Michigan's finest cheeses.

Why not take a break and treat yourself to the down-home comforts at Rummel's Tree Haven? Carl and Erma will make you feel right at home.

Beechwood Resort

Houghton Lake, Michigan
Telephone: 989-366-5512

Located in Region 2

Owners:	Rick and Rochelle Jurvis
Accommodations:	Cottage resort on Houghton Lake, 6 cabins (2-3 bedrooms)
Extras:	Private baths, CATV, fully equipped kitchens with microwaves. Some with fireplace and screened porch. Coin-operated laundry. Firepit, sea wall, dock, boats, play area, lighted walkways. Picnic tables. Gas BBQ grills.
Rates/Payment:	Weekly $600; Nightly $90. Check.
Miscellaneous:	No pets. One cabin with limited handicap access. Bring linens. In season bring paper products and towels.
Open:	Year around

Like a shiny new nickel in a pocket of pennies, Beechwood Resort clearly stands out among the many resorts in Houghton Lake. Through the hard work of Beechwood's new owners, Rick and Rochelle Jurvis, the cozy cottages have undergone major renovations that have brought this older, traditional resort back to life.

Sitting along Houghton Lake, this cozy, family-friendly resort is in beautiful condition and highly recommended for the area.

The 3 newly built cottages are fresh and comfortably styled.

They began their big renovation project a few years back with their focus on "Safety, Cleanliness and Function". At the time of our visit, the last of the three older log cabins were in the process of final restoration with the construction of three new cabins com-

plete. We were delighted at the changes.

In the older log cabins, all existing plumbing and electrical had been replaced. Kitchens and bathrooms were updated, knotty pine and log interiors refinished. New doors, windows, window treatments and furnishings added a cheery touch. Of course, we can't forget to mention their three newest cabins highlighted by fresh knotty pine walls, sparkling kitchens and bathrooms.

Rick and Rochelle didn't stop, however, with improvements to their lodgings. They've also made several enhancements to the grounds. Sod has been added along with new landscaping, which enhances their park-like setting. The resort sports a new 1,000 sq. ft. wood deck and a children's play set, tetherball,

Beechwood's 3 original cabins have been fully renovated including new furnishings and homey styling.

basketball and volleyball area.

Located right on the shores of Houghton Lake, no doubt some water action is in your future. Take advantage of one of the available rowboats and enjoy some fishing. A seawall offers easy access to the lake, which has a safe, gradual incline making it good for swimming. You may want to bring your aqua shoes, however. Depending on the time of year and weather conditions, the lake bottom can get a little pebbly.

Houghton Lake has long been one of Michigan's most popular vacation spots with outstanding fishing and boating. Because of its popularity, many of the area's old-time resorts are showing wear. However, Beechwood's recent renovations has made this traditional cottage resort our newest *favorite place* in Houghton Lake.

East Tawas Junction
Bed & Breakfast

East Tawas, Michigan

Telephone: 989-362-8006

Website: www.east-tawas.com

Located
in
Region 2

Innkeepers:	Don and Leigh Mott
Accommodations:	Bed & breakfast, 5 rooms with private baths
Extras:	Full breakfast. In-room CATV. Ceiling fans. Refreshments available daily.
Rates/Payment:	Nightly $99-$149. Check, major credit cards.
Miscellaneous:	No pets/smoking.
Open:	Year around

What should an active, vibrant couple do when they retire...especially if golf makes them angry, sailing makes them sick, and reading makes them fall asleep? Well, in the case of the high-energy Motts, it was simple. They opened a bed and breakfast. As Leigh explained, they enjoy cooking and people, so it seemed like a natural next step. Of course, the fact that Leigh is also an interior designer doesn't hurt either.

Winter, summer, spring or fall, East Tawas Junction B&B is a lovely retreat for those special getaways.

The bright white, turn-of-the-century home sits back on a large expanse of neatly groomed land. Just across the street lies East Tawas Park and Lake Huron with its great sandy beach and harbor. Leigh really enjoys the park. It's a lovely spot to spend a lazy summer afternoon.

From the porch, you'll enjoy a picturesque view of the property with Lake Huron and East Tawas Park across the street.

East Tawas Junction carries an interesting history. It was originally the home of the Pinkertons. A prominent family in the community, they owned the all-important railroad. The railroad, in fact, is still in operation with the train passing through their grounds once a day, Monday through Friday.

The home is attractively styled, from the light, airy enclosed porch to the warmth of the front parlor. We were particularly impressed with the parlor's beautiful hard wood floors, relaxing furniture and fireplace, which create a homey ambiance. Sunlight streams from windows and a scattering of lovely floral arrangements add to the room's freshness.

A sunny disposition is certain while relaxing in the sun-filled parlor.

Breakfasts are served in the dining room or deck (weather permitting). Speaking of breakfast, Leigh has developed a reputation in this area. Her skillful preparation and presentation of food, tantalizing both sight and taste, were acquired during her extensive stay in Italy. In this romantic country, Leigh tells us, meals are an event not just an afterthought. She enjoys creating an inviting visual presentation when serving, and uses large platters with entrees delicately displayed with fresh fruits to entice.

Leigh is happy to work around your special dietary needs but, otherwise, *mama mia*! Rome taught her that fresh and pure is what makes a meal. Guests are particularly fond of her crepes that are customarily filled with fresh raspberries, blueberries or other seasonal fruit. When asked about our choles-

Style and comfort are the theme of five guest rooms, all with private baths.

A picket fence is the appropriate headboard for the 1st floor Garden Room. This mini-suite has a private entrance.

terol, calorie-counting life-style of today, she responded that special weekends are just that...*special*, and guests should allow themselves to indulge. For your convenience, meal hours are from 8:00 a.m. to 10:00 a.m.

Each room is uniquely styled, with warm colors, floral prints and attractive window treatments. In addition, they feature private baths and cable TV. For those preferring a little privacy or first floor accommodations, the Garden Room is a delightful little suite with a private entrance off the deck. The remaining three rooms are on the second floor and offer views of Lake Huron or the surrounding grounds. Another feature of the second floor is a community center with coffeepot and refrigerator. It's a convenient spot to store your refreshments or enjoy one of the soft drinks available in the fridge.

This historic bed and breakfast is located in East Tawas, known for its wonderful beaches, water sports, fishing and leisurely paddleboat tours. Four blocks from the center of town, it's easy for guests to take advantage of the quaint shops, boutiques and Farmer's Market.

The East Tawas Junction B&B is a welcoming, relaxing spot in the great sunrise area of our state. Give Don and Leigh a call ... don't miss another fabulous Lake Huron sunrise.

Timberlane Resort

East Tawas, Michigan
Telephone: 248-647-9634
          248-797-0208
Website: www.timberlaneresorts.com

Located
in
Region 2

Owners: Wayne and James Hill

Accommodations: Cottage resort on Lake Huron, 7 cottages (2-3 bedrooms)

Extras: Equipped kitchens with microwave. Linens provided
                 (summer only), 1-2 baths. Gas BBQ, firepit. Boat wells
                 to rent. Some units with: dishwasher, whirlpool tub,
                 fireplace (gas or wood burning), enclosed screened
                 porch or patio. 220 ft. beachfront.

Rates/Payment: Nightly $90-$310; Weekly $880-$1,550. Check, major
                 credit cards.

Miscellaneous: $100 refundable cleaning/security deposit. Pets allowed
                 with extra charge. Smoking permitted, one cottage
                 smoke-free. Handicap accessible.

Open: Year around

The East Tawas/Tawas area has long been a major vacation spot in Michigan,
known for its incredible beaches and equally incredible fishing. In fact, the
name Tawas comes from a famous Michigan Chippewa Chief named "O-TA-
Was", who was known for his fishing prowess on the Huron. The area was
settled in the 1830's and, with the turn-of-the-century, became noted as a
popular tourist destination.

Sunrise at Timberlane offers a marvelous display of *the "Water of Light"*

Timberlane Resort wasn't there in the early days. In fact, in the history of the county, Timberlane is just a baby having been around for only 50 years or so. Like mortal humans, however, after 50 years resorts may experience a little mid-life crisis. Fortunately under its current owners, Wayne and James Hill, Timberlane has found the Fountain of Youth. It took the family four long years, but the Hills have refreshed, renewed and rejuvenated each cottage so that, at 50-plus years, Timberlane looks great.

Varying sized cottages sit back about 200-300 ft. from the sandy shoreline.

The units range from large (sleeps about 10) to small (sleeps 4). To keep their up-north feel, the Hills have kept knotty pine interiors. They have also added new appliances, furniture, carpeting, tile, cabinets, countertops and wood flooring. These cottages are a real treasure, and the decor really sets the mood for your *sunrise vacation*. Carpeted living rooms have comfortable colonial or contemporary country sofas and chairs with matching accessories. Larger

Timberlane's luxury cottage, The Hickory, (pictured here) is spacious, and impressively decorated. It features a modern kitchen and two baths, one with a whirlpool tub.

units include fireplaces. There are no TV's, so bring your own, but they do have stereo and CD players in several cottages.

Kitchens are fully equipped, including microwave, with track or recessed lighting, ceramic tile floors and lots of cupboards. The two larger cottages (Aspen/Hickory) even have a dishwasher. Remodeled bathrooms are tiled and have showers. The Hickory features two bathrooms (one with whirlpool tub) and private patio. The expansive Aspen is a loft unit with colonial decor, fireplace and screened porch providing a fabulous view of the lake. Smaller cottages don't have some of the extras, but are still very cute and comfortably styled. They're a perfect size for a family of four to six.

The Aspen features an inviting fireplace, colonial styling and a great view of the lake from its screened porch.

Grounds at the resort are tree-covered and sit back about 200 ft. to 300 ft. from the water. Gazing from the shoreline, the trees appear to dwarf the cottages. Timberlane's fabulous sandy beach is a real treasure, with lawn chairs and picnic tables dotting the sand and, of course, the ever-popular firepit. The water is perfect for swimming and the beach great for volleyball, Frisbee or just relaxing in the sun. For early risers, you will not be able to resist taking that cup of coffee, and maybe a camera, down by the water to watch daylight pierce the sky. Sand, briefly broken by a grassy knoll, extends far into the deep blue of Lake Huron. If you want to bring your boat, adjacent to the resort is a harbor where you can dock it for a small fee.

East Tawas, in Iosco County (Indian name meaning *Water of Light*) has attracted vacationers with its beautiful beaches and clear, clean waters year after year. Of course, we shouldn't let Lake Huron overshadow the nearby AuSable River, which has built its reputation around great fishing and canoeing. From lazy rippling currents to a little white water action, the AuSable brings paddlers from across the country and is home to a number of summer races and events. Most notable of these is the annual AuSable River Run from Grayling to Oscoda.

The Hill families have spent a lot of time, money and effort to make sure you can play hard and then relax at Timberlane. We recommend you book early.

Drummond Island Getaway

Drummond Island, Michigan
Telephone: 616-240-GOLD
616-850-8360

Located in Region 3

Owners:	James and Larry Goldman
Accommodations:	Private home on Sturgeon Bay, 5 bedrooms
Extras:	Three baths, fireplace, ceiling fans, CATV/VCR. Equipped kitchen, microwave, garbage disposal, dishwasher. On 7.8 acres. 300 ft. waterfront, swimming beach, patio, firepit, BBQ, hot tub.
Rates/Payment:	Weekly $2,450 (plus tax). Credit cards, check.
Miscellaneous:	No pets/smoking
Open:	Year around.

Drummond Island is frequently referred to as *The Gem of the Huron* because of its natural beauty and remote setting. With that in mind, it's safe to say the Drummond Island Getaway is *The Gem of the Island*. James and Larry Goldman have a truly unique home ... spacious, comfortable, luxurious, and *oh what a view.*

Overlooking Sturgeon Bay, the Goldman's two-story, 3,000 square foot red cedar home rests on nearly 8 acres of natural grounds. A canopy of trees skirt the roadway to the home, making it at first difficult to see. As you pass through

Drummond Island Getaway ... a luxury home with a fabulous view.

to the clearing, however, the beauty of the Getaway is suddenly revealed. The home's fresh red cedar exterior is framed by a kaleidoscope of sapphire and jade from sky, water, and trees punctuated by the white brilliance of clouds and seagulls. It's truly a vision.

Along water's edge, Sturgeon Bay reflects its undisturbed beauty.

A wooden porch runs across the home's front. In the back, facing the water, there's a large patio bordered by landscape. For your outdoor pleasure, the Goldman's have included lawn furniture and hot tub, a fine place to watch nature.

Off the patio, about 15 steps takes you to the grassy, sandy grounds leading to the bay. Stur-

The backyard patio is a great place to enjoy the view.

geon Bay, protected by the land, is warmer than much of Superior's deep, open waters. This is a good swimming area with a sandy bottom and a gradual slope. Spend the evening warming yourself by the firepit, while the salmon you caught earlier simmers on the grill.

After being overwhelmed by the exterior views, step inside and be awed by the rustic upnorth luxury that encompasses you. The great room, with its towering 20-foot ceiling, and massive stone fireplace, sets the stage for the entire house. The front wall has two columns of windows that run floor to ceiling and directly overlook the Bay. From the comfort of your chair you won't see a finer view.

The Goldman home is carpeted with knotty pine interior throughout. Its spacious great room is impressively furnished with plush sofa and chairs, heavy wood tables and pine entertainment center that includes CATV/VCR. In addition to the great room, the main floor holds a full, tiled bath and master bedroom. There's also the dining area with formal table sitting before a door wall with picturesque view of the bay.

The spacious great room features a 20 ft. ceiling, impressive stone fireplace and floor-to-ceiling windows with a perfect view.

The kitchen has all the conveniences of home and possibly more. Some of its amenities include quality appliances, microwave, garbage disposal, and dishwasher. A snack bar and small breakfast table provide additional seating. One interesting point, wherever you sit in the house, you are by a window with a view. There are lots of cupboards and counter space. Recessed lights highlight the matching wood floor, cupboards and breakfast table.

A large master bedroom and tiled full bath are found on the first floor, with the remaining four bedrooms and two additional bathrooms located on the second floor. The upstairs rooms are a little smaller, uncluttered with bed and end table, some with dresser. Five bedrooms have king, queen, double or

Bedrooms and sleeping areas are immaculate and very comfortable.

twin beds. There's no air conditioning, but with mild summer temperatures and the off-shore breeze, it's really not needed. However, virtually all rooms have a ceiling fan and that should keep temperatures nice and pleasant for you.

The Drummond Island motto is "A Place for All Seasons" and there's a reason for that. With 147 miles of shore line, 40 lakes and 50 outer islands, Drummond Island is paradise for swimmers, boaters, nature enthusiasts, and people who enjoy fishing and hunting in spring, summer and fall. It's located on the southwest end of the North Channel and separated from the UP by the De Tour Passage and the St. Mary River. The mouth of the river is famous for its salmon and big game fish. In a one or two week vacation it would be impossible to see and explore everything. During the year there are golf tournaments, Easter egg hunts, Fourth of July events, spring and summer arts and crafts, mountain bike races, and boating events.

Winter time is filled with snowmobile races, carnivals and excellent ice fishing. You must experience one of the island's truly unique winter features, the "Ice Bridge to Canada". Each winter the island locals plot a 15-mile trail, marked by Christmas trees on the ice. This 'safe trail' will take you to thousands of miles of trails in Canada.

You'll enjoy the island any time of the year, and there is no doubt that you'll love the home. If you are interested in getting away, try the Drummond Island Getaway. It's a real *Island Gem.*

Drummond Island Resort & Conference Center

Drummond Island, Michigan
Telephone: 800-999-6343

Located in Region 3

Contact:	Reservation/Main Office
Accommodations:	Hotel/lodge and cottage resort.
Extras:	TV, ceiling fans, private baths. Some with limited cable TV, VCR, fireplaces, full kitchens, whirlpool tubs. On 2,000 acres of woods/waters. Golf course, "The Rock", clinics and private lessons. Sporting clay rifle course. Tennis/volleyball courts. Swimming pool, hot tub, sauna. Fitness room. Hiking and cross-country ski trails. Boat, pontoon, snowmobile rentals. Complimentary bicycles, kayaks, sailboats, snowshoes, ice skates, sleds. Video library. Gift shop. Casual/fine dining. Conference/banquet facilities.
Rates/Payment:	Nightly $114-$600. Major credit cards, check.
Miscellaneous:	Former Domino's Pizza executive retreat. Accessible via car ferry (800-999-6343).
Open:	Year around

Carved out of the wilderness on Drummond Island is the former executive retreat of Domino's Pizza founder, Tom Monaghan. Initially created by Mr. Monaghan for his company's private use, this impressive example of luxury in the wilderness is now open for all to enjoy. Whether it's a romantic couple's

Drummond Island is a nature-lovers paradise.

ALL RATES SUBJECT TO CHANGE

43

getaway, family reunion or corporate meeting, Drummond Island Resort and Conference Center provides the setting and amenities.

The resort boasts a diverse range of accommodations within its scenic 2,000 acres, from standard hotel rooms to

A diverse range of lodgings are available, each maintaining a definite upnorth ambiance.

spacious, five bedroom/five bath homes. Whatever your choice, you'll enjoy the continuous theme of rustic comfort found throughout all their lodgings.

Similar to a motel, the log-styled lodge holds 40 rooms. Their standard units are small and simple. Two-level loft rooms offer more space. Dark wood floors, walls and ceiling along with simple, red wool bed covers and furniture designed from tree branches create a north woods atmosphere. In addition to the TV/VCR, rooms also include mini-refrigerators and coffeemakers.

We were most impressed with the diverse selection of cottages and homes. From simple, one-bedroom cabins to massive waterfront homes, each offers remarkable diversity in style. The Bayside waterfront cottages, overlooking Potagannissing Bay, are one of the newer additions to the resort. With a

Two-level loft rooms are available at the lodge.

contemporary design, these two bedroom, two level waterfront accommodations feature fireplaces, spacious living areas and well-equipped kitchens. Their light pine interiors with cheerful furnishings are fresh and appealing. Deer Track Fair Cottages, located near the 18th hole of the golf course, are another of the newer additions. More spacious, these cottages include fireplace, three bedrooms/three baths with equipped kitchens and whirlpool tubs in the master bedroom.

Authentic full-scribe log homes are more rustic in design and comfortably decorated with antiques and relaxed styling.

The resort's collection of full-scribe log homes is in direct contrast to the more contemporary design of Bayside and Deer Track. Their massive log construction and natural fieldstone fireplaces create the ambiance of a true north woods

cabin. Earthy colors of deep brown, cream and red are accented with interesting artifacts and woodsman styling. Though successfully creating the *cabin in the woods* atmosphere, they are still furnished for comfort with three to four bedrooms and an equal number of bathrooms, full kitchens or kitchenettes. Also, like all of the resort lodgings, each includes TV, VCR and telephone with voice mail.

Unfortunately, during our visit, we were unable to visit Tom Monaghan's former home. We were told it was designed and built in the Frank Lloyd Wright tradition with extensive stonework and glass throughout. The Monaghan Home has five bedrooms, each with private bath, a children's playhouse, and plenty of room for entertaining.

Bayside and Deer Track cottages offer more contemporary design and amenities.

Certainly there's more to Drummond Island Resort than its lodgings. It is also home to an impressive 18-hole championship golf course called *The Rock*. Considered one of Michigan's top 10 courses, *The Rock* is part of the Audubon Nature Preserve System with woods surrounding its secluded, well-groomed greens. Golfers often see whitetail deer or other wildlife peak through the foliage (so take care with those hooks or slices). If you want to improve your golf swing, take in one of the resort's special golf clinics or schedule a private lesson.

Non-golfers need not fret, golf is not all that's happening at Drummond Island Resort. Bring your rifle and sharpen your eye at the Cedars, their professionally designed sporting clays course.

"The Rock" is the resort's premier golf course.

The resort also holds a well-maintained tennis court, volleyball court and heated outdoor swimming pool. An outdoor whirlpool and Scandinavian sauna are particularly appealing on those blustery fall or winter days or cool summer nights. In addition, guests have full access to mountain bikes, canoes, sailboats and kayaks to explore the resort's extensive trail system or enjoy the surrounding waters. In the winter, cross-country skis, ice skates, snowshoes and sleds are made available along with on-site snowmobile rentals.

Equipment and gear for many outdoor activities are complimentary at the resort.

Dining is yet another pleasure at the resort. The Pins Bar and Grill offers casual, family-styled dining throughout the day and evening. The Pins is aptly named after its well maintained bowling lanes opened to the public. In the evening, if

you're seeking a special culinary experience, make reservations at the Bayside Restaurant and Lounge. Sitting on a bluff, in a cover of cedars overlooking Pota-gannising Bay, this lovely restaurant serves a variety of finely pre-pared cuisine created by their imaginative chef.

Drummond Island Resort and Conference Center, nestled in the island's wilderness, is a wonder-ful retreat where you can getaway from it all without leaving all the nice things behind. Contact the resort's information desk to learn about their many special rate packages.

Rainbow Lodge

(at Two Hearted River)
Newberry, Michigan
Telephone: 906-658-3357
Website: www.exploringthenorth.com/
twoheart/rainbow.html

Located
in
Region 3

Owners:	Richard and Kathy Robinson
Accommodations:	Resort with 6 rooms, 2 cabins, 1 trailer, 47 campsites.
Extras:	Most units with full kitchens or kitchenettes. Private baths. Located in Lake Superior State Forest. Canoe trips. Livery and canoe rentals. On-site store with essentials. Cafe operating in the winter. Gas pump. Grass airstrip.
Rates/Payments:	Weekly $267-$510 (double occupancy). Checks.
Miscellaneous:	Rooms use gaslights. Electric hairdryers and appliances are not permitted. One unit handicapped accessible.
Open:	Year around

"There was nothing but the pine plains ahead of him, until the far blue hills that marked the Lake Superior height of land.... While Nick walked through the little stretch of meadow alongside the stream, trout had jumped high out of water."

Excerpts from: Big Two-Hearted River by Ernest Hemingway

Rainbow Lodge's small store (left) also houses their winter-time cafe.

Lodgings include motel rooms and small apartments with kitchenettes (below) and cabins.

Immortalized by Ernest Hemingway for its wilderness and beauty, Two Hearted River runs along the shoreline of Lake Superior between Grand Marais and Whitefish Point. You will not find a Walmart, Sears, or McDonalds nearby. There is no church, police station or paved roads. This, my friends, is a naturalist's dream vacation. A resort built from the land that takes you far away from the maddening crowds, but still keeps you close to the action...if you want it.

How the Robinson family started the Rainbow Lodge is a fascinating story. They came to the area some 37 years ago, cleared the woods and built the resort and store. There was really nothing there but nature, so they setup a totally self-sufficient place with its own water system and generator for electricity.

Today Richard and Kathy have a telephone in the store, which they allow guests to use (don't worry about your cell phone, it ain't gonna work). The generator has been expanded in size and is housed in a large building in the back. Windmills have been added for extra power. Richard designed and maintains this mini-power plant, a marvel in engineering. Even with this added power, however, there is limited electricity at the resort.

Getting to the lodge is a little adventure in itself. Dirt roads take you deep into wilderness where the sounds of nature and little else surround you. Just when you think you're the only person left on earth, the trees part and there,

Rooms are very clean, simple and well-kept. All have private baths, but don't expect TV's or phones. At night, gaslights provide illumination.

like an oasis in the desert, rests the resort. Roads to Rainbow are drivable with a regular car. For city-slickers like us, we would have preferred a four-wheel drive vehicle (Kathy laughed). There is also a grass airstrip for small planes. All of this adds up to an intriguing resort for people who want to be one with nature.

Rainbow Lodge is the focal point for people living in the area. The store attracts the locals and Kathy even tries to bring in a minister or priest monthly to offer services for area residents. In the winter, part of the store is turned into a cafe serving hearty soups and sandwiches to warm their guests.

Wilderness surrounds Rainbow Lodge making it a true naturalist's retreat.

The units range in size to accommodate two to six people. They do not contain TV's or phones. Furnishings and interiors are clean but simple. Bathrooms and kitchens tend to be small but very functional. Since electricity is limited, rooms are brightened with gaslights. Appliances in many cases are new and also gas operated. Electric blankets, hairblowers, etc. are not permitted ... come on now, this is a *wilderness* experience. Handmade wooden tables and chairs, found in some bedrooms, add to the rugged atmosphere.

Richard offers a variety of fishing/hunting tours and canoe trips, from novice to experienced, on the Two Hearted River. These trips can be as short as 1-1/2 hours or up to 3 days. Whichever you choose, you will never forget the experience. The river is also considered to be one of the *top ten* in the country for trout and is also known for salmon and steelhead.

After a day on the river or Lake Superior, you may want to do something a little different. Head over to Sault Ste. Marie to visit one of the area's biggest attractions, the Soo Locks. An engineering marvel, freighters, some over 1,000 feet long and 105 feet wide, are lifted and lowered by water as they pass through the narrow channel.

A trip to the region wouldn't be complete without visiting the Seney Wildlife Refuge. A 96,000-acre refuge, it's the largest east of the Mississippi. This area is also known as 'big snow country', with snow falls up to 200 inches annually. Rainbow Lodge just happens to be in a snow belt, with hundreds of miles of groomed snowmobile trails starting right at your front door.

Because of its wilderness setting, The Rainbow Lodge may not be a spot for everyone. For the true outdoor enthusiast, however, it will be a unique adventure at one of our most beautiful and natural rivers.

Sunset Cabins

Grand Marais, Michigan 49839
Telephone: 906-494-2693

Located in Region 3

Owner:	Craig Winnie
Accommodations:	Cottage resort on Sucker River (overlooking Lake Superior), 4 cottages (1-3 bedroom)
Extras:	Newly renovated. Private baths, equipped kitchen, CATV. Firepit, charcoal grills. Decks, picnic tables.
Rates/Payment:	Weekly $480-$540; Daily $80-$90. Credit card, check.
Miscellaneous:	Pets O.K.
Open:	Year around

Sunset Cabins rest along a quiet river.

Tucked along a quiet river overlooking Lake Superior sits Sunset Cabins, a pleasant discovery we recently made while exploring the little village of Grand Marais in Michigan's UP. A relatively small four-cabin resort, it's easy to overlook on your journey to the beautiful Tahquamenon Falls or Pictured Rocks National Lakeshore. However, for those interested in a simple but remarkably clean stay in a cozy, laid-back environment, you may want to take note.

Sunset is not exactly new. In fact, it's the oldest resort in the area. What's new is the owner, and that makes the difference. A few years back, Craig Winnie and his two small daughters, Rachael and Stormi, took ownership. Since then, under Craig's skillful hands, all four cabins have been completely remodeled. It's the recent updates, Craig's friendly, helpful attitude and his two young, rosy-cheeked daughters that distinguish the resort from others.

During our visit, all cabins were occupied except for the small, one bedroom. With Craig's oldest daughter, Rachael, off playing with friends, he was about to do the cleaning and invited us to join him. As we strode along the natural treed grounds, we couldn't help but smile as his little helper, Stormi, merrily followed ...her own special little cleaning bucket in hand.

We were immediately pleased with the immaculate two-person, one bedroom cabin that was compact but still offered all the basic comforts. The primary room combined kitchen and sitting area and was furnished with small dining table and single futon. Most impressive were the warm wood cabinets and

Newly renovated, Sunset's traditional cottages are immaculate with nicely equipped kitchens.

tongue-and-groove pine floors, ceiling and walls, all constructed by Craig. The kitchen's bright ceramic tile countertops were also new as were the full size refrigerator and stove. Perched atop a cabinet was the all-important cable T.V. The bathroom was pretty small, but we were very pleased to see a well-constructed, fully remodeled room with toilet, sink and shower. A single bedroom contained a very comfortable queen bed. We weren't able to visit the other remodeled cabins (two bedroom and three-bedroom), but Craig informed us they had also undergone extensive renovation with some new tongue-and-groove wood as well as fully updated kitchens and bathrooms.

Sunset is conveniently located in the historical community of Grand Marias, which is the gateway to some of the U.P.'s most scenic attractions. In addition

Simply furnished, the new pine interior of the smallest cottage (seen here) adds a clean freshness.

to Tahquamenon Falls and Pictured Rocks National Lakeshore, Grand Marias offers miles of sandy beaches, sand dunes, cross-country skiing, snowmobile and wilderness hiking trails. Boating, sea kayaking, fishing and hunting are also very popular activities in the area.

If you're unfamiliar with this region of Michigan, then your stay at Sunset offers another bonus. Craig is very familiar with the area and is more than happy to provide information to help you enjoy your U.P. adventure. Sunset Cabins, a nice choice for those seeking a clean, homey stay at a very good price. Craig, Rachael and Stormi are waiting to hear from you.

Big Bay Point Lighthouse

Big Bay, Michigan
Telephone: 906-345-9957
Website: www.bigbaylighthouse.com

Located
in
Region 4

Innkeepers:	Jeff and Linda Gamble, John Gale
Accommodations:	Bed and breakfast, 7 rooms with private baths
Extras:	Full breakfasts. Ceiling fans. Some rooms with fireplaces, whirlpool tub. Sauna on premises. Spa services. Secluded, scenic grounds overlooking Lake Superior. Special seasonal programs include dog sledding and chocolate-lover weekends.
Rates/Payment:	Nightly $115-$183. Check.
Miscellaneous:	Operating lighthouse. Listed on the National Register of Historic Places. Caters to adult travelers. Make reservations early. No pets/smoking.
Open:	Year around

The welcoming Big Bay
Lighthouse B&B overlooks
beautiful Lake Superior.

Resting atop a craggy ridge over-looking the cool, clear waters of Lake Superior, the historic Big Bay Point Lighthouse beckons guests to its secluded serenity. For more than 100 years it has served as home to generations of keep-ers, their assistants and helpers. Today guests are invited to share with its keepers the same breath-taking views and hypnotic sounds as Superior's waves break along the coastline. One of the country's

few remaining resident lighthouses, Big Bay Point Lighthouse offers a truly distinctive experience.

Built in the mid-1880's, the lighthouse opened its doors as a bed and breakfast in 1986 and served as Michigan's first combined lighthouse and lodging. In 1991, Jeff and Linda Gamble took ownership and became its newest keepers and welcoming proprietors.

With a background and interest in historic preservation, Linda and Jeff have carefully completed extensive renovation and restoration activities. Of course they have tastefully added the needed comforts to ensure guests will enjoy their experience.

The inn's seven guest rooms, named after former keepers, assistants and helpers, are skillfully styled. Colorful quilts, cream eyelet bed covers, folk art and antiques provide atmospheric charm. The

Cheerful sunlight filters through windows adding a cozy warmth to the dining room (above) and library (left),

keepers rooms are the largest of the seven and feature sitting areas, gas fireplace or Franklin stove.

Mornings at the lighthouse will definitely add to your experience. Each day, as the sun breaks over the glistening waters of Lake Superior, you'll wake to the welcoming aroma of freshly brewed coffee and a well prepared country breakfast. Their favorite breakfast specialties include a delightfully tangy lemon-stuffed French toast and delicious oatmeal raisin pancakes.

Tucked away in this quiet, remote section of Michigan's Upper Peninsula, you'll want to savor the peaceful, relaxed atmosphere of the lighthouse. Ascend the winding staircase of the light tower. Stand 120 feet above the lake, and enjoy the panoramic view only a few have seen. Meander along the grounds, enjoy the gardens and the newly built pond or hike through the surrounding 40 acres of woods, meadows and a half-mile of lakeshore. Should the cool breezes bring a chill, the warmth of the inn's sauna will take it away.

Colorful quilts, eyelet bedspreads, folk art and antiques highlight rooms.

If you're looking for adventure, book a guided tour for sea kayaking, mountain biking, snowshoeing or dog sledding. In fact, the inn offers a very special dog sledding weekend in the winter. This day-long adventure begins

with an expert guide providing detailed instructions on running a full-team dogsled. Soon after, you'll find yourself gliding along a snow covered trail leading your own team (guide supervised) into the UP wilderness. At midday you'll stop for a trailside lunch where the warmth of the fire will be as welcoming as the conversation of your fellow adventurers. Then it's back to the lighthouse and the comfort of your room.

Of course there's plenty of tamer adventures to enjoy in this outdoor wonderland. Take the day to explore waterfalls (there are 10 within 10-15 miles of the lighthouse). Gift shops, boat and bike

Join Big Bay in the winter for their special dogsledding weekend.

In the summer, book a guided sea kayaking or mountain biking tour.

rentals, along with tennis courts, swimming beaches and restaurants can be found in the friendly nearby town of Big Bay.

Whether you're one of the many lighthouse devotees or simply someone needing the solace of nature and the exhilaration of the great outdoors, Big Bay Point Lighthouse Bed and Breakfast offers an experience unlike any other. The lighthouse books up quickly. We highly recommend making reservations at least several months in advance.

Deer Lake Bed & Breakfast

Boyne City, Michigan
Telephone: 231-582-9039
Website: www.deerlakebb.com

Located in Region 5

Owners:	Shirley and Glenn Piepenburg
Accommodations:	Bed and breakfast on Deer Lake, 5 rooms/private baths.
Extras:	Full breakfast. Individual room heating and A/C. In-room hair dryer. Two rooms with private balconies, 3 with shared balcony. Swimming pond. Paddleboat and sailboat available. Massage package, jewelry-making classes available.
Rates/Payment:	Nightly $95-$115. Major credit cards, checks.
Miscellaneous:	No pets/smoking. Family-friendly.
Open:	Year around

Deer Lake B&B is, quite literally, a dream come true for innkeepers, Shirley and Glenn Piepenburg. It began with a series of unfinished dreams for Shirley. In her dreams, she wandered through a massive construction project, never knowing what was going on. It perplexed her for years. Then one night, while she and Glenn were staying at a bed and breakfast, she finished the dream. The next morning, as Shirley was about to tell Glenn, he excitedly broke in to explain his own dream. Surprisingly, it was the same as Shirley's...they were

Fabulous views in a serene setting ... Deer Lake B&B offers guests casual luxury in the popular community of Boyne City.

Swim in the quiet pond or explore Deer Lake in a paddleboat or sailboat.

building a bed and breakfast! Shirley and Glenn made their dream a reality by expanding their lovely home on Deer Lake and opening it as a bed and breakfast around 1994. They've enjoyed sharing their home with guests ever since.

During our visit, it was difficult to say what impressed us most. Initially, it was the home's fresh, beautifully maintained exterior tucked in a scenic, wooded lot. Upon entering the home, we were delighted with the well-designed and elegantly furnished interior. Then, as our eyes swept to the rear window and the view beyond, we were held in awe as we took in the breathtaking scene of well-groomed lawn slopping around the reflecting swimming pond and onto the crystal waters of Deer Lake ... a truly remarkable vision.

The home features five impressively designed guest rooms with private baths. Each maintains individual styling. The North Room is one of our favorites with partial canopy and four-poster queen bed. Elegantly decorated in tones of burgundy and dark green, it features a cathedral ceiling and French doors

The beautifully designed living room is a perfect spot for friendly conversation.

leading to a private balcony with a wonderful view of the lake. The South Room is another of our favorites. Its design is bright and airy with light colors and fresh sea green highlights. This room also features a chalet ceiling and

Rooms offers private baths and are tastefully styled. The North and South Rooms (pictured here) have private balconies.

French doors that lead to a private balcony and another fabulous view.

Breakfasts at the inn are an eagerly awaited luxury for returning guests. Skillfully pre-pared and imaginatively presented, it's certain to be a memorable event.

Served by candlelight on fine china, guests are treated to what we like to call the Piepenburg Culinary Experience. Over the years, Shirley has accumu-lated quite a collection of recipes from which she chooses. From fresh breads and muffins to her specialty pancakes, omelets and quiches, each is a sump-tuous surprise. Glenn then adds his special, imaginative touches in presenta-tion … apples, fresh melons, strawberries or an assortment of other goodies, combine to create a cheery face, an angel, sailboat or other highly original design. It's certain to brighten your morning.

Later, after a fun-filled day that ended up being a little *too fun*, take advantage of the inn's special massage packages, which include a variety of options from full body massage to facials and scalp treatments. Yet another special program at Deer Lake is their jewelry-making classes. Glenn, a skilled jewelry designer, holds 1 to 1-1/2 hour sessions. During the class, guests will create their very own ring and leave with a much greater knowledge of jewelry design and care.

Certainly part of your stay must include some time by the lake or swimming pond. It should be noted the swimming pond is not a wadding pond. It actually reaches a depth of about 10 ft., which makes it safe for shallow dives. If you'd

Served in the lovely dining area, delicious breakfasts are skillfully prepared and imaginatively presented.

like to explore Deer Lake, a paddleboat and sailboat are available. For first time sailors, Glenn will be happy to provide a lesson or two.

If you do decide to venture out from the comforts of Deer Lake, you'll find plenty to do. Boyne, of course, is one of Michigan's most popular downhill ski areas during winter months. In the summer, beaches and water activities abound. Nearby Traverse City, Interlochen, Charlevoix and Petoskey are noted for scenic drives, artisan galleries and exceptional golf.

Whether it's a brief weekend getaway or a week-long vacation, the Piepenburg's are happy to share their dream home with you. We highly recommend Deer Lake B&B for its amiable innkeepers, sumptuous breakfasts, unique special packages and, of course, its incredible view.

House on the Hill

Harbor Springs, Michigan
Telephone: 231-539-8909

Located in Region 5

Owners:	Zulski Brothers
Accommodations:	Private home, 3 bedrooms
Extras:	Fully equipped kitchen, microwave, dishwasher, satellite TV/VCR, washer/dryer, 2.5 baths. Outdoor deck, firepit, gas grill. On 400 acres with trails.
Rates/Payment:	Weekly $800
Miscellaneous:	No pets/smoking
Open:	Year around

The three Zulski brothers built their 3,000 sq. ft. vacation home on a hill overlooking their expansive 400-acre property. The fields and woods are filled with trails for hiking, biking or snowmobiling. It's a very natural, uncrowded and private setting for your enjoyment.

Entering the home, we were immediately struck by its open and clean lines. Small touches like wallpaper trim and woodworking add to the visual appeal. Much of the wood is northern Michigan white ash milled right in the area. There has been considerable attention paid to details ensuring guest comfort.

Resting on a hill, this lovely home overlooks 400-acres of woodland.

View from the deck ... 400 acres of scenic woodlands and trails.

The living room's large window will direct your attention down the hill to the field and trees beyond. To one side, not to block the view, there's a satellite TV and a VCR. There's even a list of videos available for your enjoyment. Floral print sofa and love seat are carefully placed to enjoy the view or take a

The sofa is particularly nice for taking a little nap before your next adventure.

little nap after a hard day of play. Rich, hardwood floors and trim are found throughout the home.

The dining room has a formal table in the center framed by teal covered chairs. A truly inviting place for meals, which will be fun to prepare in the fully equipped kitchen. Appliances are very contemporary and the refrigerator even includes an icemaker. Who has time to make ice? The

kitchen cupboards have enough dishes, eating and cooking utensils to serve a seven-course meal, and there's still enough storage space left over for all the other stuff we bring. To make sure big meals won't be a chore, the dishwasher will make clean-up simple. For your added convenience, there's also a washer and dryer.

Tucked into a little corner of the kitchen, next to a window with a view of the scenic grounds, there's a cozy little table and two chairs. What a beautiful spot for a couple to relax in the morning.

Like the rest of the house, the master bedroom is lovely, with a teal and white quilt draped over the king size bed. Casting gentle light, a large window, trimmed with a delicate white lace valence, frames the natural grounds. Similar window treatments can be found throughout the house, lending a light, open feel. The master bedroom has its own bath. In addition, there's a half bath off the living room.

Traveling upstairs, tall-peaked ceilings are found in the two large bedrooms. Each contains a queen and twin bed wrapped in striped or patchwork quilts. End tables and dressers add the final touch. These sleeping areas create an expansive, open feel, much like the land. The second floor is fully carpeted and contains a full bath located between the two rooms. Contemporary bathrooms, upstairs and down, have light countertops and ceramic tile floors.

The full basement has plenty of space to store vacation toys like skis, snowshoes, bicycles and the like. Since our visit, however, the Zulskis have begun finishing the large lower level to make a rec room for family fun. The 28'x 16' room will have several bunk beds for the little ones and a large area for playing and table games. It should be complete by early 2003. From the basement a door takes you outside, so you can start exploring.

Master bedroom (above) has a private doorwall to the balcony.

Winter or summer you'll have fun on the grounds. There's a gas grill and firepit (wood is provided), for those all important s'mores. The trails are great for hiking or biking in the warm months and excellent for cross-country skiing or snowshoeing in the winter. Snowmobilers will be pleased to know several major Michigan trails can be picked up right from the property. There's an abundance of wildlife in this natural playground, especially spring and fall, so bring your camera and binoculars to capture their beauty. Hunting is not permitted on the grounds.

Not far from Traverse City, Petoskey and Mackinaw City, there is plenty to do in this region of Michigan. Great beaches, nightlife, festivals and fine dining make this area a very popular spot. Naturally, this is a winter wonderland resplendent with slopes, trails and some great snow. This Harbor Springs hilltop home is ideally located at a really good price. Highly recommended.

R&H Chalet

Boyne Falls, Michigan
Telephone: 734- 676-1405

Located in Region 5

Owners:	Dan and Barb Richards; Mike and Susie Hurley
Accommodations:	Private chalet on Deer Lake, three bedrooms.
Extras:	Fully equipped kitchen, microwave. CATV/VCR, fireplace, washer/dryer. Two baths. Swimming beach, boat included.
Rates/Payment:	Weekly $1,000; nightly $200. Check.
Miscellaneous:	No pets, smoking allowed
Open:	Year around

Let's go up north. In and around the Midwest, that's a phrase heard all year long. What do we do when we go up-north? Why do we drive in traffic almost as heavy as rush hour to go up north? It's rather simple, really … to escape. And what better way than by savoring the beauty of a Michigan lake, retreating to the wilderness, or enjoying the chilled rush of snow as we edge down a ski slope. Regardless of your reason to *go up-north*, R&H Chalet won't be far from your adventure.

Homey, well-maintained chalet on Deer Lake.

Located on a quiet road in Boyne Falls, dotted with vacation homes and pines, rests the white chalet owned by Richard and Hurley families. The home is ideal for a family up to eight.

Cheerful light and scenic views from the master bedroom (1 of 3 bedrooms).

Entering from the street side of the house, you'll find yourself on the second floor with two bedrooms and full bath. A doorwall provides access to the balcony and a fabulous view of Deer Lake. This is a great area to relax over your morning coffee as the sounds of nature and scenic view surround you. Of course, the master bedroom has all the basic comforts and, an arms-length away, a TV/VCR and stereo. This homey room also features a sitting area with sofa for leisurely discussions of today's experiences and tomorrow's adventures. The smaller second bedroom has two twin beds and, just down the hall, a bathroom with shower stall.

The fireplace is the focal point of the main living area.

Stairs take you down to the first floor. A focal point of the living room has to be the fireplace. To be sure, it's a perfect location to warm yourself after a long winter's day on the slopes. Surrounding the fireplace are two plush, deep blue sofas that will certainly soothe the weariest O!ympic hopeful's body. Naturally an entertainment center completes the room with cable TV and VCR. Just behind the main living area is another bedroom and full bath. There's even a washer/dryer in the back.

Scenic view from R&H Chalet's sandy beach.

Off the living room, a rustic-wood dining table and benches are nestled in the corner. A fully equipped kitchen, not large, has ample room and counter space to prepare your favorite foods. Large windows offer a nice view of the lake and a doorwall gives access to the small patio and sandy beach.

Décor in the home is simple and fun with a Michigan sports theme that reflect the Richards' and Hurleys' interest. Framed photographs, newspaper clippings and other sport memorabilia are found throughout the home, each highlighting special moments for Michigan teams and players.

The small but beautiful sandy beach is great for relaxing or taking a dip in the warm, shallow waters. Deer Lake is a scenic, very private lake surrounded by trees with only a few homes visible from the shoreline. A boat is available for a leisurely tour of the lake. Enjoy the scenery or try your hand at fishing.

Once you've had enough beach sand, check out the sand traps at some of Michigan's best golf courses. About a 15-minute drive in a golf cart and you could be at Boyne or Boyne Highlands infamous courses, just to name a few. The entire region is prime for tournament quality golf.

Point your car in any direction from R&H and, in an hour or less, you'll be at a premiere vacation destination. Traverse City is one of Michigan's most popular communities with great shopping and excellent restaurants. Don't miss the quaint resort towns of Charlevoix, Petoskey, Harbor Springs and Mackinaw City. Take a step back in time and ferry across to Mackinac Island where cars aren't permitted and homemade fudge will make your mouth water.

Several of Michigan's best golf and ski resorts are nearby.

Of course we can't forget the winter. When the winds blow and the snow falls, this region turns in to a paradise for skiers. There are several prime ski resorts in the area. Boyne Mountain is one of Michigan's hot spots in cold weather. Boyne Highlands is another boasting a 550-foot vertical drop. Both offer miles and miles of groomed cross-country ski trails and snowshoeing...now that's an experience. Not far away, pick up the snowmobile trials and winter life is good.

R&H Chalet is a comfortable home in one of Michigan's prime vacation areas. With a complete range of features, an ideal location, and a good rental price, it's a very nice choice for the region.

Up North Getaway

Wellston (Manistee), Michigan
Telephone: 248-668-9925
Website: www.upnorthgetaway.com

Located in Region 5

Owners:	Trevor and Dennis Wisnewski
Accommodations:	Private chalet on Pine Lake, two bedrooms with sleeping alcoves (six beds)
Extras:	Equipped kitchen, microwave, dishwasher. 2 full baths. Ceiling fans. TV, VCR, fireplace, wood-burning stove, radio/CD player; wraparound deck; outdoor firepit, charcoal BBQ. Linens included.
Rates/Payment:	Weekly $780-$1,050; weekends $365-$475. Checks.
Miscellaneous:	No pets
Open:	Year around

Amidst a peppering of trees overlooking Pine Lake in the Manistee National Forest, the lovely Up North Getaway awaits. This contemporary, multilevel, chalet offers plenty of room with a stunning view of the lake. It's a real standout, and one of our favorite new properties.

Spacious, contemporary home overlooks Pine Lake in the Manistee National Forest.

You'll enter the home through its rear porch and hallway. Here you'll find a nicely maintained full bath with tub/shower and a simply furnished bedroom with comfortable double bed and single dresser (closet not available to guests).

As you continue on, be prepared for the real surprise in this home ... the great room. This wonderful area is spacious with an open design that combines dining, kitchen and living room. Tall, chalet ceiling with beautiful floor-to-ceiling windows and

Floor to ceiling windows/doorwalls offer cheerful light and a great view of the lake.

doorwalls bookend the fireplace and surround the room with cheerful light and great views. A TV (no cable) and VCR sit in one corner with sofas facing the fireplace and doorwalls.

Nicely equipped kitchen includes a dishwasher.

The dining area has a table that seats up to 6. We were pleased to find the island-style kitchen fully equipped, including microwave and dishwasher. A stairway to the back of the great room takes you to the upstairs loft that holds the second (master) bedroom with private full bath, and two open sleeping areas. The master bedroom is simply furnished with comfortable queen bed, a single dresser and a rack to hang clothes. The sleeping alcoves have twin and double beds. There aren't many places to store your

clothes, so if you're a larger family or group of eight, you'll need to do some creative unpacking.

A second stairway, found down the hallway, takes you to the home's lower level. Here you'll find a partially finished, walkout basement furnished

Two bedrooms plus sleeping alcoves accommodate up to eight people.

with sofas, table, two full beds and a cozy wood-burning stove to take away the chill on those cooler evenings. A doorwall gives you access to the grounds and lake.

Stroll down to water's edge where you'll find a sandy lake bottom with gradual incline … great for swimming. Rent a boat (available just a couple of cottages down) or bring your own. For you fishing enthusiasts, the lake is noted for its coho, steelhead, salmon and trout.

Of course, as is true with many places where guests frequently come and go, there are things that need to be refreshed, replaced or repaired. Owners, Trevor and Dennis Wisnewski, do a good job at keeping after those on-going updates. Most recently they've replaced carpeting in the kitchen and hope to have the exterior professionally stained in the near future.

While here, if you can pull yourself away from the lake, take some time to enjoy the surrounding communities. For those interested in a little casino action, try the Little River Casino (on U.S. 23 and M-22 in Manistee). It's one of Michigan's newest gaming establishments and only a few minutes

Nearby Nordhouse Dunes is the only "designated wilderness area" in Michigan's lower peninsula.

away. Also nearby is the Nordhouse Dunes Wilderness area. Located in the Huron-Manistee National Forest, it is unique in that it's the only "designated wilderness area" in Michigan's lower peninsula.

Of course, you'll have to visit Manistee with its historic downtown district. Along River Street, you'll find several interesting shops and historic buildings. Stroll the Manistee River Channel and its 1.5-mile Riverwalk to Lake Michigan. Take a trolley ride or book a tour of historic homes and churches. Stop by one of the many riverfront eateries where you can watch Great Lakes freighters, cruise ships and pleasure craft pass as you leisurely enjoy your lunch or dinner.

Fall is an equally terrific time to visit. During this season, the Manistee National Forest's foliage becomes a brilliant palette of colors. In the winter, downhill skiers will enjoy the slopes at nearby Caberfae Peak in Cadillac, or Crystal Mountain Resort in Thompsonville.

Throughout the year, there's plenty of adventures to be enjoyed in this scenic region of Michigan. The Up North Getaway is a lovely home and a nice place to relax after an active day. We suggest making your reservations early.

Woodland Acres Lakehome

Manistee, Michigan
Telephone: 708-460-3113
Email: jbielecki1@aol.com

Located in Region 5

Owners:	John and Brigid Bielecki
Accommodations:	Private condo on Lake Michigan, 3 bedrooms
Extras:	Equipped kitchen, microwave, dishwasher. Three baths. Gas-log fireplace, CATV, VCR, DVD, stereo. Washer/dryer. Ceiling fans. Enclosed veranda. Outdoor hot tub, gas grill. Sandy swimming beach.
Rates/Payment:	Weekly $1,200-$2,300. Checks.
Miscellaneous:	No pets/smoking
Open:	Year around

You'll experience luxury living at this incredible Lake Michigan lodging, which is part of the new and exclusive Woodland Acres Lakeshore Condominiums. Located in the scenic Manistee area, this condominium community is set on 3.65 acres of land that rests along 260 ft. of private Lake Michigan shoreline. The beach is sandy, the sunsets spectacular and the comforts of this impressively designed condo unquestionable. If that's not enough, it's

Luxury living on Lake Michigan's shoreline.

Well styled interiors with scenic views ensure a comfortable stay.

also close to five championship golf courses, artisan galleries, gift shops, wineries, casinos and premiere ski resorts.

John and Brigid have furnished their 2,300 sq. ft., multi-level condo to maintain the utmost in comfort and style. Ceiling fans and central air conditioning keep things cool on those warmer days. Walls are painted with deep, contrasting colors. Mantel, shelves and walls are accented with wildlife and folk-art woodcarvings. Lighthouse pictures and framed photographs of Michigan scenes add to the up-north ambiance. This condo offers the best of vacation living at a price that's fairly competitive for this region of Michigan.

You'll enter the unit from the street-side, passing by the foyer with laundry room (includes washer and dryer) and small but immaculate bathroom with shower. The home opens to the main area that combines kitchen with dining and living rooms. Earthy, ceramic tile floors blend

A well equipped kitchen includes a dishwasher.

well with dark wood cabinets in the kitchen, natural stone (gas-log) fireplace and overstuffed furniture in the living room. High ceilings sweep upward to the second-story loft. An abundance of windows ensure cheerful light and pictur-esque views from all levels of the home.

Private deck features a hot tub.

The home's con-temporary kitchen is stocked with all the goodies, includ-ing a dishwasher. Just beyond is the dining area with country-styled oak china cabinet and table comfortably seating six. Moving into the living room, an over-stuffed sofa and chair sit opposite the fabulous stone fireplace with an entertainment cabinet (cable TV and VCR) to the side. From there, French doors open to the private deck with hot tub and an unobstructed view of well-groomed lawn, sandy shoreline and the blue waters of Lake Michigan.

Also on the first floor is the master bedroom with king-size bed. This room features a very spacious private bath with 6 ft. tub and separate shower. It has a private doorway to the outdoor deck. You'll fall asleep to the sound of Lake Michigan and awake to the sound of birds and the reflection of morning light skimming off waves.

We can't forget the second level, which offers more treasures. The cozy loft area holds a small den with sleeper-sofa and entertainment unit containing cable TV/VCR/DVD. This might be an ideal spot for the kids to hang out as the grown-ups chat downstairs or in the outdoor hot tub. There

The upstairs loft has a sleeper sofa, with CATV, VCR, DVD, and Mr. Bear to watch over you.

are also two additional bedrooms and full bath with tub shower.

We've saved the best for last. Perhaps the nicest surprise sits in the front-most portion of the second level. John and Brigid call it their "checkers room". Indeed, there is a table setup, ready for a tournament-level challenge. The checkers room, however, is really a wonderful glassed veranda with high-peaked ceiling and a wall of windows offering an incredible view of the lake. This is definitely the place to read, share quiet conversation, and enjoy a Lake Michigan sunset.

Lake Michigan sunsets are best viewed from the upstairs veranda.

Certainly what makes this lovely condo even better is the location. Its sandy Lake Michigan shoreline is shallow and great for swimming. And, as mentioned earlier, it's centrally located to five championship golf courses including Arcadia Bluffs, Manistee National and the Heathlands, to name a few. Nearby are charter fishing tours and boat rental facilities for a day on the lake. The Traverse City area, with great shopping and casinos, is only 1.5 hours away. We can't forget that one of Michigan's most popular scenic attractions, Sleeping Bear Sand Dunes National Park, is just a short drive away. It's also not far from several of our best ski resorts.

Close to the popular Sleeping Bear Sand Dunes.

Whatever time of the year you plan your vacation, we highly recommend John and Brigid Bielecki 's Woodland Acres Lakehome. It will not disappoint. Book well in advance.

The Candlewyck House

Pentwater, Michigan
Telephone: 616-869-5967
Website: www.candlewyckhouse.com

Located in Region 6

Innkeepers:	John and Mary Jo Neidow
Accommodations:	Bed and breakfast, 6 rooms with private baths.
Extras:	Full breakfasts. A/C. In-room CATV, some with VCR, microwave and fireplace. Ceiling fans. Complimentary guest bicycles. Video and book library.
Rates/Payment:	Nightly $99-$129. Major credit cards, checks.
Miscellaneous:	No pets/smoking. Well-behaved children welcomed. Child care available.
Open:	May - November

What fun our stop was at Candlewyck House in historic Pentwater. Built in 1868 and restored in country and colonial American fashion, it's a little like walking into one of those wonderful American folk art gift shops. Rich patriot blue, deep red, hunter green and cream pleasantly combine with antiques, period memorabilia, handmade baskets, dolls, unique folk art and country collectibles.

Built in 1868, The Candlewyck House is a delightful example of Americana-styling in historic Pentwater.

Americana
folk art styling
creates a
delightful
ambiance.

Candlewyck's delightful appearance is the work of John and Mary Jo Neidow, friendly inn-keepers since 1989. Both John and Mary Jo have a keen interest in early American culture and style. In fact, Mary Jo, with a Master's Degree in colonial American history, is particularly knowledgeable on that period and has paid close attention to selecting wallpaper, room colors and décor reminiscent of the period.

The open guest areas of the home, like all of Candlewyck, invite relaxation and mingling. Equally homey are the six nicely sized, varying-themed guest rooms. We enjoyed the cozy warmth of the Seaside Cottage, the homey Fireside suite, and the bright colors

The English Ivy room, with sitting area and private entrance, is a real favorite.

and patriotic vision of colonial America represented in The Patriot room. Hanna's Hideaway, the smallest, is a little nugget of coziness and is tucked under the eaves of the home. One of our favorites is the very appealing English Ivy room. Dark woods and cream walls trimmed with accents of hunter green and cinnamon are distinctively reminiscent of an English country home. Two overstuffed chairs sit before the warming gas-log fireplace and cheery light sparkles from side windows.

Most rooms have sitting areas with fireplaces. Some include multiple beds, VCR's, coffeemakers and microwaves. To meet the comforts of today's guests, all have private baths (two rooms with claw-foot tubs offer hand-held showers), air conditioning, cable TV and in-room (or access to) mini-refrigerators.

Very inviting, the Fireside room is one of our favorites.

A hearty farmer's breakfast is prepared each morning and served family-style in the dining room decorated in colonial farmhouse fashion. Here guests mingle around the large pine table as they eagerly enjoy one of the Neidow's well-prepared meals. Over the years, Mary Jo has developed quite a collection of delicious recipes that are tried-and-true successes among her guests.

Situated on East Lowell Street in Pentwater, The Candlewyck House is centrally located to many of Pentwater's restaurants, unique antique and gift shops, as well as several artisan galleries along Hancock and Second streets. In addition, the ever-popular Silver Lake State Park is just a short drive away. The park is well known for its miles of dunes and great beaches. Visit the Little Sauble Point Lighthouse, or simply while-away the hours on the beach with a good book.

Enjoy the charms of Candlewyck House while you explore this interesting and very scenic community. John and Mary Jo are waiting to meet you.

Dutch Colonial Inn

Holland, Michigan
Telephone: 616-396-3664
Website: www.dutchcolonialinn.com

Located in Region 6

Innkeepers:	Bob and Pat Elenbaas
Accommodations:	Bed and breakfast, 4 rooms with private baths
Extras:	Full breakfasts. A/C, in-room TV, phones with data ports, gas or electric fireplaces, whirlpool tubs.
Rates/Payment:	Nightly $110-$160. Major credit cards, checks.
Miscellaneous:	Caters to adult travelers. No pets/smoking. Corporate rates.
Open:	Year around

Built in 1928 as a wedding gift, the elegant and inviting Dutch Colonial Inn is a lovely reminder of what attracts visitors to the Dutch community of Holland. Located in a residential section of the city, this 8,400 sq. ft. home is tastefully styled and carefully maintained with just the right touch of hominess to make your stay comfortable.

Bob and Pat Elenbaas are certainly part of what make the Dutch Colonial Inn one of Holland's most popular bed and breakfasts. Gracious and caring, the Elenbaas' and their staff are committed to maintaining a welcoming environment. Their motto "Our Home is Your Home" shows in their attitude and manner.

"Our Home is Your Home" is the motto of Bob and Pat Elenbaas, the gracious proprietors of Dutch Colonial Inn.

We visited each of the inn's four guest rooms and were immediately impressed with their spacious, tastefully decorated interiors. Light floral prints, family heirlooms, antiques and lace accents combine with inviting colors of country blue and cream or dusty rose and raspberry to create a relaxed, calming atmosphere.

Romantic and elegant, the Master Suite features a sitting area with gas-log fireplace.

One of our favorite rooms is the Master Suite. Elegantly romantic, its lace trimmed, open canopy queen bed sets the mood. A gas-log fireplace, sitting area and private bath with double whirlpool tub add a special touch. Another favorite is their 700 sq. ft., two-level loft, Tulip Suite, featuring a tall chalet ceiling. The first floor is brightly furnished in white wicker with a gas-log fireplace adding its warm glow. Other amenities include a full entertainment center with cable TV and stereo. A stairway leads to the upstairs loft with king size bed and additional bath featuring a double whirlpool tub. This suite is particularly appealing for those seeking more space and privacy.

Enhancing the Dutch Colonial's appeal is the upstairs Common Room. Its open area is great for mingling with others. A large, cherry wood dining table and tasteful collection of furniture and antiques along with a welcoming fireplace create a tranquil atmosphere. The room also offers a small kitchen.

Guests may prefer to relax in the elegant yet comfortably styled main floor living

**The two-level Tulip Room is wonderful for that very special occasion.
A two-person whirlpool tub is tucked away in the upstairs bathroom.**

room with its impressive array of antiques including Bob and Pat's special collection of Ruby Flash King's Crown Thumbprint glassware. Off the living room is the cheery sunroom perfect for enjoying a little quiet time.

Certainly, we cannot overlook the delicious breakfasts that are an important part of the Dutch Colonial experience. Breakfasts may be brought to your door or, if you'd like to mingle, served in the formal dining room. Brightened by surrounding windows, touched by lace, fresh flowers and warmed by the deep cherry wood dining table, it's a lovely spot to begin your day.

Breakfast always starts with a fresh fruit cup (and a dollop of creamy yogurt), juices and freshly baked muffins. Main course specialties include quiche, ham and egg casseroles or French toast. Their mouth-watering fresh baked

Full breakfasts are served in the formal dining room.

desserts include their very popular cranberry crumble cake and Swedish Kringle (a light almond pastry).

After your delicious breakfast, get ready for a full day of fun exploring this wonderful area of Michigan. Holland is best known for its May Tulip Festival.

During the holidays, Dutch Colonial adds decorative touches to create cheerful memories.

Holland's Windmill Island is a popular attraction.

In spring, the Tulip Time Festival should not be missed.

The community nurtures its incredible collection of these brilliant perennials to ensure their colorful blooms greet visitors as the festival begins. Parades, live entertainment (including traditional Dutch dances) and other events add to the celebratory atmosphere.

Throughout the year, Windmill Island continues to be a popular visitor's stop with its 235-year-old Dutch windmill and more than 36 acres of gardens. A short drive away is picturesque, Saugatuck. Saugatuck's nostalgic downtown area is noted for its unique variety of gift shops, many offering the work of area artisans.

The Dutch Colonial Inn is a very nice choice for those seeking a welcoming respite from daily life while enjoying the adventures and beauty along Michigan's west shore. It's nice to know that Pat, Bob and their friendly staff are there to welcome you home.

The Lake House

Mears, Michigan
Telephone: 313-886-8996

Located in Region 6

Owners:	Ron and Theresa Mack
Accommodation:	Vacation home, 3 bedrooms
Extras:	Two baths. Fully equipped kitchen, garbage disposal, microwave, bread maker. Ceiling fans, TV and VCR. Wraparound deck with screen porch. Outdoor hot/cold shower. BBQ.
Rates/Payment:	Weekly $800-$1,200. Checks.
Miscellaneous:	One block from Lake Michigan beach access. No pets/smoking.
Open:	Year around

Just four miles from Pentwater off North Lakeshore Drive, you'll find Ron and Theresa Mack's 1,400 sq. ft. vacation retreat, The Lake House. Decorated in a blend of antiques, 1930's-1950's memorabilia and contemporary furnishings, the home's open styling is ideal for sharing laughter and stories with friends and family.

The main room is a spacious 24'x26' area that combines kitchen, dining and living rooms. Rocking chairs and sofa surround the TV/VCR near the home's entrance. To the back is a well equipped kitchen, which even includes a bread-maker. Down a short hallway are three bedrooms with double and/or twin

The open-styled Lake House is just off North Lakeshore Drive.

A 17 ft. chalet ceiling increases the spacious atmosphere of the great room that combines kitchen, dining and living room.

beds. The master bedroom has its own private bath with the second bath sitting across from the other rooms.

A particularly appealing aspect of the home is its very large, wraparound porch that includes both open and screened sections. The screened portion is simply furnished with

The three bedrooms vary in size with the master bedroom (above) being the largest.

picnic table and 1950's styled dinette set. Surrounded by trees in a park-like setting, this is a good spot to enjoy your morning coffee, relax after a busy day, or play games during rainy times. Exiting the screened section, the porch opens to the home's front with a peak-a-boo view of the sparkling lake between trees and homes beyond.

Just down the quiet road, a stairway takes you to the lake.

An enclosed sunroom is part of the home's large wrap-around deck.

Of course, we would be remiss if we omitted mentioning the home's namesake ... *the lake*. Just a short walk down the quiet street is your access to Lake Michigan. A well-made stairway takes you to a beautiful, 700 ft. stretch of Lake Michigan shoreline complete with sand and waves.

Should you need a break from the beach, Pentwater is just a few miles away. You'll enjoy the New England charm of this cozy little community with an assortment of cheery cafes, fine restaurants, antique and gift shops. Throughout the seasons, visitors adventure out on the nearby Hart-Montague trails that run 23 miles through scenic farmland and woods. Fishing enthusiasts can charter a boat for the big-fish experience. Silver Lake Dunes at Silver Lake State Park are a very popular attraction. Take a wild ride in a dune buggy as you explore the expanse of crystal sands that stretch three miles long, 1-1/2 miles wide and 350 ft. high.

Enjoy the New England charm of nearby Pentwater.

The Lake House ... think of it as your home-away-from-home with Lake Michigan as your incredibly large in-ground pool. Add to that the charm of Pentwater with the excitement of the dunes and you've got yourself one fine vacation experience.

Mason House

Saugatuck, Michigan
Telephone: 847-498-2938
Email: patkresq@msn.com

Located in
Region 6

Owner:	Patricia Rotchford
Accommodations:	Private cottage, two bedrooms
Extras:	Central A/C, fireplace, TV/VCR, telephone/ computer hook-up. Two baths. Laundry facilities. Four-seasons room. Linens provided. Equipped kitchen with dishwasher and espresso/cappuccino machine. Private deck, grill, outdoor cabinet/sink. Victorian sitting garden. Shared in-ground pool.
Rates/Payment:	Weekly from $750; weekends from $345. Check.
Miscellaneous:	No smoking. Ask about pets.
Open:	Year around

In the Wizard of Oz, Dorothy immortalized the phrase "There's no place like home." The word home conjures up all sorts of warm, fuzzy thoughts. Patricia Rotchford's vacation home is the epitome of all these things.

During our trip to the Mason House, we had spent most of the day driving in one of Michigan's worst late summer storms. After a long day, we turned down the quiet residential street and there, protected by a cluster of tall oak

The Mason House ... an inviting, homey retreat.

trees, sat the Mason House. With its country maize exterior, bright white trim and picket fence, the home was a bright spot on our dark, waterlogged trip.

A stone walking path takes you to the backyard's furnished deck with grill. Especially handy is an outdoor cabinet with sink where you can store your cooking paraphernalia and conveniently wash-up, rinse food or utensils before and after the meal.

The backyard deck features a handy, outdoor cabinet with sink next to the grill.

An in-ground pool, shared with a few neighbors is near the yard, and just the right touch for those warm summer days. Pat told us her guests are just about the only ones she has ever seen in the pool. A Victorian garden surrounds the home. Intimate sitting areas are strategically placed so that, at any time of the day, you can relax in the garden with your choice of sun or shade.

Once inside this vacation retreat, you'll feel right at home. It is meticulously decorated and picture perfect, but always with your comfort in mind. The Mason House is large enough to handle the 10 person maximum, but can still be called cozy. Pale daffodil colored walls accent the living room with warm cranberry window treatments, carpeting, chair, floral sofa and love seat. The room's blend of colors and decor create a captivating ambiance. Furnishings surround the fireplace, perfect for those chilly evenings, and an entertainment center holds a TV and VCR.

A fully stocked kitchen has nearly every conceivable item you would need. There's even a popcorn maker,

The kitchen has a dishwasher and espresso machine.

Charming decor and comfortable furnishings make the home very inviting.

cappuccino maker and, of course, dishwasher. With stripped wallpaper, cream tile and skylight, it's a cheerful place to prepare your favorite dishes. The bright white four-season room is off the kitchen. Filled with plaid sofa, hunter green wicker chairs and an eclectic mix of accents, this would have been one of our favorite rooms. However, the Mason House has so many favorite rooms, it's hard to pick one.

The rich-blue walls of the home's lovely master bedroom, with private bath, are accented with cream wallpaper and trim. Furnishings and overall decor seamlessly blend for that perfect touch. The second, smaller bedroom is cream colored with the bed's headboard resting against a deep raspberry wall. It comes complete with patchwork quilt.

It should be noted that, since our visit, Pat has made some changes. This is her doll house, and she is constantly redoing, redesigning and redecorating.

Her most recent changes include some fresh landscaping. For the interior, a new table and chandelier in the dining area were added and a popular area designer has enhanced the walls with some dry brush painting.

For a day of adventure, head over to Saugatuck. Enjoy the many art galleries and shops. Stroll along the harbor boardwalk lined with historic buildings and quaint parks. Frequent visitors to Saugatuck seldom miss an opportunity to stop by the 75-year-old drugstore notorious for the best hand-creamed sodas and malted shakes in the world.

Appealing decor extends to the master bedroom.

For a little fun and adventure, head west to tour the dunes or take a dune ride. If you enjoy boating, rentals are plentiful or enjoy a cruise on the historic *Queen of Saugatuck* stern-wheel riverboat.

What vacation in Saugatuck would be complete without a day at the world-famous Oval Beach? The beach is known for its beauty and incredible expanse of crystal sand that stretches deep into Lake Michigan. It's hard to find better beaches anywhere. Many travel magazines have recognized Saugatuck's main beach. In fact, it has been placed in the "Top 25 Beaches in the World".

Regardless of how you spend your time, Patricia Rotchford's Mason House is the great spot to start and end each day. You will always feel welcome and at home in this charming abode, at a price very easy to handle.

Rosewood Resort

Saugatuck, Michigan
Telephone: 616-396-1502

Located in Region 6 ⑥

Owner:	Brent Kleinheksel
Accommodations:	7 cottages on Lake Macatawa (2 to 8 bedrooms)
Extras:	Fully equipped kitchens with microwaves. TV/VCR, bed linens. Some cottages include fireplace, washer/dryer, dishwasher, CATV, screened porch, deck, patio, water view. Also available, firepit, BBQ, volleyball, large sandy beach.
Rates/Payment:	Weekly $1,400-$4,200. Major credit cards, check.
Miscellaneous:	Meeting room holds 20-30 people. Meeting equipment (slide projector, screen, flip chart). No pets.
Open:	Year around

An intimate wedding, just for your closest family and friends, under a canopy of old oak, or on the beach of a shimmering lake. Seems almost too good to be true. But it's possible at the Rosewood Resort. Rosewood can handle that special moment, family reunion, corporate off-site or church retreat in a relaxed and private setting. Owner, Brent Kleinheksel, has taken

The diverse size of Rosewoods' cottages and the great beach make it ideal for group gatherings.

seven very different cottages and created a resort great for a single family of four or a family reunion of 50, give or take a few. At Rosewood, there is plenty of room to work, play or just relax on the beach.

Oak and pine trees provide a natural cover for the cottages and grounds that break away to an expansive, glistening beach. The pale blue, shallow waters of Lake Macatawa are very safe for children and much warmer than Lake Michigan. Yet if you like the big lake, it's just down the road.

Completely remodeled cottages range in size, amenities and decor. Most have large living rooms, new furniture, attractive kitchens and bathrooms. Floor coverings vary and consist of tile, wood, carpeting and linoleum. For the most part, bedrooms are simple but functional.

There is one large home, the Retreat House, that accommodates up to 30 people. Other units range in size and sleep from 4 to 11. Brent keeps his homes and cottages in good condition because, unlike some resorts, he doesn't overcrowd them. At Rosewood, when a cottage sleeps 6, people will have plenty of room. Four of the units face the water and three others sit behind them. Cottages can be rented separately or as one unit, when available, to handle large groups.

At the three-story Retreat House, the living room's inviting appeal starts with a large, contemporary sofa, chairs and tables around the fireplace. Bright white walls and dark-beamed ceilings are a dramatic touch. The long enclosed porch and wicker furniture off the living room make this a comfortable gathering place for family or co-workers. To accommodate all, there are two kitchens. The large one is contemporary and the smaller functional.

There are also two dining rooms and 3.5 bathrooms. The large dining area can be used as a conference/meeting room to easily handle 25 to 30 people.

Not too big, not too small, the comfortably styled Kiwi House (pictured here) was our favorite.

Brent even has some of those AV items needed for meetings, such as flip charts, slide projectors and screens. To handle the crowd, the Retreat House has a washer and dryer.

The second and third floors contain all the bedrooms. There's nothing fancy in these rooms, but the beds are certainly comfy. The third floor is one long room with five twin beds set-up barrack style and one bunk bed. Kids would love it.

Our favorite cottage is the Kiwi house. Its 1,400 sq. ft. can comfortably handle 11 people. We were attracted to a couple of features that set it apart from many cottages. First, it faces the water and the first floor living room has a wall of glass that gives you a spectacular, panoramic view of the lake and beach. Second, uncluttered, contemporary living rooms are found on the upper and lower levels of the home, ideal for two families. The upper level has light wood floors with curved sectional, glass tables and recessed lighting.

Cottages range in size with decor and style varying significantly.

One side of the room has a fireplace and the other overlooks the lake. Dining and kitchen are behind the sofa and maintain a contemporary style, as does the bathroom. The lower level living room offers similar styling, with carpeted floor and fireplace. We noted that the dining/ kitchen areas look as if they have been completely redone. There are two bedrooms on the lower level and one on the main floor. Queen, full, bunk beds and sofa sleeper accommodate the crowd.

The beach has volleyball, firepit and fine white sand that's groomed regularly. It's a large beach made for active team sports. Each cottage has a BBQ grill and picnic table, with a couple of extra picnic tables on the grounds.

Just a few hours from Detroit, Lansing, Chicago or Toledo, it's an easy destination from many major urban areas. Rosewood Resort is in a great location with well-managed cottages and homes. Able to accommodate a wide range of needs, Brent's property is worth looking into.

Schoenberger House
Bed & Breakfast

Ludington, Michigan
Telephone: 231-843-4435
Website: www.schoenbergerhouse.com

Located in Region 6 ⑥

Innkeeper:	Tamara Schoenberger
Accommodations:	Bed and breakfast, 5 rooms with private baths.
Extras:	Expanded continental breakfasts. Five fireplaces, library, music room.
Rates/Payment:	Nightly $145-$245. Major credit cards, checks.
Miscellaneous:	Included in *Historic Homes of America* and *Grand Homes of the Midwest*. Caters to adult travelers. Corporate rates. No pets/smoking.
Open:	Year around

One step inside the Schoenberger House of Ludington and you'll be wrapped in the incredible aura of opulence during turn-of-the-century America. There are few homes built in recent years that can compare to the workmanship and attention to detail found in this exquisite 1903 mansion.

The original owner of this grand home was a gentleman by the name of Warren Cartier. A wealthy lumberman, he chose only the most skilled carpenters and

Built by a wealthy lumber baron in 1903, the Schoenberger House is an excellent example of opulence in the early 20th century.

selected only the finest woods to create this home. Today one is awed not only by the quality and intricacy of design, but also by the diverse selection of wood. From warm white oak, rich cherry and black walnut to rare mahogany and American sycamore, each room is a tribute to

Mr. Cartier designed the home's balcony in the hope it would be used for giving his acceptance speech as Michigan's new governor.

the remarkable craftsmanship of its original designer and builders. The impressive oak staircase just off the main hallway turns onto a dramatic second floor balcony. From what we understand, Mr. Cartier had the balcony designed in the hope it would be used for his acceptance speech as Michigan's new governor. As it turned out, however, voters decided otherwise.

Around 1950 the home was purchased by the Schoenbergers and has since remained in the family. It became a bed and breakfast in 1995.

The exquisitely detailed interior is a tribute to the workmanship of its original builders.

ALL RATES SUBJECT TO CHANGE

Bedrooms are spacious and retain a distinct 1920's style.

Family portraits, heirlooms and antiques are found throughout the home, including the five upstairs guest rooms. Each has a private bath, is spacious and comfortably appointed with queen or king beds. Their two-room suite includes a private balcony. Of particular note, four of the five private baths are more recent additions to the home. The fifth (original) bathroom retains its historical authenticity with deep tub, open ribbed shower (currently not used), toilet and bidet. We were amazed at its design, which was certainly a leader of its time.

Around 9:00 a.m. each morning, guests are treated to an expanded continental breakfast, which is served in the elegant dining room. Meals are carefully planned with a focus on visual presentation. Breakfast treats include such

Unique use of sycamore wood in the elegant dining room adds a distinguishing touch.

items as fresh croissants or other baked goods, a variety of cheeses, seasonal fruits and beverages.

The Schoenberger House is located in the delightful community of Ludington where you'll find plenty to do throughout the year. Perhaps one of the area's most visited attractions is Historic White Pine Village. This little community of 21 buildings recreates Mason County's history with events throughout the year. During the warmer days, explore miles of shoreline at Ludington State Park. If you're a lighthouse enthusiastic, visit The Big Sable Point Lighthouse, offering daily tours. Of special note, this area is *dunes country,* so head on out to Hamlin Lake or Silver Lake ... just a short drive away.

Catering to adult guests, the Schoenberger House offers a rare experience in early 20th Century luxury. Make reservations early.

REGION 1

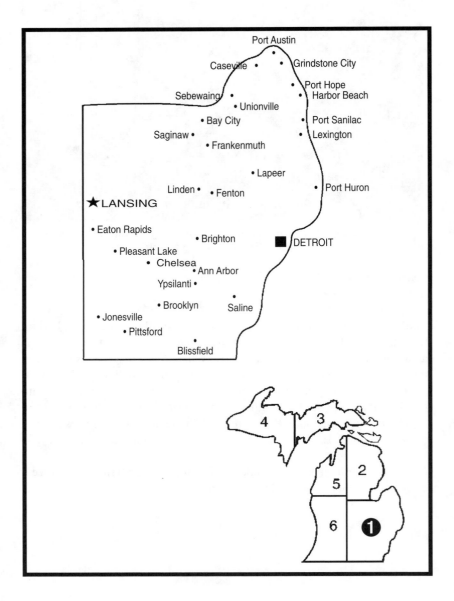

BLISSFIELD & THE IRISH HILLS AREA

INCLUDES: BROOKLYN • JONESVILLE • PITTSFORD

Surround yourself with the beauty of the **Irish Hills,** a unique blend of modern and historic. Visit the Croswell Opera House, in Adrian, the oldest continuously operating theater of its kind in Michigan. It features live theater productions as well as special art exhibits. Michigan Futurity is the place to be for horse racing excitement.

Picnic by one of the Irish Hills' 50 spring-fed lakes, ride amongst its beautiful rolling hills, and take a trip to historic Walker Tavern in Cambridge State Historic Park. Enjoy a nature walk through the 670-acre Hidden Lake Gardens at Michigan State University. Of course, there's always the fun of Mystery Hill. Ready for more? Then step back in time to the 1800s and enjoy the pioneering spirit that lives on at Stagecoach Stop U.S.A. Sit back with a sarsaparilla in the saloon, pan for gold, or take a train ride ... but be careful ... we hear there's masked bandits in the area.

Join the excitement of Indy and stock car races each summer (June-August) at the Michigan International Speedway in the Irish Hills. While enjoying the beautiful fall colors, don't forget to stop in **Brooklyn** and join the fun at Oktoberfest or their arts and crafts festival. Anyone for cross-country skiing or snowmobiling? No matter what time of year, the Cambridge State Historic Park and the Irish Hills are always waiting.

BLISSFIELD

HIRAM D. ELLIS INN

(517) 486-3155
BED & BREAKFAST

All rooms in this 1880's 2-story brick Victorian inn offer CATV, private baths, spa services available with reservation. Come, relax and enjoy the many antiques and specialty shops in the area. Full breakfast served each morning. 4 rooms. Business discounts.

Nightly $90-$110 (Corporate/Business $65)

BROOKLYN (IN THE IRISH HILLS)

CHICAGO STREET INN   (517) 592-3888 • EMAIL: chiinn@aol.com
CARL & MARY MOORE   BED & BREAKFAST

Antique furnishing, European stained glass windows, and a wicker filled veranda decorate this 1800's Queen Anne Victorian home. Full breakfasts featuring homemade baked goods are unexpected treats! Minutes from lakes, golfing, antiquing. 4 suites with Jacuzzi, 3 include fireplaces. 6 rooms with private baths, A/C. *Website: www.chicagostreetinn.com*

Nightly $85-$155

Editor's Note: Well established, reputable B&B catering to adult guests. Appealing antique styling and period pieces.

DEWEY LAKE MANOR   (517) 467-7122 • EMAIL: deweylk@frontiernet.net
THE PHILLIPS FAMILY   BED & BREAKFAST

★ EDITOR'S CHOICE ★

Sitting atop a knoll overlooking Dewey Lake on 18 scenic acres, a "country retreat" awaits Manor guests! Picnic by the lake — enjoy evening bonfires. Hearty breakfast buffet served on the glass enclosed porch (weather permitting). At night, snack on popcorn or sip a cup of cider...there are always cookies! Five rooms with private baths, fireplaces and A/C. *Website: www.getaway2smi.com/dewey*

Nightly $72-$130

Editor's Note: Very comfy, well maintained and nicely appointed B&B. Located on spacious, rolling grounds with fabulous lake views.

DUANE LOCKE   (734) 971-7558
PRIVATE COTTAGE

Lakefront cottage on Wamplers Lake, in the Irish Hills, sleeps up to 6. Features gas fireplace, TV/VCR, modern private bath with tub/shower (soft water). Excellent swimming, fishing, boat included. Near MIS. Available year around. No pets.

Weekly $900

JONESVILLE

THE MUNRO HOUSE   (517) 849-9292 • (800) 320-3792
MIKE & LORI VENTURINI   BED & BREAKFAST

★ EDITOR'S CHOICE ★

Located at Highways 12 and 99 in South Central Michigan. Historic Greek
Revival Mansion was once a Station on the Underground Railroad. Queen
beds, private baths, fireplaces, Jacuzzi tubs, CATV, VCR. Full breakfast. 100%
Air Conditioned and smoke free. *Website: www.munrohouse.com*
Nightly $99-$179

*Editor's Note: The history associated with this lovely B&B along with uniquely
styled rooms make this a nice choice.*

PITTSFORD

THE ROCKING HORSE INN   (517) 523-3826
MARY ANN & PHIL MEREDITH   BED & BREAKFAST
Guests love spending peaceful moments on the wrap around porch of this
Italianate-style farmhouse while sipping lemonade and eating the dessert of
the evening. Freshly prepared full breakfasts. Close to Hillsdale College, shop-
ping, golf, 15 minutes to Michigan Speedway. Four rooms with AC, TV,
VCR, private baths. Corporate rates.

Nightly $50-$80

*Editor's Note: Homey atmosphere with charming decor. Another nice choice for
the area.*

ANN ARBOR/CHELSEA • BRIGHTON • SALINE • YPSILANTI

Ann Arbor, home of the University of Michigan. This cosmo-
politan area offers year around activities for its visitors,
from arts and crafts to live theater and entertainment. While here, be
sure to stroll the many unique shops. Visit the University of Michigan planetarium. Canoe, swim or hike in Gallup Park. In late July, arts and craft enthusiasts never miss the Ann Arbor Art Fair featuring noted artisans from
across the country. Only 10 miles from Ann Arbor rests **Saline.** Well known
for its historic homes and antique shops, the area hosts nationally recognized
antique shows from April through November. **Ypsilanti**, home of Eastern

Michigan University, is also a city of diverse activities. Among its many points of interest include Wiard's Orchard which offers fresh cider, tours and hayrides. Enjoy the festivities for a yearly Heritage Festival (celebrated each August) commemorating its early French settlers.

Surrounded by lakes, the **Brighton** area offers excellent golf courses, parks, downhill and cross country skiing. In the summer, Independence, Folk Art and Farmer's Market festivals abound at Mill Pond located in the heart of the city.

ANN ARBOR AND CHELSEA

THE URBAN RETREAT BED & BREAKFAST   (734) 971-8110
BED & BREAKFAST

Contemporary ranch-styled home, antique furnished, set in a quiet neighborhood, minutes from downtown and UM/EMU campuses. Adjacent parkland with walking trails. Breakfast served overlooking the garden. Member National Wildlife Federation "Backyard Wildlife Habitat." Resident housecats. A/C. 2 room. Inspected and approved. By reservation only. *Website: www.theurbanretreat.com*

Nightly $60-$75

WATERLOO GARDENS BED & BREAKFAST   (734) 433-1612
EMAIL: gary.offenbacher@prodigy.net
BED & BREAKFAST

Contemporary ranch home located on the north end of Chelsea near Ann Arbor. Guest rooms offer private and shared baths. Large Jacuzzi, video library, fitness equipment and great sunsets. A/C. Full breakfasts. No smoking. We have Golden Retrievers. *Website: www.waterloogardensbb.com*

Nightly $85 (single) - $135 (2 bedroom suite)

BRIGHTON

BRIGHTON HOME   (810) 227-3225
PRIVATE HOME

Built in 1990, this home sleeps 8 and is completely furnished. Located in a secluded area. The balcony overlooks the water only 10 ft. away. Features fully equipped kitchen, microwave, freezer, dishwasher, washer and dryer, use of rowboat and dock.

Weekly   (summer) $900   (off season rates available)

ISLAND LAKE RESORT   (810) 229-6723 • EMAIL: ebabrawski@email.com
EDMUND BAPRAWSKI   DUPLEX/COTTAGES
Fronts Briggs and Island Lakes. Year around resort offers 1-3 bedroom housekeeping cottages and duplex units. Furnished and equipped (bring bed linens
and towels). Use of boat is included. Beautiful sandy beach, playground, picnic tables. 50% deposit required. Pedestrian underpass below Academy Road.
Weekly $225-$500   (duplex units less)

SALINE

THE HOMESTEAD BED & BREAKFAST   (734) 429-9625
SHIRLEY GROSSMAN   EMAIL: homestead_b_b@msn.com
                                               BED & BREAKFAST
1851 circa brick farmhouse filled with period antiques, features comfort in
Victorian elegance. Cross-country ski, stroll or relax on 50 acres of farmland.
Only 10 minutes from Ann Arbor. A/C. Corporate rates. 5 rooms.
Nightly $40-$75

YPSILANTI

PARISH HOUSE INN   (800) 480-4866 • (734) 480-4800
CHRIS MASON   BED & BREAKFAST
                     ★ EDITOR'S CHOICE ★
1893 "Queen Anne" styled home first constructed as a parsonage. Extensively
renovated in 1993. Victorian styled with period antiques. Fireplace, Jacuzzi,
CATV, central A/C, and telephones. Hearty breakfast. Enjoy near-by golfing,
antiquing, biking and restaurants. No smoking. 9 rooms w/private baths.
Nightly $89-$150 (Corporate Rate $85)
*Editor's Note: Appealing rooms and knowledgeable innkeeper make this a nice
choice for vacation or business travelers. See our review in this edition.*

LANSING

INCLUDES: EATON RAPIDS • PLEASANT LAKE

Lansing has been our State Capital since 1847. Visiting the Capitol
building is an absolute must for travelers in the area. Guides
conduct free tours daily! Also take some time to visit the Michigan
Historical Museum and explore the state's dynamic and exciting past. Relax
on a riverboat cruise of the Grand River. There's also plenty of excellent

golfing, shops, galleries, live theater and restaurants. The Boars Head Theater (Michigan's only resident theater) and Woldumar Nature Center are additional attractions.

If you're looking for an intimate and distinctive dining experience, you'll want to try Dusty's English Inn in **Eaton Rapids** — only a short drive from Lansing. For simpler yet well prepared homemade meals, you'll enjoy *Ellie's Country Kitchen* on East Grand River in Williamston for breakfast, lunch and dinner. Just down the street, is the *Red Cedar Grill* with its casually upscale atmosphere.

LANSING & EATON RAPIDS

Dusty's English Inn
(517) 663-2500 • (800) 858-0598
Bed & Breakfast

Resting along the Grand River, amidst lovely gardens and woodland trails, this elegant English Tudor-style home is decorated throughout with antiques and reproductions. Its intimate restaurant offers fine dining and cocktails in the European tradition. Full English breakfast is served each morning.

Nightly $105-$175 (dbl., plus tax)

PLEASANT LAKE

Rockfish Inn
Heidi/Mike Ritchison
(517) 769-6448
Private Cottage

★ EDITOR'S CHOICE ★

Vacation cottage on all sports lake with sandy bottom. 3 bedrooms, sleeps 5-7, one bath, fully carpeted, with large fully equipped kitchen. Walk to fine dining, playground and 27 hole golf course (x-country skiing in winter). Enjoy fabulous sunsets, grassy sunbathing area, private dock, boat hoist, TV with VCR. Grill provided. Open year around.

Weekly $500-$600

Editor's Note: Well maintained cottage on narrow lot. The wood deck offers a great view of lake.

PORT HURON • LAPEER

Port Huron joins Lake Huron's waters with the St. Clair River. This port town is the home of the Blue Water Bridge, arts and craft fairs, waterfront dining and wonderful views from the shoreline. While in the area, visit Fort Gratiot Lighthouse and the Knowlton Ice Museum. In July, enjoy the excitement of the Blue Water Festival and the 3-day Port Huron to Mackinac Island Yacht Races.

Approximately 35 miles west of Port Huron is the scenic countryside of **Lapeer**. Surrounded by orchards, the area is known for its blueberry farms. The many lakes and streams in this region offer good fishing. In the winter, enjoy one of Lapeer's groomed cross-country ski trails.

LAPEER

HART HOUSE   (810) 667-9106
ELLIE HAYES   BED & BREAKFAST
Listed on the National Historic Register, this Queen Anne B&B was home of the first Mayor, Rodney G. Hart. Full breakfasts served each morning. Private baths. 4 rooms. No smoking.

Nightly $40-$50

PORT HURON

THE VICTORIAN INN   (810) 984-1437
MARVIN/SUSAN BURKE   BED & BREAKFAST
Queen Anne styled inn, authentically restored, offers guests a timeless ambiance. Each room uniquely decorated. Enjoy the Inn's classically creative cuisine, fine wines and gracious service. Pub in cellar. One hour from Detroit. 4 rooms, private/shared baths.

Nightly $100-$150

LEXINGTON • PORT AUSTIN • CASEVILLE

INCLUDES: GRINDSTONE CITY • HARBOR BEACH • PORT HOPE
PORT SANILAC • SEBEWAING • UNIONVILLE

Known for its historic homes, **Lexington** has excellent boating, fishing and swimming. Visit the general store (dating from the 1870's) and indulge in the tasty nostalgia of their "penny candy" counter. Walk to the marina and visit the old lighthouse which was built in 1886.

Further north is Port Hope, home of the Bottom Land Preserve. The Lighthouse County Park, just outside town, is an ideal spot for scuba diving enthusiasts to view under water wrecks of 19th Century vessels.

Take the turn off to Huron City and stroll among the historic recreations of a 19th Century village. Visit and see if you can spot some of the original grinding wheels made from sandstone. We understand the general store in Grindstone serves ice cream cones big enough to satisfy the hottest and hungriest of visitors.

Celebrate both outstanding sunrises and sunsets at the tip of the thumb in **Port Austin**. Stop at Finan's Drug Store's nostalgic soda fountain in the area's restored business district. Discover the rolling sand dunes hidden behind the trees at Port Crescent State Park. Relax on its excellent 3-mile beach. This is also a bird watcher's haven with abundant numbers of hawk, oriole, osprey and bluebird populations. Moving around the thumb is **Caseville**. Drive along its half-mile stretch of Saginaw Bay Beach. Here's a great area for perch fishing, boating, swimming and just plain relaxing.

For a unique dining experience in Port Austin, try *The Bank* on Blake Street ... a little pricey, but worth it. This historic former bank is now an excellent restaurant, noted for its sourdough bread with herb butter and freshly prepared meals. Another excellent dining treat is offered at the *Garfield Inn* on Lake Street that serves as both a B&B and elegant restaurant. *The Farm Restaurant,* off M25, is another well known, reputable eatery. For more casual, relaxed dining you'll want to stop at the *Port Hope Hotel Restaurant* (in Port Hope) where we understand they prepare some hearty and very tasty hamburgers and other basics at affordable prices. In the Port Sanilac area, fresh perch is served up daily at *The Bellaire Lodge*. Check out *Mary's Diner* for good, old-fashion family-style meals. Craving pizza? Then head over to the *Dry Dock*. *Eric's Landing Restaurant* is one of the newer eateries found by the marina in Port Sanilac.

CASEVILLE

BELLA VISTA INN & COTTAGES
(989) 856-2650
COTTAGE/EFFICIENCY/MOTEL RESORT

1 bedroom efficiencies with kitchenettes, 2 bedroom cottages with full kitchens. Motel and cottages have lake views from picture windows and include screened porch, linens, tiled bath, CATV w/HBO. Heated outdoor pool, grills, picnic tables, sun deck, shuffleboard courts, swings, 400 ft. of beach.

Nightly $79-$89 (motel)   Weekly $950 (cottages)

THE LODGE AT OAK POINTE
(989) 856-3055
BED & BREAKFAST

Five deluxe guest rooms with private baths, each with 2-person whirlpool tub, gas log fireplace, queen canopy bed and private screened porch overlooking pond. All in this 11,000 sq. ft. log lodge on 30 wooded acres. Handicap access. Continental Plus breakfast. *Website: www.oakpointelodge.com*

Nightly $79-$109

GRINDSTONE CITY

WHALEN'S GRINDSTONE SHORES
(989) 738-7664
CABIN/GUEST ROOM RESORT

Located in Historic Grindstone City at the top of the thumb on a scenic harbor waterfront. Five efficiency units with kitchen facilities and CATV. Five guest sleeping rooms. Gift shop. Laundry room. R.V. Park. Boat docks. Good fishing. Charters available. Call for reservations.

Nightly $45-$85

Editor's Note: Nice spot for fishing enthusiasts. Clean, small, basic cottages, closely spaced. Scenic harbor. Comfortable sleeping rooms at the main house.

HARBOR BEACH

ANGEL VIEW COTTAGE
(810) 359-2140
DENISE & CURT MANNINEN
PRIVATE COTTAGE

Clean, cozy cottage, remodeled in 2002. On Lake Huron near Harbor Beach. Two bedrooms, walk-in shower. Bed linens provided, bring towels. Complete kitchen, living room with TV-VCR, fireplace. Outside patio, BBQ, firepit. Birdwatchers' paradise. Fishing, swimming, boating nearby. Pets OK. No smoking. Open year around.

Weekly $700 (3 days/$375)

LEXINGTON

BEACHCOMBER RESORT MOTEL & APARTMENTS

(810) 359-8859
COTTAGE/MOTEL RESORT

Spacious grounds, sandy beach, swimming pool, tennis court, barbeques, comfortable rooms, A/C, TV, family units, efficiencies, cottages, special occasion suite with fireplace and kitchenette facing beach. No pets. 4 miles north of Lexington on M25 on Lake Huron.

Nightly $51 (and up)

COZMA'S COTTAGES

(810) 359-8150 • (313) 881-3313
COTTAGE RESORT

Located on 2 acres in a secluded, beautiful, park-like setting along 200 ft. of private, sandy beach. Volleyball/badminton court, shuffleboard, horseshoes, kiddie swings, stone BBQ grills, picnic tables, ceiling or wall fans. Showers in all units. Bonfires on the beach nightly. Ideal for family reunions.

Weekly $420 (and up)

LITTLE WHITE COTTAGES

(616) 669-5187
PRIVATE COTTAGES

Right on Lake Huron! Experience a real old-fashioned cottage with a comfortable blend of antique and modern furnishings. Swing serenely on our beautiful, shady bank as you contemplate the majesty of Lake Huron only steps away. Low bluff and excellent beach for swimming. Delightfully unique cottages have large screened porches, fireplaces, and are completely furnished, except linens. Relax and unwind and let the Seadog or Nymph be your "place on the lake" this summer! No pets/smoking. Sleeps 4-6.

Exterior of Nymph

Weekly $450-$895

Editor's Note: On a small but quiet lot. Owners continue to make significant upgrades to add to the comfort and appearance of these older cottages.

LUSKY'S LAKEFRONT COTTAGES

TOLL FREE: (877) 327-6889 • (810) 327-6889

COTTAGE RESORT

Voted "Michigan's Best Family Resort" in 2002, *The Detroit News.* Cozy and comfortable, ceiling fans, CATV, picnic tables, BBQ grills, fully equipped kitchens, private bathrooms. Screened porches have good view of lake and play area. Play area features airplane swings, play boats, tire swirl, gymset with tube slide, large sandbox. Also volley ball, basketball, shuffleboard, paddle-boats and rowboats. Stop at our novelty store for candy, pop, ice cream and trinkets galore — at old fashioned prices! All this makes for a fun, relaxing and affordable family vacation place where memories are made and treasured. Rentals available daily-weekly. Pets allowed for an additional charge. *Website: www.luskys.com*

Weekly $325 (and up)   Nightly $60 (and up)

Editor's Note: New owners in 2000. Basic, traditional cottage. Very nice beach.

THE POWELL HOUSE

NANCY POWELL

(810) 359-5533

BED & BREAKFAST

★ EDITOR'S CHOICE ★

Warm and gracious 1852 Victorian architecture and decor; resting on 4 acres, tree-shaded and gardened, The Powell House is a peaceful escape. Walk to the beach, relax in the gardens or wander in town. Comfortable beds and delicious breakfasts awaits all guests. Private baths. Open all year. Nightly $85-$90

Editor's Note: Historic home, relaxed ambiance, maintained in very good condition by a caring owner. Nice choice.

MARLENE WILSON   **(989) 635-2911 • (866) 586-7851**
PRIVATE HOME

3,000 sq. ft. home on 4 acres with stairway to 250 ft. of beach front. Four bedrooms (sleeps 8), furnished with equipped kitchen, washer and dryer, shower, full and 1/2 bath. CATV and VCR, picnic tables and grill. Enjoy spectacular sunrises or scenic night views of The Blue Water Bridge, or views of the grounds and waters of Lake Huron from the fully enclosed porch. Advance security deposit and payment required.

Weekly $1,250-$1,500 (seasonal rates May-Oct.)

Editor's Note: Older home on a scenic bluff overlooks the lake and offers plenty of room for those who crave it. Beach with mix of pebbles, rocks and sand.

PORT AUSTIN

CAPTAIN'S INN   **(989) 738-8321 • RES. 888-277-6631**
DAVID & DEBBIE RAMEY   BED & BREAKFAST

★ EDITOR'S CHOICE ★

Impressively renovated, this spacious Pre-Civil War home offers an inviting blend of antiques, period styling and modern conveniences. CATV. 5 charming guest rooms (3 with private bath; 2 share a bath). Continental Plus breakfasts. Just blocks from restaurants/shops. Open year around. No pets/smoking.

Nightly $64-$125

Editor's Note: One of the area's newest B&B's. Beautifully restored and tastefully styled. A new favorite and highly recommended. See our review in this edition.

GARFIELD INN   **(800) 373-5254 • EMAIL: garfield_inn@hotmail.com**
BED & BREAKFAST

Visited by President Garfield in 1860. Inn features period antiques and premier restaurant. For that special occasion ask about the "Presidential Room". Rooms feature double and queen size beds. Complimentary bottle of champagne. Breakfasts served between 9 am-10 am. Six rooms (private/shared baths). *Website: www.garfieldinn.com*

Nightly $110-$120

KREBS BEACHSIDE COTTAGES
MARV & SALLY KREBS

(989) 856-2876
COTTAGE RESORT

★ EDITOR'S CHOICE ★

8 cottages (1-4 bedroom) on open, landscaped grounds with a scattering of trees. Fully furnished with living area, private baths, equipped kitchens with microwaves. Picnic tables and grills. Large wooden deck overlooks 200' of sandy beach with a great view of Saginaw Bay. Open May-Nov. 15. Heated. Hunters welcome. Pets allowed off-season.

Weekly $650 (and up) Reduced/daily rates spring/fall

Editor's Note: Simple, clean, comfortable cottages on spacious grounds, affordably priced with warm and caring owners make this a choice spot to stay — reserve early.

KREBS LANE COTTAGES

(313) 886-5752 • (989) 738-8548
COTTAGE RESORT

Set vertically to the water, these 5 clean, well maintained cottages sit on a 300 ft. x 50 ft. lot of sandy beach on Saginaw Bay. Includes equipped kitchens with microwaves and hook-up for cable TV. All units accommodate 6. Some offer lake views. No pets.
Weekly $575-$675

LAKE STREET MANOR

(989) 738-7720
BED & BREAKFAST

Historic brick Victorian. Furnished with antiques and features large bays, high peaked roof and gingerbread trim. Hot tub, in-room movies, private and shared baths. Brick BBQ's and bikes for guests' enjoyment. Fenced 1/2 acre. 5 rooms, AC. *Website: www.hometown.aol.com/lakestreetmanor*

Nightly $55-$65 ($65-$75 Weekends)

Editor's Note: Homey accommodations close to the center of town.

LAKE VISTA MOTEL & COTTAGE RESORT
RON & MARY GOTTSCHALK

(989) 738-8612
MOTEL/COTTAGE RESORT

On the shores of Lake Huron and Saginaw Bay. All units have queen beds, air, CATV. Fully equipped cottages. Heated pool, snack bar, bait and tackle. AAA. Major credit cards.
Weekly $615-$800

TOWN CENTER COTTAGES

(989) 738-7223
COTTAGE RESORT

In the heart of it all! Comfortable two bedroom cottages with fully equipped kitchens, CATV, screened front porch and a very private outdoor area with picnic tables, grills and a fire ring for family fun. Short stroll to beach, shopping, dining, and all the fun.

Weekly $395   Nightly $69

OSENTOSKI REALTY/LAKEFRONT   **(888) 738-5251 • (989) 738-5251**
ACCOMMODATIONS   **PRIVATE CONDOS/COTTAGES**
INCLUDES: HARBOR PINES & NORTH SHORE BEACH CONDOS

★ EDITOR'S CHOICE ★

Spacious condos and cottages located on the beautiful shores of Lake Huron and Saginaw Bay. 1-2 bedroom/1-2 bath units feature fireplaces, CATV, fully equipped kitchens, some with A/C, VCRs, and much more. Open all year.

Weekly $800 (and up)

Editor's Note: Contemporary condominiums with lake views ... very nice.

PORT HOPE

STAFFORD HOUSE   **(989) 428-4554**
GREG & KATHY GEPHART   **BED & BREAKFAST**

Only one block from Lake Huron, this nicely maintained B&B sits on an attractive open treed lot with a lovely backyard wildflower garden. Open year around. Full breakfasts served each morning. 4 rooms with private baths (one suite overlooks garden), CATV and AC.

Nightly $65-$90

PORT SANILAC

RAYMOND HOUSE INN   **(800) 622-7229 • (810) 622-8800**
GARY & CRISTY BOBOFCHAK   **BED & BREAKFAST**

★ EDITOR'S CHOICE ★

500 ft. from Lake Huron and lighthouse, 1871 Victorian Home. 7 large, high-ceiling bedrooms, 5 private baths/2 shared baths, A/C. All in period furnishings. CATV-VCR, in-room phones. Old fashioned parlor/dining room adds to charm. Open year round. Harbor Light Gallery and Gift Shop attached. No smoking/pets. *Website: www.bbonline.com/MI/raymond*

Nightly $65-$115

Editor's Note: Antiques and lovely decor highlight the Raymond House. A very nice choice for the area. See our review in this edition.

SEBEWAING

RUMMEL'S TREE HAVEN **B&B**   **(989) 883-2450** • EMAIL: erummel@avci.net
CARL & ERMA RUMMEL, JR.   BED & BREAKFAST

A 2 room bed & breakfast with full breakfast. Features private baths, cable TV, A/C, refrigerator and microwave. Fishing for perch and walleye. Very good area for hunting duck, goose, deer and pheasant. Personal checks accepted. Open all year. Pets allowed in garage area.

Nightly $40-$55

Editor's Note: Homey lodging with friendly innkeepers who enjoy nature and their guests. Carl knows all the best hunting spots and Erma makes wonderful breakfasts. See our review this edition.

UNIONVILLE

FISH POINT LODGE   **(989) 674-2631**
    LODGE

Near Fish Point game reserve this lodge, built in 1902, offers 4 bedrooms, shared bath and a huge fireplace. Kitchen facilities are available. Lodging accommodates up to 20 people. Breakfast included. Two cabins. R.V. sight also available. Credit cards. Open year around.

Call for Rates

BAY CITY • FRANKENMUTH • SAGINAW

Bay City, well known for its water sports, features a variety of events including speedboat and offshore power boat races. Tour the city's historical sites and view the many stately homes on Center Avenue, Wenonah and Veterans Memorial parks. Come south from Bay City and explore the historic district of **Saginaw**. Take a four-mile river walk, visit a museum or the zoo and stroll among the fragrant rose gardens in downtown parks.

Traveling south from Saginaw, you'll reach the historic town of **Frankenmuth**. The classic Bavarian styling of its original settlers can be seen throughout the town's homes, buildings and craft shops. For many it has become a traditional yearly visit. They come to the more than 100 shops and attractions, stroll the streets, tour the scenic town, sample traditional German cuisine or their famous *all you can eat* chicken dinners. The *Bavarian Inn* and *Zehnder's* still reign as the area's most popular eateries ...and beware, the bakeries are too tempting.

One of the newest shopping adventures in Frankenmuth is The Riverplace Shops. Located on Main Street, visitors can explore 30 specialty shops offering a unique range of gifts and handcrafted items. The Riverplace Shops is also the place to enjoy a nostalgic tour of the Cass River onboard the Bavarian Belle paddle wheel boat. At the close of each night, a special laser light show is given for all to enjoy.

While you're in Frankenmuth, be sure to take a horse-drawn carriage ride through the charming town. And, of course, you must visit Bronner's Christmas Wonderland where holidays are celebrated year around. Spend the night and start shopping early the next morning at the area's largest designer outlet shopping mall, Birch Run.

BAY CITY

CLEMENTS INN
DAVID & SHIRLEY ROBERTS
(800) 442-4605
BED & BREAKFAST

This 1886 Victorian mansion offers 6 comfortably elegant rooms with private bath, TV/VCR and phone. Six fireplaces, central A/C. Enjoy a romantic evening in 1 of 2 whirlpool suites with in-room fireplaces. *Website: www.clementsinn.com*

Nightly $75-$190

KESWICK MANOR   (989) 893-6598 • EMAIL: inkeepers@keswickmanor.com
BED & BREAKFAST

Relax in the comfort of a traditional English inn. Enjoy stylish decor and unsurpassed personal amenities. Four rooms furnished with heirlooms. Includes multi-room Jacuzzi suite and luxury suite with fireplace. A/C. Full breakfasts. *Website: www.keswickmanor.com*

Nightly $89-$189

FRANKENMUTH

POINT OF VIEW   **(989) 652-9845**
ED AND BETTY GOYINGS   PRIVATE COTTAGE

★ EDITOR'S CHOICE ★

Completely remodeled one-room cottage plus Florida Room ... has lots of history. Features open great room with original maple floors and paneled walls, fireplace, bar, dinette, furnished kitchen, private bath. Includes CATV, phone, A/C, grill and picnic table. Linens included. No pets. Children under 12 FREE.

Weekly   *$400 (based on 1 person/$35 each add'l. person)

* Rate based on single occupancy

Editor's Note: Betty has a talent for interior design and it shows in this delightfully cozy one room cottage. Lovely location.

SAGINAW

BROCKWAY HOUSE BED & BREAKFAST   **(989) 792-0746**
DICK & ZOE ZUEHLKES   BED & BREAKFAST

On the National Register of Historic Homes, this 1864 B&B was built in the grand tradition of the old southern plantation. Near to excellent restaurants and antique shops. 4 rooms, private baths, A/C. Two-person Jucuzzi suite. Full gourmet breakfast served each morning.

Nightly $95-$225

REGION 2

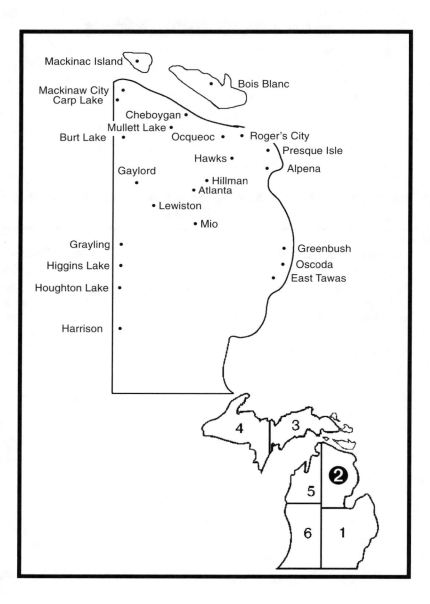

Mackinac Island

Bois Blanc

Mackinaw City
Carp Lake

Cheboygan
Mullett Lake
Burt Lake   Ocqueoc   • Roger's City

Presque Isle

Hawks •
Gaylord   Alpena

• Hillman
• Atlanta

• Lewiston

• Mio

Grayling   • Greenbush
Higgins Lake   Oscoda
Houghton Lake   East Tawas

Harrison

4   3

2

5

6   1

OSCODA & THE AUSABLE AREA

COVERS: TAWAS/EAST TAWAS • GREENBUSH • MIO

Settled where the AuSable River meets Lake Huron, these series of communities offer a variety of activities from canoeing and fishing to hiking, hunting, cross-country skiing, and snowmobiling. **Oscoda** is considered the gateway to the River Road National Scenic Byway that runs along the south bank of the AuSable River. **Tawas City** and nearby Huron National Forest offers lakes, beaches and great trails. In July the area features the Summerfest with events and food for the entire family. August is famous for waterfront art fairs, golf tournaments and car shows. September tees off with more golf and Labor Day arts and crafts. During winter season, cross-country ski enthusiasts can enjoy the well-groomed trails at Corseair. In February, the Perchville U.S.A. Festival takes place — be there to enjoy the festivities.

The quaint harbor town of Harrisville offers terrific trout and salmon fishing. The Sturgeon Point Lighthouse Museum, a summer concert series, art and craft fairs, festivals and the Harrisville State Park provide a variety of both summer and winter recreational fun.

Mio, the Heart of the AuSable River Valley, excels in canoeing and winter sport activities. In June they host the Championship Canoe Race and the Great Lakes Forestry Exposition in July. While there, tour the Kirtland warbler nesting area.

To sample some of the area's down home cooking, try *The Bear Track Inn* (AuGres) noted for outstanding breakfast buffets plus a diverse menu including, of course, excellent fish. *H&H Bakery* (AuGres) has developed a proud reputation for their delicious, fresh baked goods with one of their specialties being pizza. *Charbonneau* (on the AuSable in Oscoda) offers a waterfront setting with a diverse menu. Stop by *Wiltse's* (Oscoda) for great food and some of their own micro-brewed beer. Treat yourself to a meal on the water at *Pier 23* (Tawas), known for great fish at moderate rates. Also, in the Tawas/East Tawas area, *Falco Rosso* is known for excellent Italian cuisine. Treat the children (under 12) to free dessert at the *Red Hawk Golf Club*. If your craving a big, juicy hamburger, steak or prime rib, try out *Chums*.

GREENBUSH

SID'S RESORT
(989) 739-7638
COTTAGE RESORT

★ EDITOR'S CHOICE ★

OFF-SEASON DISCOUNTED RATES. Also, Discount Coupons available

for golf, restaurants, fishing, canoes, tube, kayak, boat rental and Dinosaur Zoo (see our website). Property reviewed and featured in the 1997/98 *Michigan Vacation Guide* as a *"highly recommended Premiere Resort"*. 11 cottages set along a sandy

stretch of Lake Huron. 1, 2 or 3 bedroom cottages sleep 2-8. Renovations include cathedral ceilings, knotty pine walls, lofts, color coordinated furnishings and remodeled kitchens. Amenities include CATV, gameroom, shuffle-

board, badminton, playgrounds , picnic areas; watercraft rentals. Open May-Oct. No pets. *Website: www.sidsresort.com*
Weekly $550-$1,325   (Call for nightly/off-season rates, spring and fall specials/packages)

Editor's Note: Sid's continues to be a favorite of ours on Michigan's sunrise side. Highly recommended. Make reservations early.

SUNNYSIDE COTTAGES
JOHN & DONNA WITTLA
(989) 739-5289
COTTAGE RESORT

★ EDITOR'S CHOICE ★

On the sunny side of Michigan these charming, knotty pine cottages offer equipped, tiled kitchens, microwaves, stove, refrigerator, coffeemaker and utensils. Large living room (some with sofabed), 2 bedrooms or 2 bedrooms and loft. Gas heat. CATV, VCR, BBQ, picnic table and lawn furniture. Close to area activities.
Weekly $500-$1,250
Editor's Note: Comfortably updated resort. Nice choice for the area.

MIO

HINCHMAN ACRES RESORT
(800) 438-0203 (MI) • (989) 826-3267
COTTAGE RESORT

★ EDITOR'S CHOICE ★

AAA Rated Family Resort. A place for all seasons ... something for everyone. Summer—weekly family vacations. Rest of year — secluded getaway weekends. 11 cottages (1-2-3 bedrooms), CATV, A/C, fireplaces, phones, kitchens,

cribs, swimming, beach, fishing. Enjoy campfires, playground, gameroom, hiking and mountain bike trails. Canoe trips on AuSable River, canoe, tube, raft and kayak rentals. Cross country ski on groomed tracked trails, ski and snowshoe rentals. Golf, horseback riding, antique shops and Amish community nearby. 3 hours from Detroit. No Pets. Brochure. *Website: www. hinchman.com*

Weekly $325-$575   Nightly $50-$150

Editor's Note: Spacious grounds in a natural setting. The resort offers diverse activities with very clean and well maintained lodgings. Good location for a very good price.

OSCODA

AUSABLE RIVER RESORT
(989) 739-5246
COTTAGE RESORT

Located on the AuSable River. Two bedroom cottages with kitchen and color TV. Only a half mile west of downtown Oscoda and five blocks from the lake. Boat dockage available. No pets.

Call for Rates

ANCHORAGE COTTAGES
JIM & SUE MURTON

(989) 739-7843
COTTAGE RESORT

Unpack and relax on our sugar sand beach on Lake Huron. Six clean, comfortable, fully furnished cottages (2-4 bedrooms) with fully equipped kitchens. Swim, fish, canoe, golf, hunt, snowmobile, cross-country ski. Grills, picnic tables, bonfire pits, volleyball. Open year around. No pets.

Weekly $450-$800 (Nightly winter rates available)

EAST COAST SHORES RESORT
ROY WENNER

(989) 739-0123
COTTAGE RESORT

★ EDITOR'S CHOICE ★

Major renovations completed in 1993-94. Resort rests on 200 ft. of sandy beach, fully furnished, 2-3 bedroom beach front cabins with equipped kitchens (includes microwave, automatic coffeemaker), CATV with HBO, ceiling fans and screened porch. Enjoy volleyball, badminton, bonfires and swimming. No pets.

Weekly $525-$742   Nightly $75-$115

Editor's Note: Owners have done a very nice job renovating this traditional resort.

EL CORTEZ BEACH RESORT

(989) 739-7884
COTTAGE RESORT

On Lake Huron, these 1-2 bedroom cottages offer equipped kitchens, gas heat, city water. Some cottages have CATV w/HBO. Linens provided. Enjoy the family fun area, BBQ's, picnic tables and large sandy beach. Fish cleaning station on premises. Wave runner rentals. No pets.

Weekly $500-$1,130   Nightly $65 (and up)

Editor's Note: Owners have put major effort into updating this resort with good results. The new beach homes are a favorite of ours. Great beach.

Mai Tiki Resort
Marina & Robert Stock

(800) 231-1875 • (989) 739-9971
Condo/Cottage Resort

NEW OWNERS ...
Unique *tropical setting*
on Lake Huron. 1-4
bedroom cottages, 2-
bedroom condos.
Equipped kitchens,
CATV, some cottages
with fireplace. All
units face the beach
and lake. Condos have
A/C. Enjoy miles of

sugar sand beach, panoramic sun-
rises/moonrises. Picnic tables, grills,
firepit, horseshoes, swingset, game/
snack room. Kayak rentals. Handicap access. No pets.

Weekly $800 (Condos)
              $475-$1,200 (Cottages)

*Editor's Note: New owners are work-
ing hard to renovate this long-time resort. They hope to have half the updates completed by summer of 2003
and full renovation by 2004. We'll look
forward to seeing what transpires.
Great beach area.*

Shenandoah on the
Lake Beach Resort

(989) 739-3997 • (941) 352-4639 (winter)
Cottage Resort

Six cottages, 2 miles south of Oscoda on Lake Huron w/300' sandy beach.
Features 1 and 2 bedroom cottages and 3 bedroom beachhouses. Each has
fully equipped kitchen (some w/fireplaces), decks, CATV, recreation area,
campfires. Open May-October.

Nightly $55-$175 (call for weekly rates)

HURON HOUSE
(989) 739-9255
BED & BREAKFAST

★ EDITOR'S CHOICE ★

Located between Tawas and Oscoda on a beautiful stretch of sandy Lake Huron beach. Accommodations feature panoramic views of Lake Huron, fireplaces, private hot tubs, in-room Jacuzzis and continental breakfast at your door. Glorious sunrises, romantic moonrises. Perfect romantic getaway!
Website: www.huronhouse.com
Nightly $120-$185
Editor's Note: Beautifully designed rooms, most with exceptional lake views. Charmingly landscaped courtyard. Treat yourself! Highly recommended.

THOMAS' PARKSIDE COTTAGES
(989) 739-5607
COTTAGE RESORT

On Lake Huron with 333 ft. of private beach, the cottages are near the AuSable River. Includes 2, 1 bedroom and 11, 2 bedroom cottages facing the lake with enclosed porches, kitchen with stove and refrigerator, CATV. Bring radio and linens. $100 deposit. No pets.
Weekly $475-$575

TAWAS/EAST TAWAS

CHICKADEE GUEST HOUSE
DON & LEIGH MOTT
(989) 362-8006
PRIVATE COTTAGE

A few steps from Tawas Bay, the park, playground and beach, and a short walk to lovely shops, restaurants, theatre and pier, this recently renovated turn-of-the-century arts and craft home is a vacationer's delight. Master bedroom (queen bed, chair bed), a second bedroom (twins, convertible-to-king), a glassed-in front porch with bay view (trundle daybed) accommodates 7. The open plan including a fully equipped kitchen, breakfast bar and dining area, living room, telephone, CATV, and fireplace encourages group activities. Linens, basics provided. Open year around. Website: *www.east-tawas.com*
Weekly $950 (and up)   Nightly $150 (and up)

East Tawas Junction B&B
Don & Leigh Mott
(989) 362-8006
Bed & Breakfast

Lovely turn-of-the-century country Victorian home overlooking Tawas Bay rests on an acre of well-groomed grounds. Five tastefully decorated guest rooms feature private baths, CATV. Enjoy freshly prepared full breakfasts elegantly presented in the dining rooms or on the bay view deck. A charming parlor with fireplace and piano, an inviting library, family room, glassed-in wraparound porch and lovely garden seating encourage relaxation. A hop and a skip to the beach and a few blocks to elegant shops, restaurants, library, theatre and pier. Seasonal activities, festivals, concerts, community theatre and scenic tours. *Website: www.east-tawas.com*
Nightly $99-$149

Editor's Note: Invitingly styled home on scenic, park-like setting. Train buffs will enjoy the operating railroad that passes through their front grounds once a day, Mon.-Fri. See our review in this edition.

Riptide Motel & Cabins
Emma & Larry, Managers
(989) 362-6562
Motel/Cabin Resort

On Tawas Bay, this year around motel/cabin resort features large sandy beach, picnic tables, play area, CATV and BBQ grills. In addition to motel rooms, Riptide offers 4, 2-bedroom cabins with equipped kitchens, private baths, linens provided. No pets in summer.

Weekly $270-$540 (cabins assume 6 days)   Nightly $45-$90

Sand Lake Inn Waterfront Motel & Stone Cabins
Don & Kelly Kammer
(989) 469-3553
Motel/Cabin Resort

On Sand Lake ... great beach...great fishing! All units have fully equipped kitchens, CATV, BBQ grills and picnic tables. Row and paddle boats included. Nearby golfing, hiking, bicycling, canoeing, snowmobile and ORV trail. 3 Mile North of M55 and 9 miles west of Lake Huron. *Website: www.sandlakeinn.com*
Weekly $350-$650

Editor's Note: Friendly owners at this quiet, cozy little waterfront lodging. Nothing fancy but clean with panoramic view of Sand Lake. A few steps takes you down to the sandy beach area.

TIMBERLANE RESORT   (248) 647-9634 • (248) 797-0208
                                                     COTTAGE RESORT

★ EDITOR'S CHOICE ★

Eight renovated cabins on Tawas Bay, 2-4 bedrooms, 1-2 baths, knotty pine interiors. Sleeps 6 - 12. Some with dishwashers, gas or woodburning fireplaces, whirlpool tub. Equipped kitchens with new appliances. Picnic tables, gas grills. Open all year. Pets extra. *Website: www.timberlaneresorts.com*
Weekly $880-$1,550   Nightly $90-$310

Editor's Note: Impressively renovated cabins. A diverse selection. From luxurious to simple, all are fresh ... even their smallest is cute and welcoming. See our review in this edition.

ALPENA & THUNDERBAY

INCLUDES: ATLANTA • HAWKS • HILLMAN • OCQUEOC •
PRESQUE ISLE • ROGERS CITY

Located on the beautiful sunrise side of Michigan, visitors can enjoy a variety of activities in the **Thunder Bay** area. It's know for underwater ruins of sunken ships from another era. Or, for something a little less exerting, enjoy **Alpena's** "live" theater which presents year around plays and musicals. The area also offers a wildfowl sanctuary, lighthouses, and excellent hunting, fishing, cross-country skiing, and golf. Don't miss July's Brown Trout Festival which lures (excuse the pun...) over 800 fishing contestants to this nine-day event featuring art, food concessions and nightly entertainment.

While in the area, don't forget to visit one of the Lower Peninsula's largest waterfalls, Ocqueoc Falls, in **Rogers City**.

ALPENA

GLORIA HASSETT   (989) 734-2066 (AFTER 4 P.M.)
                                                   PRIVATE COTTAGE

One, two-bedroom cottage located on US 23 South. It is midway between Alpena and Rogers City on Grand lake.
Weekly $300

TRELAWNY RESORT

(989) 471-2347
COTTAGE RESORT

Resort features 9 attractive, clean and comfortable cottages. They have 200 ft. of white sugar sand beach on Lake Huron's beautiful Thunder Bay with 3 acres of restful grounds and tall pines. On-site laundromat and game room. Cottages have full kitchens and shower-bath. No pets. *Website: www.trelawny-resort.com*

Weekly $430-$525

ATLANTA

BRILEY INN
CARLA & BILL GARDNER

(989) 785-4784
INN

Redwood inn with impressive windows overlooking Thunder Bay River. Rooms are decorated in Victorian Antique. Great Room, cozy den with fireplace, Jacuzzi, full country breakfast. Canoes and paddleboat available. Central A/C, CATV. Minutes from Thunder Bay Golf Course, Elk Ridge, Garland. Golf packages available. Private baths. 5 rooms. *Website: www.yesmichigan.com/brileyinn/*

Nightly $65-$75

HAWKS

NETTIEBAY LODGE
MARK & JACKIE SCHULER

(989) 734-4688
COTTAGE/LODGE RESORT

★ EDITOR'S CHOICE ★

Year around on beautiful Lake Nettie. One to 4 bedrooms with full kitchens, living room, private baths (linens available) and lake views. Into bird watching? NettieBay is where you want to go. Join them in classes, seminars and their birding walks. Also enjoy excellent fishing and x-country skiing. No pets.

Weekly $400-$675

Editor's Note: Excellent programs on birding and other outdoor activities. Natural and picturesque setting. Accommodations basic, clean and comfy.

HILLMAN

THUNDER BAY RESORT

(800) 729-9375
CONDO/VILLA RESORT

★ EDITOR'S CHOICE ★

Golf resort featuring luxury suites, whirlpool suites, villas and chalets with kitchen, living room and deck overlooking golf course. Two restaurants. During winter, Elk viewing sleight ride with gourmet dinner packages, cross-country skiing, snowmobiling, ice skating and romantic getaways.

Weekly $900 (chalets) ;   Nightly $66 (per person & up)

Editor's Note: Premiere golf resort with and interesting year around package programs. Wintertime Elk viewing/gourmet dinner program is highly recommended.

OCQUEOC

SILVER ROCK RESORT ON OCQUEOC LAKE
STEVE & VICKI KELLAR

(810) 694-3061
PRIVATE COTTAGE

Ocqueoc Lake is a 132 acre lake twenty miles north of Rogers City and three miles west of Lake Huron. Secluded 2 bedroom cottage with boat, color TV. ORV and snowmobile trails nearby. Great fishing for bass, walleye, pike, trout and salmon. Open all year. No pets.

Call for Rates

PRESQUE ISLE

FIRESIDE INN

(989) 595-6369
COTTAGE/LODGE RESORT

Built in 1908, 17 cottages/cabins with private baths, some with kitchen/ fireplace. 7 lodge rooms with private/shared baths. Tennis, volleyball, ping-pong, horseshoes, shuffleboard. Price includes 2 meals daily, in-season. Open spring to fall. Pets OK.

	Rooms	Cottages/Cabins
Weekly	$242*	$286*

* Per adult/children less. Daily Off-season rates available.

Editor's Note: Historic resort located in a quiet, wooded setting. Cottages range in size with several maintained in rustic condition - sparse/basic furnishings.

ROGERS CITY

MANITOU SHORES RESORT **(989) 734-7233**
BRUCE & COLLEEN GRANT **COTTAGE/MOTEL RESORT**
12 acre resort on 600 ft. of Lake Huron. 4 cottages, 4 motel units, 3 log cabins with wood decks. Cottages/cabins include fully equipped kitchens. Log cabins with microwave, dishwasher, fireplace with glass sliding doors. A/C and TV/VCR. Limited handicap access. No pets.
Weekly $450-$900   Nightly $85-$200

MACKINAW CITY • MACKINAC ISLAND

Near the tip of the mitt, **Mackinaw City** is located at the southern end of the Mackinac Bridge and offers ferry service (May-October) to **Mackinac Island**. Known for its sparkling waters and natural beauty, it is visited by thousands of vacationers each year. While in the City, be sure to visit Fort Michilimackinaw. Built in 1715, the Fort was initially used as a trading post by early French settlers before becoming a British military outpost and fur-trading village. Today its costumed staff provide demonstrations and special programs. You'll also want to stop by Mill Creek Park (just east of town). Visit the historic water-powered sawmill and gristmill that re-create one of the first industrial sites. You'll also find ongoing archeological digs and reconstructed buildings here.

One of **Mackinaw City's** most popular attractions is Mackinaw Crossings and the Center Stage Theatre. It's northern Michigan's largest entertainment complex. This brightly painted, Victorian-themed outdoor complex boasts over 50 retail shops, six restaurants, a five-plex theatre, unique butterfly house and an arcade. Every hour (during the season) the outdoor amphitheater offers live entertainment plus a free laser light show every night. To add to this is the 850-seat Center Stage Theatre which features live, Broadway-style shows (tickets: 231-436-4053). If you enjoy miniature golf, check out the one right next to the Crossings. The whole family will love it. Then, for another unique treat, try the century-old *Detroit-to-Mackinac Depot Pub & Grill* which has been charmingly restored to reflect the railroad era of yesteryear.

If you're a walker, don't forget the famous Mackinac Bridge Walk on Labor Day. Join in the joy and celebrations with Michigan's Governor and thousands of others who walk the world's longest total suspension bridge.

Visit **Mackinac Island** and step back in time. This vacation land is a haven for those seeking a unique experience. Accessible by ferry, the Island allows only horse-drawn carriages and bicycles to be used as transportation. Historical and scenic, the Island is filled with natural beauty and boasts a colorful past. Explore Old Fort Mackinac where costumed staff perform period military reenactments and demonstrations. In addition, the Fort has an interpretive center that traces military life on the island during the 1800's. Stop for a refreshment or lunch at the fort's *Tea Room* which offers a wonderful, panoramic view of the straits.

Take a carriage tour, visit nearby historic buildings and homes, browse the many shops, and dine at the many restaurants. Enjoy nightly entertainment, golfing, swimming, hiking, horseback riding, and just relaxing on this Michigan resort island. There are also several fine restaurants on the island. For an elegant dining experience, try the 107 year old Grand Hotel's formal dining room. Or, on the northwest side of the island, *Woods* is the spot for a romantic, candlelight dinner (located in Stonecliffe, a mansion built in 1905). For more casual dining with very good food, try the *Point Dining Room* at the Mission Point Resort. Hangout with the locals, and try the down-to-earth *Mustang Lounge* (one of the few places open year around). Enjoy your trip to the island ...oh, by the way, don't forget to bring home some fudge.

MACKINAW CITY

THE BEACH HOUSE
(800) 262-5353 • (231) 436-5353
COTTAGE RESORT

Situated on 250 ft. of Lake Huron frontage, view the Bridge and Island from these 1-3 bed cottages in Mackinaw City. Units include kitchenettes (no utensils), electric heat, A/C, CATV w/HBO. Coffee and homemade muffins available each morning! Playground, beach, indoor pool and spa on the premises. Small pets O.K.

Nightly $39-$125

Editor's Note: Good, clean, comfortable accommodations.

CEDARS RESORT
(231) 537-4748
COTTAGE RESORT

Four, 1-2 bedroom cottages on Paradise Lake, just 7 miles south of Mackinaw City. Each unit includes full housekeeping, equipped kitchen, bathroom, gas heat and CATV. 2 units with fireplace (wood furnished). Sandy beach - great for swimming. Boat and dock included. Open year around. $100 deposit.

Weekly $355 (and up)

CHIPPEWA MOTOR LODGE - ON THE LAKE (800) 748-0124 • (231) 436-8661
COTTAGE/MOTEL RESORT

Motel and 2 bedroom cottage units (double/queen size beds) offered. Features sandy beach, CATV, direct dial phones, indoor pool/spa, sun deck, shuffleboard, picnic area. 1 block from ferry docks.

Nightly $29-$99 (Based on dbl. occ.) Seasonal rates

Editor's Note: Clean and very nicely maintained.

NORTHERN LAKES PROPERTY MGMT. (800) 641-8944
PRIVATE COTTAGES/CONDOS

Several waterfront condominiums, cottages and houses in Mackinaw City, Burt Lake, Mullett Lake, Black Lake, Long Lake, Lake Huron and Lake Michigan. From 1-5 bedrooms, fireplaces, king/queen/full beds. No pets/smoking. Availability year around.

Weekly $400-$3,800

WATERFRONT INN (800) 962-9832 • (231) 436-5527
COTTAGE/MOTEL RESORT

Sitting on 300 ft. of sandy beach, this facility offers full housekeeping cottages along with its motel units. Amenities included CATV w/HBO, A/C and indoor pool. Picnic and playground area on premises. Bridge and Island view.

Weekly $250-$750*   Nightly $29-$99*

*Based on double occupancy. Rates will vary depending on season.

MACKINAC ISLAND

BAY VIEW AT MACKINAC (906) 847-3295 • EMAIL: bayviewbnb@aol.com
DOUG YODER   BED & BREAKFAST

★ EDITOR'S CHOICE ★

Victorian home offers grace and charm in romantic turn-of-the century tradition. The only facility of its type and style sitting at water's edge. Deluxe continental breakfast served from harbor-view veranda. Private baths. Open May 1-Oct. 15. 17 rooms. Major credit cards. *Website: www.bayviewbnb.com*

Nightly $95-$345

Editor Note: Located in a quiet section on the Island's main road. All rooms have water views. It's a bit of a walk from the docks...but that's Mackinac.

CLOGHAUN (906) 847-3885 • (888) 442-5929
JAMES BOND   BED & BREAKFAST

This large Victorian home is convenient to shops, restaurants and ferry lines. Built in 1884, it was the home of Thomas and Bridgett Donnelly's large Irish family. Today guests enjoy the many fine antiques, ambiance and elegance of a bygone era. Open May-Nov. 11 rooms.

Nightly $100-$165 (plus tax)

GREAT TURTLE LODGE
JOHN & JUDY

TOLL FREE: (877) 650-4600
B&B/CONDOS/APARTMENTS

Nestled among tall cedars, the lodge is located in one of the most peaceful spots on the island, around the corner from the Grand Hotel and moments from downtown activities. Rooms/suites vary with private entrances, 1 or 2 bedrooms, full kitchens, TV/VCR, Jacuzzis. Open year around.

Nightly $59-$459

HAAN'S 1830 INN   SUMMER (906) 847-6244 • WINTER (847) 526-2662
NICHOLAS & NANCY HAAN   BED & BREAKFAST

Historic home, built in Greek Revival style, furnished in period antiques. The earliest building was used as an inn for Michigan and Wisconsin. Continental breakfast on the wicker filled porch. Featured in <u>Detroit Free Press</u>, <u>Chicago Tribune</u>, <u>Chicago Sun Times</u> and <u>Sears Discovery Magazine</u>. Open May 21-Oct. 18. 7 rooms (5/private baths, 2/shared baths).

Nightly $90-$180

JOE'S ISLAND GETAWAY
JOE DRESSLER

(800) 631-5767
PRIVATE CONDO

Enjoy your romantic Mackinac Island stay in our luxurious condo. Old World charm with all of today's amenities. Breathtaking view, Jacuzzi, fireplace, balcony. Hiking, biking, tennis and Grand golf course nearby.

Call for Rates

THE ISLAND HOUSE HOTEL &   (906) 847-3347 • RES. (800) 626-6304
HARBOR PLACE APARTMENTS   HOTEL & APARTMENTS

Historic hotel perched on a hilltop overlooking Mackinac harbor. Accommodations feature indoor pool, spa, bar and fine dining. Harbor Place Apartments located separately on Main Street, sleep 4, and feature queen bed, equipped kitchen, washer/dryer, TV and full bath.

Nightly $145 & up (Hotel)*; $200-$250 (Apartments)*
*Reduced rates off-season

LAKEBLUFF CONDOS AT STONECLIFFE   **(800) 699-6927 • (888) 847-0487**
MARIANNE O'NEILL/PATRICIA HELD   EMAIL: **marianneoneill@mindspring.com**
PRIVATE CONDO

PENTHOUSE STUDIO SUITE:
Located high atop the West
Bluff of Mackinac Island.
Beautiful one room suite
sleeps two with a solarium
overlooking a breathtaking
view of the Straits of Lake
Huron and the Mackinac
Bridge. Cathedral ceiling
with skylights, Jacuzzi next
to fireplace, private balconies, queen size bed. Small

dining area. Kitchen with microwave, bar refrigerator, CATV, TV/VCR. Golf
course. Daily maid service. No smoking. *Website: www.yesmichigan.com/
lakebluff*

Nightly $225 (In Season); $205 (Off Season) Mid-week, 2 Night Minimum

LAKEBLUFF CONDOS AT STONECLIFFE   **(800) 699-6927 • (888) 847-0487**
MARIANNE O'NEILL/PATRICIA HELD   EMAIL: **marianneoneill@mindspring.com**
PRIVATE CONDO

GARDENVIEW STUDIO
SUITE (OAKWOOD BLDG.)
Located high atop the
West Bluff of Mackinac
Island. Charming one
room suite, sleeps two,
features small kitchen-
ette, wet bar, microwave
and small refrigerator.
Queen size bed, sofa,
Jacuzzi with separate
shower. Bayed sliding
patio doors take you to

balcony and overlook of Stonecliffe's gardens and grounds. CATV, TV/VCR.
Golf course. Daily maid service. No smoking. *Website: www.yesmichigan.com/
lakebluff*

Nightly $165 (In Season); $135 (Off Season) Mid-week, 2 Night Minimum

LAKEBLUFF CONDOS AT STONECLIFFE   **(800) 699-6927 • (888) 847-0487**
MARIANNE O'NEILL/PATRICIA HELD   EMAIL: **marianneoneill@mindspring.com**
PRIVATE CONDO
1, 2 & 3 BEDROOM SUITE

Enjoy panoramic views of the Lake or Bridge from our 1, 2 and 3 bedroom luxurious Mackinac Island suites. Each features bay windows in dining area, sliding glass doors leading to private balcony or patio, well appointed living room with fireplace. Private bath with Jacuzzi and separate shower. Fully equipped kitchens include microwaves and coffeemakers. Available May 22 through October 15. *Website: www.yesmichigan.com/lakebluff*
Nightly $225-$245 (1 Bedroom); $325-$365 (2 Bedroom); $425-$475 (3 Bedroom)

METIVIER INN   SUMMER **(906) 847-6234** • EMAIL: **metinn@light-house.net**
KEN & DIANE NEYER   BED & BREAKFAST
Originally built in 1877 and recently renovated, the Inn offers bedrooms with queen size beds, private baths, and one efficiency unit. Relax on the large wicker filled front porch and cozy living room with a wood burner. Breakfast served. Open May-October. 22 rooms. *Website: www.mackinac.com/metivier*
Nightly $115-$285

HOUGHTON LAKE • CHEBOYGAN • BOIS BLANC ISLAND

INCLUDES: BURT LAKE • CARP LAKE • GAYLORD • GRAYLING •
HARRISON • HIGGINS LAKE • LEWISTON • MULLET LAKE

H oughton Lake is where fishing enthusiasts and vacationers thrive on one of Michigan's largest inland lakes. Enjoy hunting, boating, water skiing, cross-country skiing, and snowmobiling. Ice fishing for walleyes, bass and bluegill is so good it merits its own annual event. Each year, the Tip-Up-Town U.S.A. Festival (held mid to late January) offers a variety of events including contests, parades and games for the entire family.

Known as the "Alpine Village", **Gaylord** has more to offer than just great downhill and x-country skiing or groomed snowmobile trails. Try their championship golf courses or terrific year around fishing. Nearby, in the Pigeon River State Forest, roams the largest elk herd east of the Mississippi.

Grayling's historical logging background is preserved at Crawford County Historical Museum and Hartwick Pines State Park. Grayling is also the area for canoeing and trout fishing enthusiasts. In fact, the area is known as the Canoe Capital of Michigan. It is the spot for the internationally famous Weyerhaeuser Canoe Marathon which takes place the last week of July. During this event, up to 50 teams of paddlers attempt to finish a gruelling 120-mile course which can take up to 18 hours to complete. This event is considered one of the most demanding endurance races in any sporting event. Televised broadcasts reach over 150 countries worldwide. The popular AuSable River Festival takes place the week of the Marathon. The festival abounds with numerous activities which include a major parade, juried art shows, antique car shows, ice cream socials, special canoe tours, and several amateur and youth canoe races.

Cheboygan continues the chain of great year around fishing, skiing, snowmobiling, swimming and golf. Be sure to visit Cheboygan's Opera House built in 1877. This restored Victorian theater still offers great entertainment on the same stage that once welcomed Mary Pickford and Annie Oakley.

Seeking an island retreat without all the crowds? **Bois Blanc Island** is your spot. Referred to as Bob-lo by the locals, this quiet, unspoiled island is only a short boat ride from Cheboygan and Mackinac Island. One main road (unpaved) takes you around the Island (cars are permitted). Great for nature hikes, private beaches, boating and relaxing. Here is a community of century homes and a remote lighthouse. While visiting, stop at the Hawk's Landing General Store or the Bois Blanc Tavern and meet some of the warm and friendly year around residents. The island is accessible via ferry boat service (runs several times per day). Be sure to call ahead and reserve a spot if you plan on bringing your car (Plaunt Transportation: 231- 627-2354).

139

BOIS BLANC ISLAND

BOIS BLANC ISLAND RETREAT   **(616) 846-4391**
GRAM & LINDA MCGEORGE   **PRIVATE COTTAGE**

★ EDITOR'S CHOICE ★

Secluded, four bedroom, waterfront cottage on quiet protected bay. Surrounded by white pines and cedar forest. Beautiful view of Lake Huron and the Straits Channel. Cottage offers all the conveniences in a private setting — just bring groceries and fishing pole. Relax, fish, hike, swim, explore. Mackinac Island 30 miles by boat. Open May-Nov. Car ferry. No pets.

Weekly $600-$895   (Call for off-season weekend rates)

Editor's Note: Comfortable and clean cottage with renovations completed in 1995. Nice island retreat with natural grounds and sandy beach.

BURT LAKE

MILLER'S GUEST HOUSE ON BURT LAKE   **(231) 238-4492**
JESS & PAM MILLER   **PRIVATE HOME**

Spacious Burt Lake cottage. Built to exacting standards for our personal friends and family. Available for up to 4 non-smoking guests. Complete kitchen, private sandy beach. Brilliant sunsets, quiet wooded atmosphere. Ideal for swimming, sailing, kayaking, bicycling. No pets. Open year around. *Website: www.upnorthlakes.com*

Weekly $850 ($425 off-season)

SHARON PRESSEY   SUMMER (TOLL FREE) (866) 313-6543 • WINTER (772) 229-1599
PRIVATE COTTAGES

One and 2 bedroom cottages on 150' of Burt Lake's west shore. CATV, gas grills, rowboat, complete kitchens, bedding provided, decks overlooking lake. Sandy bottom for great swimming, beautiful sunrises, wooded setting. Great walleye and bass fishing. Great location 20 minutes north of Petoskey, 20 minutes south of Mackinaw City. Pets OK with approval. Open May-October. *Website: my.voyager.net/~yesserp*

Weekly $550-$1,000 ($400-$575 off-season)

CARP LAKE

STARRY NIGHTS RESORT   (231) 537-3100
VICKIE POWELL   COTTAGE RESORT

Open Year around. On Paradise Lake. Great for reunions and family fun. Located 6 miles south of Mackinac Bridge. Shop till you drop and relax on our sandy beach or take a boat out. Cottages sleep 6, equipped kitchens, private baths, TV. Snowmobile, downhill and cross-country trails nearby. Pets OK.

Weekly $375-$450

CHEBOYGAN & MULLETT LAKE

LAKEWOOD COTTAGES   SUMMER (231) 238-7476 • WINTER (248) 887-5570
KEITH R. PHILLIPS   COTTAGE RESORT

Clean comfortable 2-3 bedroom cottages located on Mullett Lake, with lake frontage. Screened porches, CATV, carpeted, fully equipped kitchens, showers, picnic tables, grills, boats and motors for rent. Buoys for private boats, swimming, fishing, 24' pontoon boat and evening bonfires. Pets allowed. Open May-Sept.

Weekly $435-$515   Nightly $65-$75

THE PINES OF LONG LAKE   (231) 625-2121 • (231) 625-2145
COTTAGE RESORT

Year around resort, 1-3 bedroom cottages. 2 bedroom cabins with 2 double beds face the lake, shared shower building. 1 and 3 bedroom cottages with private showers. All have stoves, refrigerators, limited utensils, gas heat, blankets/pillows (bring linens). Bar/restaurant on premises. Pets allowed ($10 add'l).

Weekly $225-$275   Nightly $50-$60

VEERY POINTE RESORT ON MULLETT LAKE   **(231) 627-7328**
FRED SMITH & DEBBIE SOCHA   **COTTAGE/MOTEL RESORT**

Lakefront cottages, open year around. Fully furnished (except linens—linens available), includes microwave, CATV/HBO & Disney. Picnic area. Motel with efficiencies (some with A/C) across from lake, beach privileges. Docks. Good fishing, x-country skiing, skating and snowmobiling. Ask about pets.

Weekly $350-$1,200 (Motel: $25-80 Nightly)

GAYLORD

BEAVER CREEK RESORT   **(877) 295-3333**
THE NATURAL   **CABIN RESORT**

Year round all season resort. Family getaways, golf getaways, or just time to enjoy and relax. Beautiful 1 and 2 bedroom, fully furnished log cabins. 200' waterslide. 18-hole adventure golf course. No pets. *Website: www.beavercreekresort.org*

Nightly $53-$185

Editor's Note: Excellent golfing and family fun at this impressive resort featuring rustic-contemporary accommodations.

CHALET AT MICHAYWE   **(248) 649-5463**
DAVE WINER   **PRIVATE CHALET**

Fully furnished chalet at resort near Gaylord. 4 bedrooms, 2 baths, large deck, 2-car garage. Nestled in birch woods, close to a dozen resort class golf courses. Sleeps up to 10. Cross-country ski and hiking trail runs next to lot. Private and public lakes and downhill skiing nearby. Fully equipped kitchen, CATV, VCR, barbeque, fireplace. Tennis courts and swimming pools on premises. Open year around.

Weekly $700   Weekends $375

HOFFMAN CEDAR HOME   **(734) 439-7230** • EMAIL: devcat1@aol.com
    PRIVATE HOME

New cedar home on wooded lot. Minutes from top rated golf courses. Large deck with 8 person hot tub and gas grill. Fully furnished, central AC, CATV and VCR. Fully equipped kitchen with microwave, dishwasher. Washer/dryer. Five bedrooms (sleeps 12) with 2.5 baths. No pets/smoking. Weekends negotiable.

Weekly $900

MARSH RIDGE
(800) 743-PLAY
HOTEL/TOWNHOUSE/CHALET(LODGE) RESORT

A golfer's paradise in Gaylord's golf mecca. Unique decor and themes throughout. Jacuzzi rooms, king and queen size beds, microwaves, refrigerators. Townhouses with full kitchen. Outdoor Thermal Swimming Pool, Pro Shop. Jac's Restaurant and more on premises. No pets.

	Hotel/Suites	Townhouses/Lodge
Nightly	$89 (and up)	$120 (and up)

POINTES NORTH
(989) 732-4493
BETSY BERRY
PRIVATE HOMES

Five private, lakefront vacation homes for day, week or month rental. Sizes vary from 3 to 4 bedrooms. Properties vary from sophisticated country to cozy, log cabin and chalet styling. All are set in secluded locations and come fully furnished and equipped, including rowboat, CATV and telephone. No pets.

Weekly $700-$1,200

Editor's Note: Betsy's lodgings are very comfortable with good locations.

TREETOPS SYLVAN RESORT
(888) TREETOPS • (989) 732-6711
CONDO/CHALET/EFFICIENCY RESORT

Standard, deluxe accommodations—condominiums, efficiencies and chalets. 81 holes of championship golf, 19 downhill ski runs and 14 km. of groomed, x-country trails. Dining room, grill and sports bar on premises. Plus indoor/outdoor pools, spas, fitness center, state licensed day care, Edelweiss Ski and Sports Shop.

Nightly $115 (and up)

GRAYLING

BORCHERS BED & BREAKFAST
(800) 762-8756 • (989) 348-4921
MARK & CHERI HUNTER
BED & BREAKFAST

★ EDITOR'S CHOICE ★

The friendly hosts at Borchers invite you to enjoy a unique riverfront experience on the banks of the AuSable. Six rooms, twin/double beds (shared baths) and queen beds (private baths). Full breakfasts. Canoe rentals. Smoking permitted on porch. Open year around. *Website: www.canoeborchers.com*

Nightly $59-$69 (shared bath); $64-$89 (private bath)

Editor's Note: This delightful retreat will make a great place to begin your AuSable River vacation.

PENROD'S AUSABLE RIVER RESORT
(989) 348-2910
COTTAGE/CABIN RESORT

Established resort on the AuSable River. Noted for its planned river canoe/ kayak trips. 13 rustic cabins, most set along the river. All include TV, gas heat, grill and shower. Some with kitchens. Non-kitchen cabins include coffeepot, toaster and dishers. Mountain bike rentals. Opened spring-fall.

Weekly $330-$540   Nightly $55-$90

Editor's Note: One of the area's best noted spots to begin an AuSable River trip. Cabins are clean but rustic with very basic amenities.

HARRISON

LAKESIDE MOTEL & COTTAGES
(989) 539-3796
BOBBIE & GARY SAGER
MOTEL/COTTAGE RESORT

Modern, air conditioned waterfront cottages. Private beach, picnic pavilion/ grills, and campfire hearths. One room cottage (2 people) and two bedroom cottages (up to 5 people) available. Renting April-November. Boat/canoe rental also available. No pets. *Website: www.lakesidemotel.com*

Weekly $375-$475 (+ tax)

SERENDIPITY INN
989-539-6602
BILL & LORI SCHUH
BED & BREAKFAST

Four unique guest rooms, with private baths, provide comfortable, luxurious accommodations. Nestled on 16 wooded acres, walking trails, perennial/herb gardens. Relax in the outdoor Jacuzzi or by the fireplace in the common area. Large suite with fireplace, clawfoot tub. Corporate rates. Smoke free. AAA 2 diamonds.

Nightly $55-$175

SNUG HAVEN LAKESIDE RESORT AND
(989) 539-3117
WATERCRAFT RENTAL
EMAIL: snughaven@voyager.net
COTTAGE RESORT

Fully furnished housekeeping cottages on Budd Lake, a 175-acre all sports lake. Located on 150 ft. of sandy beach, all cottages have decks, picnic tables and gas grills. Open May-October. Jet skis, pontoons and fishing boats available for rent. Excellent bass, muskie and pan fishing. *Website: www.snughaven.com*

Weekly $550-$1,000

HIGGINS LAKE

BIRCH LODGE
(989) 821-6261
COTTAGE RESORT

50 year old resort on the shores of Higgins Lake. The 9 cottages (2-3 bedrooms with kitchenettes) are simply furnished, maintained in great condition and sit in a semi-circle facing the water. Sandy beach. Gathering room features TV with VCR. Open July-August.

Weekly $610   Nightly $100

Editor's Note: Well established area resort...family owned for over 50 years. Clean, simply-furnished cottages.

CEDAR SHORE CABINS
RICK DIXON
(810) 629-6657
Email: reservations@higginslake.com
PRIVATE HOME/COTTAGES

Enjoy one of the most beautiful lakes in the world! At the Cedar Shore, you can choose the cabin that's right for you. We have small, medium, or large depending on your needs. All of this located on 100 ft. of lakefront on the northwest shore of Higgins Lake. There is a gravel road that separates the cabins from the beach. *Website: www.higginslake.com*

Weekly $900-$1,900

Editor's Note: Three cottages. Diverse size and amenities offered, from small cottage to spacious home, are all nicely decorated, comfortable and clean.

MORELL'S HIGGINS LAKE COTTAGE
(989) 821-6885
PRIVATE COTTAGE

Overlooking the south end of beautiful Higgins Lake, this immaculate, cozy cottage sits on a nicely wooded lot and is fully furnished w/equipped kitchen, two bedrooms and nursery. Cottage sleeps 5-6. Includes use of rowboat and a 4000 lb. hoist. No pets.

Weekly $848 (Summer. After Labor Day thru Memorial Day — special rates)

REZNICH'S COTTAGES

(989) 821-9282
COTTAGE RESORT

Clean, comfortable 3, 2 bedroom cottages on Higgins Lake. Carpeted floors, private bath, gas heat and equipped kitchen. BBQ, picnic table and rowboat included in rental price. All cottages are close to the water, one directly overlooks the lake and features knotty pine interior.

Weekly $625-$700

HOUGHTON LAKE

BAY BREEZE RESORT & MOTEL
MANFRED & DIANE BOEHMER

(989) 366-7721
COTTAGE/MOTEL RESORT

2 large cottages (sleep 6) and spacious kitchenette motel rooms with 2 double beds on Houghton Lake. Private sandy beach, CATV, picnic tables, BBQ grills, horseshoes, boat dockage. Linens provided. Pontoon, boat/motor, wave runners and bicycle rentals available. Open year around.

Weekly $385-$600   Nightly $50-$95 (seasonal rates)

BEECHWOOD RESORT
RICK & ROCHELLE JURVIS

(989) 366-5512
COTTAGE RESORT

★ EDITOR'S CHOICE ★

6 cabins completely renovated or newly built in Sept. 1999 on north shore of Houghton Lake. Exceptionally clean, carpeted. Three rustic log cabins with fireplaces (one, three bedroom; two, two bedroom); three newly built with knotty pine interiors (2 bedroom). All feature quality double beds, sleeper sofas, color TV, private bath/ shower, refrigerators, stoves, equipped kitchens, gas BBQ, picnic tables. Coin operated laundry, sea wall, dock, boats, play areas, fire pit, lighted walkways. Minutes from public launch, state land and towns. Handicap friendly. No pets.

Weekly $600 and up;   Nightly $90 and up (off-season)

Editor's Note: Quality renovations made to this long-time Houghton Lake resort make this a standout. Fresh, attractively styled. Highly recommended for the area. See our review in this edition.

THE CREST
(989) 366-7758
COTTAGE/EFFICIENCY RESORT

Lakefront lodgings (3 cottages/3 efficiencies) feature nicely maintained, very clean facilities inside and out! Furnishings in good condition and comfortable. Complete kitchens, picnic table and grill. Ping pong, horseshoes, basketball, paddlewheeler and swim raft. No pets.

Weekly $305-$485

DRIFTWOOD RESORT   RESERVATIONS: (800) 442-8316 • (989) 422-5229
BOB & SHEILA BLESSING   CABIN RESORT

Modern lakefront resort on 2 wooded acres on the north shore. 7 housekeeping cabins (4 log cabins with fireplaces and microwaves) include porches, swings, color TV, full kitchens, electric coffeemakers, 14 ft. boat, picnic table and grill. Excellent playground with basketball, volleyball, horseshoes, swings, etc. Motor and paddle boat rental. Open all year. No pets.

Call for Rates

HIDEAWAY RESORT
(989) 366-9142
MARYANN PRZYTULSKI   COTTAGE RESORT

A clean and well kept resort on Houghton Lake features 4 cottages (2 bedrooms) with full kitchens. 3 cottages directly face the water. Sandy swimming beach. Rowboat included, dock available. No pets.

Weekly $400-$425

MILLER'S LAKESHORE RESORT   RESERVATIONS: (248) 652-4240
DOUG MILLER   EMAIL: doug@millerslakeshoreresort.com
COTTAGE/CHALET RESORT

Open all year. Good swimming, fishing, hunting, snowmobiling and ice fishing. New chalet with fireplace. Modern lakefront housekeeping cottages. Large unit with fireplace. Boats with cottages. Motor rentals. Dockage. Safe sandy beach. Large playground. Grill and picnic tables. Ice shanty. On snowmobile trails. Located at Tip-Up-Town, Zone 10. 306 Festival Drive. Visitors by approval. No pets.

Reservations: Doug Miller, 3639 Pierce, Shelby Twp., MI 49316. *Website: www.millerslakeshoreresort.com*

Weekly $440-$620

MORRIS'S NORTHERNAIRE RESORT   (989) 422-6644 • EMAIL: northernaire@i2k.com
WES & MARY MORRIS   COTTAGE RESORT

Two bedroom housekeeping cabins on Michigan's largest inland lake. Dock, 14' boat included. Cabins feature all kitchen items, microwave and drip coffeemaker, bathroom/shower, HBO TV. Open all year. Hunting, fishing, snowmobiling, cross-country skiing, water activities. No pets. Mobile Travel Club quality rated. *Website: www.morrisresort.com*

Weekly $300-$650   Nightly $50-$110

Songer's Log Cabins
Bill & Jill Songer

(989) 366-5540
Cottage Resort

★ EDITOR'S CHOICE ★

Open year around, these clean and well maintained log cabins are located on the north shore of Houghton Lake with 150' lake frontage. Each two bedroom cabin features fully equipped kitchens, cable TV, private baths, and screened porches. Several have natural fireplaces. Paddle boat, pontoon boat, tether ball, swimming and more. No pets (except for fall).

Weekly　　*$575-$675 (summer)　　Nightly　$85-$105 (winter)

*Rates reduced in winter

Editor's Note: Nothing fancy, just clean and cozy log cabins by the water. A nice choice for the area.

The Woodbine Villa

(989) 422-5349 • Email: lpress@i2k.com
Cottage Resort

Staying at The Woodbine Villa is like taking a step back in time. Experience the charm of the Old Fashion Log Cabins, yet still enjoy all the amenities of home. 9 fully equipped, two-bedroom log cabins. Pontoon boat rental, fishing boats, motors. Nearly 300 ft. beach frontage. Sauna. Expanded cable and much more. MC and Visa accepted. Open year around. *Website: www.woodbinevilla.com*

Weekly　　$595 (June-Aug.); $445 (Sept.-May); Nightly $75-$100

Tradewinds Resort
Paul & Kim Carrick

(989) 422-5277 • Email: tradewinds@i2k.com
Cottage Resort

Year around cottages are carpeted, fully furnished with equipped kitchens, private bath/showers, double beds, CATV. Boats included. Motors and pontoon boats available. Spacious grounds with sandy beach. Horseshoes, volleyball, shuffleboard, playground on premises. Provide your own linens and paper products. *Website: www.tradewindsresort.org*

Weekly　　$475-$525 (off-season rates available)

WEST SHORE RESORT **(989) 422-3117**
COTTAGE RESORT

★ EDITOR'S CHOICE ★

Nicely maintained, clean and comfortable, small 2 bedroom (sleep up to 6) cottages are fully furnished with equipped kitchens. The cottage closest to the water is more spacious with a direct water view. Provide your own linens/towels during prime season (June-Aug.). $150 deposit. No pets.
Weekly $385-$676

Editor's Note: Mostly smaller but well maintained, clean cottages. The cottage nearest to the lake is good sized and has a great view of the lake.

LEWISTON

GORTON HOUSE BED & BREAKFAST **(989) 786-2764**
LOIS & TOM GORTON BED & BREAKFAST
Relaxing, peaceful Cape Cod on Little Wolf Lake. Antique "theme" rooms. Canoe, boats, putting green, 1920 pool table, fireplaces. Gazeboed outdoor hot tub. Bountiful breakfast, chocolate chip cookies. Garland Golf package. XC skiing, snowmobiling, antiquing, mushroom hunting, nearby golf courses. Gaylord 20 miles. Six rooms with private baths. Open all year.
Nightly $75-$130

LAKEVIEW HILLS RESORT & SPA **(989) 786-2000 • (989) 786-3445**
BED & BREAKFAST

★ EDITOR'S CHOICE ★

15 rooms furnished in antiques feature different eras in American history. Private baths, CATV, individually controlled heating, A/C. Beautiful, groomed pro-croquet court, fitness center with whirlpool, sauna and exercise equipment. Full breakfast with kitchen privileges. Relax in the great room, observatory, library or 165 foot porch. In the winter, enjoy 20 km. of groomed cross-country ski trails on the highest elevation in the Lower Peninsula.
Nightly $98-$149

Editor's Note: Contemporary country styling, beautiful views in a secluded wooded setting. A professional croquet court adds an interesting touch.

PINE RIDGE LODGE **(989) 786-4789** • EMAIL: PINERIDG@NORTHLAND.LIB.MI.US
DOUG & SUZAN STILES LODGE
Grand 7 bedroom log lodge located in the AuSable Forest. Perfect for family holidays, work retreats and couples getaways. Unlimited recreation. Cross-country skiing and mountain biking on-site. Snowshoe rentals, outdoor hot-tub, pool table, fireplace, dart boards and wet bar. Full breakfasts served. Lunch/dinner service upon request. First class amenities with rustic charm. Open year around.
Nightly $54-$89

REGION 3

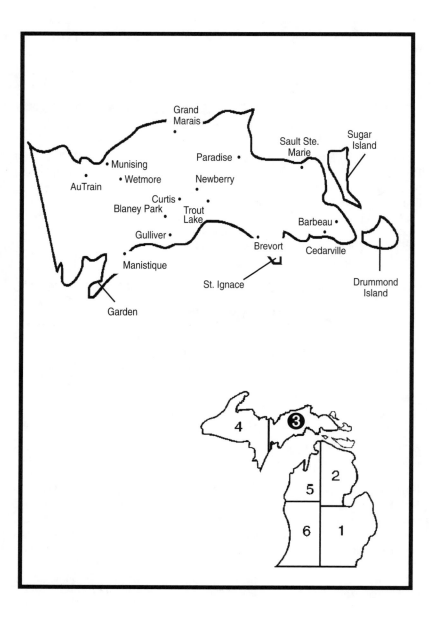

ST. IGNACE • SAULT STE. MARIE

INCLUDES: BREVORT • CEDARVILLE • DRUMMOND ISLAND • SUGAR ISLAND

St. Ignace is a community established in 1671 by the Ojibwa, Huron, and Ottawa tribes. The French Father, Jacques Marquette, was the first priest at the Mission of St. Ignace and became famous for his travels of the Great Lakes and Mississippi River. He is buried outside a 150 year old church which is now a museum in the Father Marquette State Park, located at the base of the Mackinac Bridge. Native American pow-wows are still held outside the mission church. Some are open to the public with the most popular being held Labor Day Weekend. Be sure to see the Marquette Mission Park and the Museum of Ojibwa Culture where you'll learn about Native Americans at the Straits of Mackinac.

An hour's drive north is **Sault Ste. Marie** (meaning the Rapids of St. Mary), the oldest community in Michigan. The Indians once considered this area their summer gathering and fishing place and the first Jesuit missionaries arrived in 1641. It is often referred to as the Gateway to the North.

Starting at the Sault, you will see the Great Rapids white waters as Lake Superior feeds into Lake Huron. The Soo Locks, an engineering marvel, were built in 1855 to raise or lower vessels up to 1,000 ft. in length through these white waters. Take a boat tour through the Locks, experience the feeling and wonder at the ingenuity of man.

Afterwards, walk the path to historic churches and homes and visit the Tower of History. Of course, you must take time to relax and enjoy one of Lake Superior's many sandy beaches. For all those wanting to give Lady Luck a try, this is also the home of The Kewadin Casino, one of the largest casinos in this region. In winter, this area becomes a snowmobilers' heaven. It's also the spot for many winter festivals and outdoor events.

There are several good restaurants in the Sault Ste. Marie area. *Antler's* has been a favorite among vacationers for years. The atmosphere here is fun and laid back and the decor a taxidermist's fantasy with numerous stuffed wildlife found throughout. Expect loud whistles, bells and plenty of good hamburgers (the menu is a fun read, too). If you have a taste for Mexican, try *The Palace Restaurant* or, for an Upper Peninsula flavor, *Abner's Restaurant* is the spot for a traditional "Yooper's" menu which includes, of course, their special pasty. A quieter atmosphere, with good Italian food can be found at *Ang-gio's Restaurant.*

Accessible by ferry, **Drummond Island** is a wilderness paradise. Its natural beauty and wildlife are protected by state and federal laws. The island features over 110 miles of hiking and snowmobile trails and is a wonderful experience for those seeking peace and quiet in natural surroundings. But don't expect total wilderness here. Excellent golfing and refined accommodations are available at the popular Druummond Island Resort. It served as the Domino Pizza's executive retreat for several years and is now opened to the public.

BREVORT

BREVORT LAKE COTTAGE
WENDY KUSLER

(517) 881-7311 • EMAIL: kwenco1@aol.com
PRIVATE HOME

Lakefront log home on 140' of Brevort Lake frontage. 2,600 sq. ft. home offers 3 bedrooms, 2 full baths, den, 1st floor laundry, gourmet kitchen, dishwasher, large greatroom with stone fireplace, extensive deck overlooking the lake. Satellite TV, VCR, ceiling fans. Beautiful year-round ... fall color tours, snowmobiling, sightseeing. Close to Mackinac Island, Tahquamenon Falls, Pictured Rocks, Lake Michigan beaches, casino, golf, hiking and snowmobile trails. No smoking/pets.

Weekly: Memorial Day-Labor Day $1,950 (weekly rental only, Sat.-Sat.)
Weekly: Snowmobile Season $1,500 (Off-season weekly: $1,350)

Editor's Note: This is another NEW property for the MVG. We haven't had a chance to inspect it yet. However, from photos received, this looks like a real gem in the UP.

CEDARVILLE

ISLAND VIEW RESORT, INC.
LARRY & JACKIE

(906) 484-2252 • (800) 854-0556
COTTAGE RESORT

Two and 3 bedroom cottages with carpeting, showers, electric heat and ranges, refrigerators, dishes and cooking utensils. Linens furnished except towels and wash cloths. Fish cleaning house and freezer. Children's playground. Good swimming area. Great fishing. Boats and pontoon available. Major credit cards.
Website: www.islandviewresortinc.com

Weekly $600-$715

DRUMMOND ISLAND

BRETT'S HIDE-A-WAY   **(508) 533-6087 • EMAIL: b.basa@verizon.net**
BRETT DAVIS   **PRIVATE COTTAGE**
Log cottage built in 1993. Located in a quiet wooded lot 300 ft. from the road. Fully equipped and furnished. Satellite TV, VCR, ceiling fan. Hot tub. *Website: http://members.bellatlantic.net/~vzeqhxz*
Weekly $600   Nightly $125 ($100 off-season; 3 night min.)

CAPTAINS COVE RESORT   **(906) 493-5344**
DRUMMON ISLAND REALTY   **COTTAGE RESORT**
Nine remodeled, 1- 2 bedroom cottages in a wooded area on Gold Coast Shores in the heart of Potagnnissing Bay. Some lakefront cabins with fireplaces. All are completely furnished light housekeeping cottages, automatic heat, bathrooms with showers. Boat included. $100 refundable deposit. No pets.
Weekly $370-$450 (4 people)

DRUMMOND ISLAND GETAWAY   **(616) 850-8360 • (616) 240-GOLD**
JAMES & LARRY GOLDMAN   **PRIVATE HOME**

★ EDITOR'S CHOICE ★

3,000 sq. ft. cedar home on 7.8 private acres. 300 ft. of shoreline on Sturgeon Bay. 10 rooms, fireplace, CATV, VCR. Excellent swimming, boating and water sports. Fantastic snowmobiling in winter. No smoking. Pets allowed. Open year around.
Weekly $2,450 (plus tax)
Editor's Note: Luxury home overlooking Sturgeon make ... a picture-perfect view. Pricey, but well worth it. See our review this edition.

DRUMMOND ISLAND RESORT   **(800) 999-6343**
    HOME/LODGE RESORT

★ EDITOR'S CHOICE ★

On 2,000 acres of beautiful woods and waters. Challenging golf at *The Rock*, one of the best courses in the Midwest. Eight homes with fireplaces, full kitchens and 1-5 bedrooms. The Lodge offers 40 rooms. Restaurant on premises. Boats, pontoon rentals.
Nightly $114-$600 (specials starting at $59 nightly)
Editor's Note: Former Domino Pizza executive retreat. Standard hotel rooms to luxurty condos and rustic cabins. Excellent golf and vacation resort. See our review in this edition.

FORT DRUMMOND MARINE & RESORT   **(906) 493-5471**
BLAINE & KAREN TISCHER   COTTAGE RESORT & PRIVATE HOMES
Three cottages on Whitney Bay with equipped kitchens and baths. Linens included. Dock, fish cleaning house. Also, two private homes with washer/dryer. One home is spacious (sleeps 10) with hot tub, fireplace, CATV/VCR. Second home is on a private island, sleeps 6, TV/VCR. Year around.
Weekly $340-$1,300

WA-WEN RESORT   **(906) 493-5445 • (520) 574-5244 (WINTER)**
PHIL & MARCIA STITES   CABIN RESORT
10 acre resort on Maxton Bay near the mouth of the Potagnnissing River. House-keeping cabins have 1-4 bedrooms. Equipped kitchens, electric stoves, bed linens and towels. Aluminum boat, fish cleaning house, electric scaler and freezer available. Tackle shop. Enjoy shuffleboard, fire-pit, basketball/badminton court, picnic tables, charcoal grills and outdoor pool. *Website: www.northcountryproperties.com*
Weekly $330-$530 (prices subject to change, off-season rates available)

ST. IGNACE

BALSAM'S RESORT & MOTEL   **(906) 643-9121 • SEPT.-JUNE (313) 791-8026**
STEVE & SARA MAKOWSKI   COTTAGE/MOTEL RESORT
Close to many U.P. attractions. 40 acre woods, sandy Lake Michigan beach, playground, nature trails and streams. Real log cabins equipped and furnished. Motel rooms include microwave and fridge. CATV. Pets allowed. Open June-October. *Website: www.balsamsresort.com*
Weekly $650 (in-season)   Nightly $45-$95

COTTAGE ON THE STRAITS   **(651) 646-2915 • (651) 690-0590**
JIM & DIANNE MASTERS   PRIVATE COTTAGE
Old world charm, modern amenities, and a spectacular view of the Mackinac Bridge and Island from 100 ft. of private lakeshore. Antiques, wicker, quilts, fireplace, screened porch. Sleeps 6. Close to shops, restaurants, ferry. Open year around. No pets/no smoking. *Website: www.upnorth.biz*
Weekly $950 June-Aug. (Call for other rates/times)
Editor's Note: Clean and cozy interior decor. Owners had fun styling the kitchen with memorabila from the '50's. Exterior wood deck offers a great view of the lake and Bridge.

SAULT STE. MARIE

RIVER COVE CONDOS /HOUSEBOAT RENTALS,   **(906) 632-7075**
SCENIC & FISHING CHARTERS   CONDOS/HOUSEBOAT

★ CONDOS: EDITOR'S CHOICE ★

Waterfront, two bedroom condos completely furnished in nautical themes. Handicap access. Also, 34 ft. live aboard dockside houseboat, rented nightly. Great view of passing ships. Two miles from Kewadin casino and Soo Locks. Open May-December. No pets/no smoking. Charters available. *Website: www.rivercove.com*

Weekly $600-$900   Nightly $99-$189

Editor's Note: The Tiptons' special touches will make you feel welcomed. Great spot to watch the big ships pass. Contemporary condos. Houseboat is a unique alternative.

SUGAR ISLAND

BENNETT'S LANDING   **(906) 632-2987**
COTTAGE RESORT

This fishing resort located on the shores of Big Lake George, has been newly remodeled including a new general store. Cabins are fully equipped. Rent boats, motors, bait. Propane for RVs. Open April 1-Oct. 18.

Weekly $375 (2 people)   Nightly $65 (2 people)

PARADISE • GRAND MARAIS

INCLUDES: BLANEY PARK • CURTIS • GULLIVER • NEWBERRY • TROUT LAKE

As you travel along M123, stop at Hulbert and plan a trip to the Tom Sawyer River Boat and Paul Bunyon Timber Train, or the Toonerville Trolley and River Boat. Both offer 4-1/2 hour round trips to the Tahquamenon Falls with commentary on fauna, flora and various points of interest. Then on to **Paradise**, only 10 miles from the second largest waterfall east of the Mississippi River. It is sometimes called Little Niagara, for here lies Tahquamenon Falls in all its glory. Not far away is Whitefish Point, site of an Audubon Bird Observatory. When you're in the area, be sure to tour the Great Lakes Shipwreck Museum. This is where you will find the "Graveyard of the Great Lakes" and the first Lighthouse of Lake Superior.

Grand Marais is the Eastern Gateway to the Pictured Rocks National Lakeshore. This lovely, unspoiled village offers it all — ladyslippers and trillium, white-tailed deer, black bear, Canadian lynx, moose and — even our own bald eagle resides in this beautiful Upper Peninsula wilderness. As might be expected, boating, fishing, hunting, skiing, and snowmobiling are the thing to do in this area. The Grand Marais Historical Museum, Pictured Rocks Maritime Museum, and the AuSable Lighthouse are some of its attractions. But, of course while you are here, you must be sure to explore their many scenic overlooks including the Log Slide, Munising Falls, Sable Falls and don't forget the unforgettable Tahquamenon Falls and the beautiful Pictured Rocks along Gitche Gumee (Lake Superior). This area is a photographer's dream—bring your camera!

If you're in the **Gulliver** area, enjoy a casual meal at *Fisher's Old Deerfield Inn* which features an informal log cabin atmosphere and quaint dining room.

BLANEY PARK

BLANEY COTTAGES

(906) 283-3163
COTTAGE RESORT

11 cottages, 1-3 bedrooms with fireplace, gas heat and color TV (no kitchens). Continental breakfast. Smoking/non-smoking cabins, picnic areas with gas grills and tables. On 40 acres, bike and snowmobile trails at your door. Seney National Wildlife Refuge nearby. Open all year. Pets O.K.

Nightly $40-$120

CURTIS

LOON'S NEST RESORT   **(906) 586-3525** • EMAIL: loonsnets@portuup.com
COTTAGE RESORT

Nestled along the south shore of Big Manistique Lake on 8 acres of North Country woods, 3 miles west of Curtis. This is a perfect getaway spot with a beautiful setting. There is abundant wildlife, fishing and a great centrally located base to see many UP sightseeing attractions. One, 2 and 3 bedroom cottages include private bath with showers, fully equipped kitchens, CATV, dock and firepit. Also included, 14 ft. aluminum boat. Bring linens. Open all year. No pets, Call or write for a free color brochures.

Weekly $300-$625   Nightly $60-$125

Editor's Note: Small to medium size lodgings. Clean with nicely maintained exteriors and interiors.

MANILAK RESORT   **(906) 586-3285** • **(800) 587-3285**
CHALET/HOME RESORT

Two miles north of Curtis, 11 chalets or ranch-style homes (sleep 1-8). Carpeted, fireplaces, full baths, fully equipped kitchens, linens, charcoal grills, picnic tables and decks. Overlooks Manistique Lake. Includes rowboat. Activity area. Laundry. Open year around. No pets.*Website: www.manilakresort.com*

Weekly $680-$1,070

Editor's Note: A mix of old and new accommodations. The new lodgings looked nice.

SUNSET PINES RESORT   **(800) 586-3199**
KAY   CABIN RESORT

Lovely woodland/lakeside setting. Spacious grounds, secluded, quiet. Playground, swim area. Comfortable, very clean, attractively furnished 1-4 bedroom cabins. Fireplace, TV, laundromat (seasonal), grills, posturepedic beds, carpeted. Open year around. *Website: www.curtismi.com*

Weekly $400-$660 (Off-season rates available - spring, fall, midweek)

SUNSET POINTE RESORT   **(877) 586-9531 (AM) • (906) 586-9527 (PM)**
MIKE SODER   CABIN RESORT
Manistique Lake, 3 miles north of Curtis. 4 spacious cottages on 260' of lake frontage. 2-3 bedroom cottages, fully equipped kitchens, color TV, outdoor cooker. Winter packages include cottages *and* snowmobile. Outboard motor, pontoon rentals available. *On-line store: www.fishandhuntshop.com*
Weekly $400-$650   Nightly $75-$125
Editor's Note: Clean, basic cottages with private baths/showers. Nice sitting/ play area for adults and children overlooking the lake.

TRAILS END RESORT   **(906) 586-3515**
TIM & CARMEN   CABIN RESORT
Four, 2 bedroom cabins with knotty pine interiors, private showers and TVs. Linens included (bring towels and washcloths). A 14 ft. aluminum boat included with rental (motors available). Campfire site. Open year around. Pets O.K. Great fishing for walleye, pike, perch and smallmouth bass.
Weekly $350
Editor's Note: Traditional cabins with nicely maintained exteriors. We found their location appealing ... at the end of a quiet lane overlooking Cooks Bay on Big Manistique Lake.

GRAND MARAIS

HILLTOP MOTEL & CABINS   **(906) 494-2331**
                                               CABIN/MOTEL RESORT
Five, renovated motel units (2 with kitchenettes). Also 9 furnished housekeeping cabins, 5 are brand new. All include gas heaters, showers and CATV. Outdoor fireplace, grills, picnic and play area. Open year around.
Nightly $50-$90

THE RAINBOW LODGE   **(906) 658-3357 • EMAIL: www.rbl2hrt@up.net**
RICHARD & KATHY   CABIN/MOTEL RESORT
All new, modern cabins. Full housekeeping services. Each cabin sleeps up to 6 and features a complete kitchen. Linens are furnished ... all you need to do is come! 3-4 day minimum stay required. Canoe, fishing, snowmobile. Open year around. *Website: www.exploringthenorth.com/twoheart/rainbow.html*
Weekly $267-$510
Editor's Note: Remote setting. Very clean, basic lodgings. Rooms lite by gaslight, electricity supplied by on-site generator. A true wildnerness experience. See our review in this edition.

SUNSET CABINS   **(906) 494-2693** • EMAIL: **sunset3@jamadots.com**
CRAIG WINNIE   CABIN RESORT

Four, newly remodeled, fully furnished cabins (1- 3 bedrooms), along the banks of the old Sucker River overlooking Lake Superior. Equipped kitchens, private bath, full and king si ze beds, CATV. Fire pits, charcoal grills, decks and picnic tables. Open year around. Pets O.K.

Nightly $80-$90   Weekly $480-$540

Editor's Note: If Sunset's other cabins are as appealing as the small, one-bedroom we visited, we are impressed. Bright pine interior,new kitchen, bath and appliances. Simply furnished, but still comfortable. Park-like setting. See our review in this edition.

GULLIVER

FISCHER'S OLD DEERFIELD   **(906) 283-3169**
MARILYN   COTTAGE/MOTEL RESORT

On Gulliver Lake, 21 up-to-date lakeside motel units and housekeeping cottages feature pine paneled walls, bath with shower and automatic heat. Enjoy the private, shallow, sandy beach. Stroll among the well groomed grounds and wooded nature trails. Restaurant, lounge, gift shop, fish cleaning on premises. Open May through November. No pets.

Call for Rates

NEWBERRY

NORTHCOUNTRY CAMPGROUND & CABINS   **(906) 293-8562**
CATHY CLEMENTZ   EMAIL: **cclementz@sault.com**
     CABINS, LODGE/CAMPGROUNDS

Located on 76 acres, 4.5 miles N. of Newberry on M-123, 1/16th mile to snowmobile trails. Campground includes 2 room log cabins with rustic charm and modern conveniences, plus Little Lodge. Lodge accommodates a group of up to 6 and has full kitchen, CATV and more. Bedding provided for all units. Two are partially barrier free. Open May 15 through snowmobile season.

Weekly $435-$625   Nightly $65-$100

PARADISE

BIRCHWOOD LODGES
STEVE HARMON

(906) 492-3320
CABIN RESORT

★ EDITOR'S CHOICE ★

8 modern but rustic log cabins on Lake Superior. Two lakefront cabins with fireplaces. All units carpeted with well furnished kitchens. TV/VCR and movie rentals. Individual picnic tables and grills. All units spotlessly clean, you can bring your mother, and affordable. Shallow all-sand beach with inner tubes, bikes and playground. Paradise is the center of numerous tourist and natural attractions. Check out this year around resort and its accommodating owner since 1981. Late June to September, by-the-week rentals only. No overnights. No pets. *Website: www.harmonsbirchwoodresort.com*

Weekly $360 - $725 (2 people)   Nightly $55-$90

Editor's Note: Simple but comfortable and clean. Steve does a nice job with upkeep. Great sandy beach.

SAUDER'S SUNRISE COTTAGES

(906) 492-3378
COTTAGE RESORT

Two miles north of Paradise on Whitefish Bay. Traditional, two bedroom cottages with double beds, private bath and shower. Fully equipped kitchens with microwave. Linens/towels provided. TV with VCR. Mini-kayaks, canoes and john-boat available. Pets O.K. Open all year.

Nightly $70-$80 (up to 4 people)

Editor's Note: Long, narrow lot with basic, older but clean cottages sitting along a bluff.

TROUT LAKE

TROUT LAKE RESORT

(906) 569-3810
CABIN/APARTMENT/HOUSE RESORT

Just 45 minutes from the Mackinac Bridge. Property overlooks Trout Lake. Cabins have fully equipped kitchenettes, apartments and house have full kitchens with microwave and color TV. Fishing boat is included. Open year around.

Nightly $65 (cabins); $95 (apartments); $150 (house)

TWIN CEDARS RESORT

(906) 569-3209
COTTAGE/MOTEL RESORT

Located in the heart of Hiawatha National Forest, on beautiful Frenchman's Lake — resort provides private setting. Completely furnished, two bedroom cottages, small cabin and plus motel accommodations. Three cottages are lakefront. All, except

one, have lake views. Recent additions: individual decks, complete with grill, table/chairs. Boat use included with stay. Large stone patio on water's edge with built-in firepit. Twin Cedars is a small resort and a memorable place, surrounded by Upper Peninsula atmosphere. Close to points and ports of historical interest. Three of the great lakes, entertainment, and premium shopping. Smoking units available. Sorry, no pets. Well established, family owned and operated.

Call for Rates (Portions of off-season, motel units reduced to $50 for 1 person)

Editor's Note: Nice location, friendly owners. Traditional cottages. The hotel-type accommodations located on the back lot compare to some of the nicer motel rooms we've seen.

AUTRAIN • GARDEN • MANISTIQUE
MUNISING • WETMORE

Just north of **Manistique** you'll find Palms Books State Park, home of the amazing Kitch-iti-kip (Big Spring). It's one of the most unusual water sites in the Upper Peninsula. Take a wooden raft out to the middle of the crystal clear water and watch as more than 23 million gallons of water erupt daily from the lake's bottom.

Looking for a well-preserved ghost town? Then you'll enjoy Fayette Historic Townsite in **Garden**. On the north side of Lake Michigan, Fayette was once a bustling industrial community from 1867 to 1891. Today there are 19 structures standing with a visitor's center, museum exhibits and walking tours .

For you fishermen, stop at either Big Bay de Noc or Little Bay de Noc, rated in *USA Today* as one of the top 10 walleye fishing spots in the country. With nearly 200 miles of shoreline, the bay hosts perch, smallmouth bass, northern pike, rainbow trout, salmon and fishing tournaments. You'll also find uncongested and challenging golf courses, and even a Las Vegas style gambling casino called "Chip-in-Casino". In the winter there are pow-wows and sled dog races.

In **Munising**, take a cruise along the shores of the world famous Pictured Rocks — Miner's Castle, Battleship Rock, Indian Head, Lovers' Leap, Colored Caves, Rainbow Cave and Chapel Rock. Most of these can only be seen from the water. Visiting **Au Train,** you will walk in the footsteps of Hiawatha for, according to Longfellow, here lies his home. Es'ca'naw'ba, from the Indian Eshkonabang, means flat rock. Longfellow's Hiawatha tells of the rushing Escanaba River, sometimes referred to as the land of the Red Buck.

While in the Munising/Au Train area, for good family dining at very reasonable prices, check out *Sidney's* in Munising. Just west of Autrain, *The Brownstone,* is one of the area's more popular restaurant with laid-back UP atmosphere and really great food. Another excellent restaurant is the *Camel Riders* restaurant (2 miles east of county highway 450) reservations are recommended. Just west of Manistique at Highway 2 and 13, *Maxie's* provides a simple but homey Yooper's atmosphere with pretty good steaks.

AUTRAIN

COLEMAN'S PARADISE RESORT   **(906) 892-8390**
BILL & MICHELLE COLEMAN   COTTAGE RESORT
On the west side of AuTrain Lake, this resort offers 1-3 bedroom, furnished cottages. Three bedroom cottages have fireplaces. Large deck overlooks sandy beach. Great swimming. Playground, with horseshoes, volleyball, badminton, basketball. General store and bait shop. Boats and motors available. *Website: www.exploringthenorth.com/colemans/resort.html*
Weekly $295-$600

Dana's Lakeside Resort   (906) 892-8333 • Email: info@danasresort.com
Amy & Kevin Herstad   Cottage Resort
Located in Hiawatha National Forest on the west shore of AuTrain Lake, 3 miles south of M-28. Minutes away from Lake Superior sand beaches, Pictured Rocks National Lakeshore, Grand Island National Recreation Area and Kewadin Casino. Modern 2 and 3 bedroom housekeeping cottages with cable TV hookup. Sand beach, playground, basketball court, shuffleboard. Recreation building with pool table, pinball and video games, air hockey. Washer and dryer available. Boat, motors, kayaks, canoes, and pedal boat available. Lighted boat dock and screened-in fish cleaning house. Campfires in the evenings. Pets welcome. Open all year. *Website: www.danasresort.com*
Call for Rates

Northern Nights   (906) 892-8225
Herb & Debbie Blackstock   Cottage Resort
Cabins on AuTrain Lake. Excellent fishing. Newly renovated. Laundry facilities and recreation room. Boat and motor available. Sandy beach, nightly campfires, easy access to trails for mountain biking, hiking and x-country skiing. Snowmobile from your door. No pets. Weekly rentals June-September. *Website: www.cabinsnorth.com*
Weekly $400-$700

Northwoods Resort   (906) 892-8114 • Email: edkuivanen@chartermi.net
Ed & Pam Kuivanen   Cottage Resort
Located on the northside of Autrain Lake, in the Hiawatha National Forest, 2 miles from Lake Superior, on a paved road. 1-5 bedroom, housekeeping cottages. Beautiful sandy beach, boats, motors, bait, canoe and kayak livery. Open year around. Small pets welcome. *Website: www.exploringthenorth.com/ northwoods/resort.html*
Weekly $320-$750

Pinewood Lodge Bed & Breakfast   (906) 892-8300
Jerry & Jenny Krieg   Bed & Breakfast
Massive log home overlooking Lake Superior. Relax on decks, gazebo, atrium, great room. Enjoy the sauna and stop at our craft store. Walk miles of sandy beach. Tour Pictured Rocks, Grand Island, Hiawatha National Forest, Song Bird Trail, Seney Wildlife Refuge. Full breakfasts, 5 rooms, private baths. *Website: www.pinewoodlodgebnb.com*
Nightly $105-$140

Editor's Note: On M-28. Country-styled rooms give a rustic, woodsy feel with all the modern conveniences.

SEACOAST COTTAGE

(800) 555-6792 • (877) 307-6710
PRIVATE COTTAGE

Lakefront, comfortable, 3 bedroom A-frame located 3.5 miles west of AuTrain/13 Miles west of Munising. Seacoast cottage rests on the shores of mighty Lake Superior. Accommodates 6 adults. Features new furnishings, fully equipped kitchen, CATV, stereo, linens provided. Open year around. *Website: ww.seacoastcottage.com.*

Weekly $700 and up   Nightly $110 and up

GARDEN

THE SUMMER HOUSE
MIKE & NANCY RANGUETTE

(906) 644-2457
BED & BREAKFAST

Built in 1874, this two-story farm house has been restored and decorated in Victorian style. It is located on the picturesque Garden Peninsula, just 7 miles from Fayette State Historical Park. Enjoy golfing, swimming, hunting, fishing, hiking and snowmobile trails. Explore area shops or just relax! 4 rooms.

Nightly $45-$75

MANISTIQUE

MOUNTAIN ASH RESORT

(906) 341-5658
COTTAGE RESORT

On beautiful Indian Lake, 2-4 person cabins or 2-3 bedroom deluxe cabins. Fully furnished (except bath towels). Boat included, individual fire pits. Picnic tables, BBQ grills. Grat fishng and water sports. motor and pontoon rentals. Nearby golfing, salmon fishing and casinos.

Weekly $275-$650   Nightly $45-$95

WHISPERING PINES RESORT   **(888) 772-1786 • (906) 573-2480**
MIKE HOLM   **CABIN RESORT**

Four modern, fully equipped, two-bedroom cabins on Thunder Lake. One large cabin with fireplace, deck, TV, sleeps eight. Bed linens, boats and canoe included. Fish cleaning shed, docks, firepit, barbecue, horseshoe pits, picnic tables. No pets. Open May-December. *Website: www.manistique.com/resorts/whisper/home.htm*
Weekly $350-$450

MUNISING

JOHNSON COTTAGE   **(517) 339-8762**
CHARLES JOHNSON   **PRIVATE COTTAGE**

Immaculate, tastefully decorated, 3 bedroom cottage on 16 Mile Lake, 8 miles south of Munising. Gas fireplace, wood burning stove, TV/VCR, indoor sauna, 2 bathrooms, screened porch. Enjoy all-sport lake, snowmobiling, fishing. Paddleboat and BBQ provided. Cross-country skiing, restaurant within 5 miles. Pets OK with approval. Open all year.
Nightly $80-$150

WHITE FAWN LODGE (906) 573-2949 • EMAIL: hannah@net-link.net
SANDRA & SCOTT BUTLER   CABIN/LODGE RESORT

In the heart of Hiawatha National Forest, lakeside and wooded area cabins. Rooms, suites or apartment units. All have microwaves, refrigerator, coffee makers and color TV's. Community building. Enjoy ATV, hiking and snowmobile trails, hunting, fishing, canoeing and waterfalls. Located 2 hours from Mackinac Bridge/3 hours from Green Bay.

Weekly $375-$450   Nightly $50-$125

RUSTIC RETREAT (906) 387-4971
PRIVATE LOG COTTAGE

Newly renovated, loft-styled log cabin tucked away in the Hiawatha National Forest on all-sport 16 Mile Lake. Very comfortably furnished. TV/VCR. Linens provided.

Sun porch with swing. Includes use of rowboat, paddleboat, BBQ grill, fire pit, wood burning sauna. Swimming beach. Open March-October. Pets O.K. with approval.

Nightly $100
Weekly $500

WETMORE

CABIN FEVER RESORT (800) 507-3341 • (906) 573-2372
RICK & COLLEEN JOHNSON   LOG CABIN RESORT

On 30 acres, these log cabins are fully carpeted and completely furnished with log furniture. Each has housekeeping facilities (1 or 2 bedrooms), fully equipped kitchen and private bath w/shower. Use of boat included. Excellent snowshoeing, x-country ski and snowmobile trails nearby.

Nightly   *$60 (and up) *based on 3 night minimum

REGION 4

MARQUETTE • KEWEENAW PENINSULA • SILVER CITY

INCLUDES: BIG BAY • CALUMET • CHASSELL • COPPER HARBOR •
EAGLE RIVER • HOUGHTON • KEARSARGE • L'ANSE • LAURIUM •
ONTONAGON (PORCUPINE MTNS. & LAKE OF THE CLOUDS) • PEQUAMING •
SKANEE • TOIVOLA (TWIN LAKES)

Marquette, one of the oldest cities in the Upper Peninsula, was initially founded in the 1840's by French settlers to serve the iron-ore mining and lumber industries. Visitors to the area will enjoy the 328-acre Presque Isle Park with its extensive cross country and hiking trails or its International Food Festival in July, hosted by Northern Michigan University. There are plenty of historic sites and outdoor activities to fill your day. As you leave Marquette for Copper Country, you'll want to stop at the *Mt. Shasta Restaurant* in the Champion/Michigamme area where several scenes from the 1950's movie, *Anatomy of a Murder,* were filmed. Here you'll find pictures of Jimmy Stewart, Lee Remick and other cast members adorning the walls.

Thrill to a genuine underground adventure—The Arcadian Copper Mines not far from **Houghton/Hancock**. Take a tour and see the geological wonders created eons ago deep inside the earth. Here, too, is a mecca for rock hounds. Then on to the Quincy Mine Hoist (the Nordberg Hoist), the largest steam-powered mine hoist ever manufactured. Not only is the hoist of great interest, but so is the lore of the Quincy Mining Company. You'll have to visit the area to learn more about it.

In **Calumet,** visit Coppertown USA's Visitor Center. It tells the story of mines, communities and the people of the Keweenaw Peninsula. Theater buffs must stop at the Calumet Theatre and walk with the "Greats" — Bernhardt, Fairbanks, and Sousa. While visiting the area, you'll want to stop at *The Old Country House* just two miles north of Calumet known for its fresh Lake Superior fish, prime rib and homemade bread.

Looking to explore a ghost town? Then travel further north to Mandan, between Delaware and Copper Harbor. In the woods, a block or two south of US-41, you'll find what's left of the town, once a bustling community in Michigan's early copper days. A small sign marks the road.

Then continue on, all the way to **Copper Harbor**, at the tip of the peninsula. Here you'll find a charming little village where everything is less than four blocks away. Stop at the Laughing Loon Gift Shop and from there take a tour into the countryside to view the untouched, towering Estivant Pines. Before the tour, stop for breakfast at the *Pines Restaurant* and taste one of their wonderful cinnamon rolls—a local institution — or *Johnson's Bakery* for great rolls and coffee. The aroma alone from these tasty places will add 10 lbs.

Your trip to Copper Harbor is not complete until you dine at the *Keweenaw Mountain Lodge* which provides well prepared meals in a wilderness setting. Once you've replenished yourself, take a tour of historic Fort Wilkins found along the shoreline of Lake Superior. It was initially built in 1844 to maintain peace in Michigan's Copper Country. Life at the Fort was very difficult with raging waters, frigid winters and heavy snows taking its toll. Much of the Fort's history is retold through museum exhibits, audio-visual programs and costumed interpretation.

Take a boat trip to Isle Royale National Park, a roadless land of wildlife, unspoiled forests, refreshing lakes, and scenic shores. You will find massive waves exploding along rugged coastlines, lighthouses, rolling hills, thimbleberries, vast pines and hardwood forests, a unique culture and accent. Best of all, you can view both the spectacular sunset and sunrise no matter where you are. Here is vacation land at its very best.

For your next adventure head south, back through the Keweenaw and west to **Silver City**. Get ready to experience one of Michigan's biggest and most impressive wilderness retreat, the beautiful Porcupine Mountains. In the Porkies you'll find 80 miles of marked hiking trails in the 58,000 acres of mountainous terrain and more than a dozen rustic trailside cabins. Backpacking the "Porkies" is a challenge reserved only for the strong of heart. For those seeking less challenging experiences but still wanting to savor the beauty of nature, there are driving tours. You might also enjoy the 1/4 mile hike up to The Lake of the Clouds overlook with a wonderful, panoramic view of the lake's clear waters surrounded by forest (this is a particularly breathtaking view in the fall). Of course, the Porkies also has excellent Alpine and cross-country skiing along with terrific snowmobiling, fishing, and swimming.

Ready for another ghost town? Perhaps one of the UP's biggest and most interesting is Nonesuch, which covers a number of acres in the southeast corner of the Porkies. Park interpreters often provide guided tours of the site.

BIG BAY

BIG BAY POINT LIGHTHOUSE B&B	(906) 345-9957
JEFF & LINDA GAMBLE	BED & BREAKFAST

★ EDITOR'S CHOICE ★

A secluded retreat. Seven rooms with private baths. Living room with fireplace. Sauna. 1/2 mile of lakeshore and 50 wooded acres for walking. Spa packages. Ideal area for hiking, mountain biking, snowmobiling, cross-country skiing and more. Open year around. Full breakfasts. *Website: www.bigbaylighthouse.com*

Nightly $115-$183 (May-Oct.); $99-$160 (Nov. -Apr.)

Editor's Note: This B&B represents one of the few surviving resident lighthouses in the country. Very secluded — a truly unique experience. See our review.

THUNDER BAY INN	(906) 345-9376
DARRYL & EILEEN SMALL	INN

Built in 1911 and renovated by Henry Ford in the 1940's. The Inn was used for filming scenes from "Anatomy of a Murder". 12 guest rooms furnished with antiques. Historic lobby with fireplace. Pub and restaurant on premises. Conference facilities. Gift Shop. Open year around. Private and shared baths. Continental breakfasts.

Nightly $65-$105

Editor's Note: This is a classic inn with well maintained rooms which definitely reflect an earlier time.

CALUMET

CALUMET HOUSE B&B	(906) 337-1936
GEORGE & ROSE CHIVSES	BED & BREAKFAST

In the Keweenaw Peninsula, built in 1895, B&B features original woodwork, upright piano and antique furniture. Breakfast served in the formal dining room which has an original butler's pantry. Guests can view television in the drawing room by a cozy fire with their evening tea. No smoking/pets. Adults only.

Nightly $30-$35

CHASSELL

THE HAMAR HOUSE
(906) 523-4670
BED & BREAKFAST

1903 Victorian, set on spacious grounds, features 2 rooms with adjoining sunroom and 3 rooms with shared bath. Children welcome. Enjoy the 3/5 size playhouse. Parking for snowmobiles and trailers. Close to shops, lakefront, ski/snowmobile trails. Open year around. Check or cash only.

Nightly $48-$64 (summer); $48-$58 (winter)

MANNINEN'S CABINS
(906) 523-4135 (W) • (906) 334-2518 (S)
CABIN RESORT

The 7 housekeeping cabins, located on 60 acres of land, are very accessible. The cabins, on Otter Lake (well known for outstanding fishing), come with boats. Freezer service. Open May 15-Oct. 1.

Call for Rates

NORTHERN LIGHT COTTAGES
(906) 523-4131 • (248) 212-6635 (WINTER)
GARY & MARGE WICKSTROM
COTTAGE RESORT

Three fully furnished cottages on Chassell Bay. Two bedrooms sleep up to 6, bed linens and towels provided. Sandy beach, swimming, fishing, docking space. Boats, sauna and campfire site are available. Rent weekly (Saturday to Saturday). Six miles to Michigan Tech. University.

Weekly $285 (and up)

COPPER HARBOR

BELLA VISTA MOTEL & COTTAGES
(906) 289-4213
DEAN, TODD & JENNIFER LAMPPA
COTTAGES/MOTEL RESORT

In Copper Harbor, motel rooms overlook Lake Superior with 8 cottages one block away. Cottages feature kitchens or kitchenettes, satellite TV, some with fireplaces. Next to public dock/boardwalk. Near Isle Royale Ferry. Open mid-May to mid-October. Pets O.K. *Website: www.bellavistamotel.com*

Weekly $270-$390   Nightly $42-$65

BERGH'S WATERFRONT RESORT   **(906) 289-4234**
PHYLLIS BERGH   COTTAGES

These comfortable housekeeping cottages are fully equipped. They include showers, dishes and linens, also boat with dock available. Resort overlooks harbor near Copper Harbor Marina. Open May 15-Oct. 15. Pets allowed. P.O. Box 37, Copper Harbor, MI 49918.

Weekly $260-$300   Nightly $42-$60

LAKE FANNY HOOE RESORT   **(906) 289-4451 • (800) 426-4451**
                                   COTTAGES/CHALET/MOTEL/CAMPGROUND RESORT

Lakefront rooms and cottages with kitchenettes and private balconies on Lake Fanny Hooe. Modern campground with rustic and full hook-up sites. Amenities include clubhouse, sandy swimming beach, boat/snowmobile rentals, gift shop/camp store, laundromat, LP gas, playground, fishing, hiking, cross-country skiing, snowmobiling. *Website: www.fannyhooe.com*

Nightly $65-$80

KEWEENAW MOUNTAIN LODGE   **(906) 289-4403**
                                              CABINS/LODGE RESORT

Log cabins and main lodge nestled in the pines south of Copper Harbor. One, 2 or 3 bedroom cabins, most with fireplaces, and motel rooms. Scenic golf course, hiking trails, tennis court, restaurant and lounge. Discover the tradition.

Nightly $80-$100

Editor's Note: Picturesque comfort in a wilderness setting. Older cottages are basic but comfortable and clean. The restaurant prepares excellent meals.

EAGLE RIVER

EAGLE RIVER'S SUPERIOR VIEW   **(906) 337-5110**
PAUL   PRIVATE HOME

Three bedroom vacation home overlooking Lake Superior and the Sand Dunes. Sleeps 9 comfortably, 1-1/2 baths, fully equipped kitchen, modern decor. Linens provided. Fireplace, washer/dryer. Full porch. Excellent snowmobiling, skiing, swimming beach and play area. Call for free brochure.

Weekly $650   Nightly $100

HOUGHTON

CHARLESTON HISTORIC INN   **(800) 482-7404**
JOHN & HELEN SULLIVAN   **BED & BREAKFAST**
Circa 1900 Georgian architecture. Ornate woodwork, library with fireplace, grand interior staircase, antique and reproduction 18th Century furniture. King canopy beds, private baths, TV's, telephones, A/C, sitting areas. Suites, some with fireplace, private verandas. Deluxe continental breakfast. Major credit cards. Smoking limited. Children 12+ welcome. AAA approved.
Website:www.charlestonhouseinn.com
Nightly $118-$168

KEARSARGE

BELKNAP'S GARNET HOUSE   **(906) 337-5607**
    BED & BREAKFAST
Enjoy the huge porch and 3 acres of this beautiful mining captain's Victorian home. Unchanged throughout the 1900's. Original fireplaces, fur room, leaded/beveled glass pantries, fixtures, woodwork and servants' quarters. 5 rooms (private/shared baths) are decorated with Victorian theme. Full breakfast. Open mid-June through mid-September. Adults only.
Nightly $60-$90

L'ANSE-PEQUAMING

FORD BUNGALOW   **(906) 524-7595**
ALVIN BRINKMAN, MGR.   **PRIVATE HOME**
★ EDITOR'S CHOICE ★
Henry Ford's summer home. Spacious retreat (over 5,000 sq. ft.), sitting 30 ft. above the shores of Lake Superior in a densely wooded area. 9 bedrooms/6 full baths (sleeps up to 16). Fireplace, linens provided. Rocky/pebble beach. No pets/restricted smoking.
Weekly (7 nights) $2,600; 2 Nights $950; 3 Nights $1,350
Editor's Note: An historic home with plenty of ambiance. Located on a very quiet, private back road with a bluff overlook.

LAURIUM

LAURIUM MANOR INN   (906) 337-2549 • EMAIL: lauriumanor@yahoo.com
BED & BREAKFAST

★ EDITOR'S CHOICE ★

Opulent 1908 antebellum mansion has 41 rooms, 13,000 sq. ft. (including a ballroom), 5 fireplaces, hand painted murals and gilded leather wall covering. This elegant mansion offers 17 bedrooms (15 private bath, 2 shared bath), whirlpool tubs, king and queen size beds. Tour this mansion and relive the unforgettable wealth that once was Copper Country. No smoking/pets. *Website: www.lauriummanorinn.com*

Nightly $59-$109 (winter); $69-$139 (summer) private. bath
           $55 (winter); $59 (summer) shared bath

Editor's Note: Elegant and inviting ... premiere Victorian styled B&B.

MARQUETTE

WHITEFISH LODGE   (906) 343-6762 • EMAIL: whitefishl@aol.com
KAREN & STEVE PAWIELSKI   LODGE/COTTAGES

★ EDITOR'S CHOICE ★

A quiet retreat in the U.P. northwoods on the picturesque Laughing Whitefish River. 2 and 3 bedroom lodgings, each completely furnished throughout including kitchens, bedrooms (queen beds) and baths. Enjoy our outdoor decks, grills, excellent walking and biking trails from door. Great fall colors! Five minutes from Lake Superior and close to Pictured Rocks. Open year around. On snowmobile trail and close to x-country ski trails. Gas available on property. 17 miles east of Marquette and 21 miles west of Munising, off M-28. *Website: http://members.aol.com/whitefishl/*

Weekly $350-$675   Nightly $60-$135

Editor's Note: Rustic, secluded, scenic location. Dirt roads ... 4-wheel drive cars recommended in winter. Amiable owners. We enjoyed our stay in their clean accommodations.

ONTONAGON & SILVER CITY (PORCUPINE MTNS. & LAKE OF THE CLOUDS)

LAKE SHORE CABINS   **(906) 885-5318**
                                                      CABIN RESORT
Two miles from the Porcupine Mtns. with 500 ft. frontage on beautiful Lake
Superior. Experience nature with the calm and comfort of home. Private sandy
beach. Fish, hunt, bike, ski, snowmobile and snowshoe right from your door.
All cabins offer housekeeping and include sauna bath and screened porch.

Nightly $79 (based on 2 people)

*Editor's Note: Simple but well maintained traditional cabins. Great beach. A
definite "Up North" feel. Cabins with 1/2 baths. Shower in sauna room.*

MOUNTAIN VIEW LODGE   **(906) 885-5256**
GARY & BECKY ANDERSON   COTTAGE RESORT
                    ★ EDITOR'S CHOICE ★

Contemporary lakeside cottages, 1 mile from Porcupine Mountains. Ski hill
3 miles. On snowmobile trail. Two bedroom cottages with queen beds. Fully
equipped kitchens including dishwasher and microwave. CATV with
videoplayer, fireplace. Pets allows in specific cottages. *Website:
www.mtnviewlodges.com*

Nightly $119-$168

*Editor's Note: Built in 1994, these cottages are well designed, very clean and
comfortable. Highly recommended for the aera. Great view of Lake Superior.*

PETERSON'S CHALET COTTAGES &   **(906) 884-4230** • EMAIL: petcot@up.net
VACATION HOMES (CHUCK/WENDY PETERSON)   CHALET/HOME RESORT
                    ★ EDITOR'S CHOICE ★

On the shore of Lake Superior. 13 chalets with kitchenettes (some with fireplaces)
and vacation home (with whirlpool). CATV, phones. Sandy beaches, grills, picnic
tables and Porcupine Mountain, gift shop on premises. Major credit cards. Open all
year. Some non-smoking units. No pets.

Nightly $85-$130 (Cottages); $300 (Homes)

*Editor's Note: Lodgings vary in style and amenities from small to large homes
and chalets. All well maintained and comfy...something for everyone.*

TOMLINSON'S RAINBOW LODGING
BOB & NANCY TOMLINSON

(906) 885-5348 • (800) 939-5348
CHALET/MOTEL RESORT

Overlooking Lake Superior and Porcupine Mountains. We offer our guests a variety of accommodations, all extremely well maintained with all the amenities of home. We have a two bedroom Lake Superior beach front home. Chalets, 1 with a 2-person hot tub. Kitchen equipped family suites, country decor motel units and much more.

Call for Rates

Editor's Note: Chalets and motel look very well maintained.

SKANEE

AURORA BOREALIS RESORT
ARLENE & HAROLD RIPPLE

(906) 524-5700
COTTAGE RESORT

★ EDITOR'S CHOICE ★

Four comfortably furnished cottages on the shore of Lake Superior offer a unique experience in the Upper Peninsula. They offer a variety of styles from a 150 year old log building to a traditional cedar sided dwelling. Kitchen facilities are complete and all linens, except beach towels, are provided. Three of the cottages are designed to accommodate wheelchairs. The grounds are lovely with many gardens, and a gazebo is available for use in inclement weather. You are invited to enjoy all of the property including the sandy beach and dock. Open April-December. No pets/no smoking. *Website: www.uppermichigan.com/aurora*

Nightly $60-$80

Editor's Note: From historic to new lodgings, all are nicely appointed, clean and comfy. Unique/fun wood carvings hidden on wooded grounds. A very nice choice for the area.

GABE'S SUMMER SUITE COTTAGES
BETTE & JOSEPH GABE

(906) 524-6619
COTTAGE RESORT

Three charming cottages on private grounds along beautiful Huron Bay. Attractively furnished, meticulously-cleaned. Each lodging features two bedrooms, equipped kitchens, private bath, DDS Satellite TV, fireplace. BBQ grills, picnic tables and outdoor furniture. Safe, sandy beach, dock and fish cleaning area.

Open year around. No pets/smoking.

Weekly $385-$465

Editor's Note: Well maintained with attractive interior in excellent condition. Located on quiet, very spacious grounds.

TOIVOLA /TWIN LAKES

KRUPP'S ALL SEASON RESORT

(906) 288-3404
COTTAGE RESORT

Seven units, 1-3 bedroom housekeeping cottages with full kitchens, TV and more. Located on the lake - boating, fishing and swimming. Near golf course, state park, bakery, restaurant, pasties and groceries. Open year round. Gasoline on premises. Major credit cards accepted.

Weekly $150-$550

TWIN LAKES RESORT

(906) 288-3666
COTTAGE RESORT

6 units, summer cottages and vacation homes. Kitchens, tub and showers. Sandy beach, safe swimming, fishing, sight-seeing. Boat available.. Located near a golf course and state park. Reservations appreciated. Open late May thru mid-October. Brochure available.

Weekly $400-$790

IRONWOOD & SURROUNDING AREAS

INCLUDES: BESSEMER • CRYSTAL FALLS • IRON RIVER • IRONWOOD •
LAKE GOGEBIC • WAKEFIELD • WATERSMEET

Ironwood is known as *The Big Snow Country*. But don't let that fool you, it is more than just winter fun. Here among unspoiled forest and mountains are miles of trout streams and hundreds of spring fed lakes. Visitors will enjoy their vacation on the famous Cisco Chain of Lakes, in Bergland/Marenisco. Bring your camera! Here stands "The World's Tallest Indian"—HIAWATHA. He towers 150 feet over downtown Ironwood. Also, don't miss the Copper Peak Ski Flying Hill in the Black River Recreation Area, 10 miles northeast of Ironwood.

Lake Gogebic is the area's largest lake, with 13,000 acres of prime fishing water. In June, September and throughout the season, fishing tournaments are held. Families will enjoy all sorts of summer fun, sight-seeing, hiking and water sports. Further northeast we come to the Porcupine Mountains Wilderness State Park (15 miles west of Ontonagon).

BESSEMER

BLACKJACK SKI RESORT   **(800) 848-1125**
CONDO/CHALET RESORT

Trailside lodging units offer ski-in, ski-out convenience. Cozy fireplaces, new TV systems, complete kitchens and saunas in every building. Longest run over 1 mile. PSIA Ski School, Kinderkamp and nursery. Lodgings range from studio to 1-3 bedroom. Special package rates available.

Nightly $52-$115 (per person, per night) Call for special package rates

BIG POWDERHORN LODGING   **(800) 222-3131 • (906) 932-3100**
CONDO/CHALET RESORT

Luxury to budget conscious private chalets and condos. Ice rink, horse-driven sleigh rides, x-country skiing, pool, special events, trailside decks, and live entertainment. NASTAR, ski school, ski shop, rentals, Kinderschool and cafeteria. 3 restaurants and lounges, sauna/whirlpool, and fireplace. Credit cards accepted. Call for special package and off-season rates.

Nightly   Beginning at $62 ($13 ea. add'l person)

CRYSTAL FALLS

BIRCHWOOD CABINS **(906) 875-3637**
CABIN RESORT
On Swan Lake in a park-like setting, these 5 (1-2 bedroom) cabins are completely furnished (linens included) and offer equipped kitchens, showers and gas heat. Boat included. Excellent hunting/fishing (walleye and perch), plus easy access to miles of snowmobile, x-country ski trails. Pets allowed.
Call for Rates

IRON RIVER

LAC O'SEASONS RESORT **(800) 797-5226**
RANDY & NANCY SCHAUWECKER COTTAGE RESORT
10 min. from downtown Iron River on Stanley Lake, close to Ski Brule, snowmobile trails. Indoor pool, sauna /whirlpool. 2-3 bedroom cottages, some log, electric heat, full kitchens. Some with fireplaces. Porch with grills with each unit. Boats, canoes, kayaks and pontoon rentals. *Website: www.lacoseasons.com*
Weekly $590-$1,225 (plus tax)

IRONWOOD

BEAR TRACK CABINS **(906) 932-2144**
CABIN RESORT
Deep within the west end of the Ottawa National Forest, adjacent to a designated national scenic river. Cabins include kitchens, showers, woodburning stoves, linens. Authentic Finnish wood sauna on premises. Minutes from 5 waterfalls, Lake Superior beach, hiking/mountain biking trails. Located in a true wilderness setting.
Nightly $68-$146

BLACK RIVER LODGE **(906) 932-3857**
TOWNHOUSE/MOTEL/CONDO RESORT
Located 2 miles from Big Powderhorn Mtn., near Copper Peak Ski Flying Hill with 5 waterfalls and Black River Harbor. The lodge offers motel rooms, suites, townshouses and condominiums. Indoor swimming pool, hot tub, restaurant, lounge and game room. *Website: www.westernup.com/blackriverlodge*
Call for Rates

River Rock Retreat

(906) 932-5638
PRIVATE LOG CABIN

Massive log cabin that sets the highest standard for log cabin construction with many special features including hand-hewn red pine logs. Snowmobile right outside your door and snowshoeing. Fully equipped and furnished, 3 fireplaces, 3 baths, 3 living areas, complete kitchen, jacuzzi, sauna, phone, BBQ. Open year around.

Call for Rates

LAKE GOGEBIC

Gogebic Lodge
BERQUIST FAMILY

(906) 842-3321
CHALET/COTTAGE RESORT

CHALETS: ★ EDITOR'S CHOICE ★

West side of Lake Gogebic, cottage and chalet accommodations. Cottages feature private bath, CATV, equipped kitchens, and more! The Lodge includes sauna/whirlpool, dining room/lounge. Boat and motor rentals available. Enjoy hunting, fishing, swimming, snowmobiling and skiing. Credit cards accepted. Pets allowed, extra charge.

Weekly $350-$1,100   Nightly $60-$200

Editor's Note: Very good location. Great for fishing/outdoor enthusiasts. Excellent restaurant on-site. The chalets built in 1994 and 1999 are in very nice condition and rate an Editor's Choice.

The West Shore Resort

(906) 842-3336
COTTAGE RESORT

450 ft. on Lake Gogebic. Great fishing for walleye or hunting for bear and deer. All cabins are 2 bedrooms, sleep 6, bath (towels and linens provided). Boat launch on site, docks and boat lifts. Boat and motor rentals. Pets welcome. Open year around.

Weekly $425 (dbl. occ. - $50 each add'l person) Summer Rates
Nightly $70 (dbl. occ. - $10 each add'l person) Summer Rates

Editor's Note: Small but very clean, comfortable accommodations — reasonable prices make this a good choice.

MALLARD COVE & TEAL WING
SNOW COUNTRY REAL ESTATE
(800) 876-9751
PRIVATE HOMES

★ EDITOR'S CHOICE ★

Mallard Cove: Four bedroom, two baths with cedar sauna. Accommodates 8. Features phone, fireplace, Weber grill, fully equipped kitchen with dishwasher, linens, towels. Excellent waterfront view. Lakeside deck and boat dock. Groomed snowmobile trails and skiing nearby.

Teal Wing: Contemporary, spacious lakeside home on Lake Gogebic. Four bedrooms, two baths (sleeps 8). Fully furnished and equipped including microwave, phone, TV/ VCR, stereo. Includes use of boat dock. Also overlooks Lake

Teal Wing

Gogebic and is located on snowmobile route. Available year around. Pets O.K. Private setting on the lake. *Website: www.snowcountryhomes.com*

Weekly $995 (Summer)   Nightly $195 (Winter) (Seasonal Discounts)

Editor's Note: Tom and Arlene Schneller, owners, have designed and decorated these homes with comfort and style.

NINE PINE RESORT
RON & JOANN MONTIE
(906) 842-3361
COTTAGE RESORT

A family resort, centrally located in "Big Snow Country". Snowmobile right to your door. Modern, carpeted housekeeping units (sleep 2-8) with TV. Boats and motors available for rent. 1 cottage with fireplace. Linens provided. Restaurants nearby. Open year around. Major credit cards. Pets allowed.

Weekly $400-$995 (up to 4 people)

SOUTHWINDS COTTAGE   **(906) 575-3397 • EMAIL: pat@pathansonhomes.com**
MARLINE & PAT HANSON
PRIVATE COTTAGE

Cozy, clean 2 bedroom cottage on Lake Gogebic with 220 ft. of sandy beach. Private dock. Sleeps 6. All new carpet and furnishings. Fully equipped kitchen with microwave and grill. Private, very quiet. Lovely wood deck overlooks the lake. Rent year around. Snowmobile/watercraft rentals available. No pets.

Weekly $850

SUNNYSIDE COTTAGES
SUE GROOMS

(906) 842-3371
COTTAGE RESORT

★ EDITOR'S CHOICE ★

Set along 450 ft. of Lake Gogebic, these 8 well maintained, comfortably furnished lodgings feature fully equipped kitchens including microwaves, knotty pine interiors, satellite TV, private baths, bedrooms with 1 to 2 full size beds. Doorwalls lead to private deck. Campfires-charcoal grills. *Website: www.sunnysidecottages.net*

Weekly $650-$750

Editor's Note: Spotless cabins with a "luxurious" feel. We continue to be very impressed.

THE TIMBERS RESORT
DAVID & LINDA DANIELS

(906) 575-3542 • EMAIL: ldaniels@portup.com
COTTAGE RESORT

A resort focused on family vacationing, open year around. Located on the north end of Lake Gogebic. Nine fully furnished cottages with most of the amenities of home. Resort features nightly bond fire, playground, trampoline, sandy swim area, laundromat, fish cleaning house, bait, boat and motor rentals. Pets welcome.

Nightly $59-$260

WHITETAIL LODGING
PHIL BERCOT

(906) 842-3589
COTTAGE RESORT

★ EDITOR'S CHOICE ★

Four fully furnished lodges on the east shore of Lake Gogebic. Three hold 4-6 people, one holds 8-10 people. All include knotty pine interiors, full baths, queen size beds, linens, complete kitchens, and gas fireplaces. Dock space, boat lifts, and on-site ramp available at no charge. Great walleye, bass and perch fishing, deer and grouse hunting. Gorgeous fall colors. Snowmobile trail access from the resort. Pets O.K. Open all year. *Website: www.whitetaillodging.com*

Weekly $600-$1,100 (April 16-Nov. 30)   Nightly $45 (per person-winter)

Editor's Note: Fully renovated, nicely furnished cottages with fresh, appealing interiors. Clean and comfortable.

WAKEFIELD

INDIANHEAD MOUNTAIN RESORT
(800) 3-INDIAN
CONDO/CHALET RESORT

Condos, chalets and lodge room with varied amenities including phones, color TV's and/or CATV, VCR's, dishwashers, washers/dryers, Jacuzzi or sauna. Two restaurants, 2 cafeterias, 5 cocktail lounges, indoor pool and spa, health/racquet club, full service ski shop, child care, Kids 12 and under free. Pets allowed in some units. *Website: www.indianheadmtn.com*

Nightly $75-$498 (from basic lodge room to 5 bedroom chalet)

WATERSMEET

THE ARROWS   (906) 358-4390 • EMAIL: the arrows@portup.com
DENVER & CAROLE YAKEL
COTTAGE/HOME RESORT

Six ultra-modern homes and luxury vacation homes with fireplaces, satellite TV's, double whirlpools, dishwashers, microwaves, washers and dryers, phones, decks, piers and more. On Thousand Island lake on the Cisco Chain in the Upper Peinsula. Sleep up to 15 each. Boat, motor, deluxe boat and pontoon rentals. Snowmobile from door and x-country nearby. Great off-season discounts. LVD casino coupons. *Website: www.watersmeets.org/thearrows*

Weekly $520-$1,435

Editor's Note: Cottage interiors in good condition. The newer homes are very nice. Beautiful, natural setting. Excellent fishing and boating.

CROOKED LAKE RESORT   (906) 358-4421 • Email: crookedlake@portup.com
COTTAGE RESORT

On Crooked Lake in Sylvania Perimeter/Wilderness Area. Motors allowed. Six modern, 2 and 3 bedroom housekeeping cottages. Everything furnised except personal towels. Each cottage comes with a boat or canoe. Dock space available for rent. Motor rental, bait, gas available. Open May 15-November. Pets allowed.

Weekly $515-$780

JAY'S RESORT — (906) 358-4300
COTTAGE RESORT

Lakefront cottages on Thousand Island Lake. Ten, 1-4 bedroom housekeeping cottages, including 2 new log units. Many with fireplaces. Complete kitchen, color TV, sleeps up to 15. Lund boats, deluxe boats and pontoons. Spacious grounds with play area. 20% seasonal discounts. Pets with permission, extra charge. Handicap access.

Weekly $500-$1,650

Editor's Note: Cottage exteriors new—the natural grounds were well groomed. Cute play area for children.

LAC LA BELLE RESORT — (906) 358-4390 EMAIL: the arrows@portup.com
THE YAKELS   HOME/MOBILE HOME/COTTAGE RESORT

Located on Thousand Island Lake on the beautiful Cisco Chain in Michigan's Upper Peninsula. A very modern, four-bedroom home with two baths, dishwasher, satellite TV, VCR, washer and dryer, large deck, pier. Also a modern, two-bedroom mobile home right on the water with pier. Picnic tables, grills. Boats, motors, deluxe boats and pontoon rentals. Fantastic sunsets. Snowmobile from door. LVD canio coupons. *Website: www.watersmeet.org/laclabelle*

Weekly $565-$1,100

VACATIONLAND RESORT — (906) 358-4380 • EMAIL: wsmet@portup.com
BILL & JAN SMET   COTTAGE RESORT

Housekeeping cottages, 1-4 bedrooms, some with fireplaces, on Thousand Island Lake. Linens furnished (bring towels). Boat included (motors extra). Safe swimming beach. Dock and raft, tennis, volleyball, basketball, fishing and boating. Great x-country skiing, snowmobiling and ice fishing. *Website: www.westernup.com/vacationland*

Weekly $345-$1,400   Nightly $65-$300

REGION 5

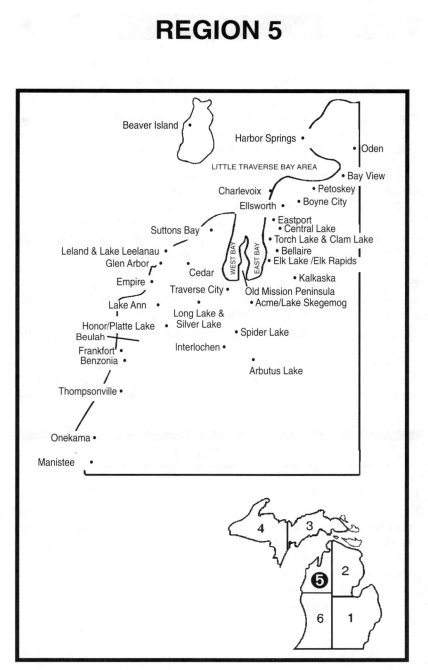

Beaver Island

Harbor Springs •

• Oden

LITTLE TRAVERSE BAY AREA

• Bay View

Charlevoix

• Petoskey

Ellsworth •   • Boyne City

Suttons Bay •

• Eastport
• Central Lake
• Torch Lake & Clam Lake

Leland & Lake Leelanau •

• Bellaire

Glen Arbor •

WEST BAY   EAST BAY

• Elk Lake /Elk Rapids

Cedar

• Kalkaska

Empire •

Traverse City •   Old Mission Peninsula

Lake Ann •

• Acme/Lake Skegemog

Honor/Platte Lake •   Long Lake &
Beulah   Silver Lake   • Spider Lake

Frankfort •

Interlochen •

Benzonia •

Arbutus Lake

Thompsonville •

Onekama •

Manistee •

BOYNE CITY • CHARLEVOIX • PETOSKEY

INCLUDES: BAY VIEW • EASTPORT • ELLSWORTH • HARBOR SPRINGS
• LITTLE TRAVERSE BAY • ODEN

T he scenic area of **Boyne, Charlevoix, Harbor Springs**, and **Petoskey** offers superb sight-seeing, unique shops, fishing, sailing, and some of the best downhill and cross country skiing in Lower Michigan.

Five linear miles of flower-lined streets, a drawbridge, and two lakes have earned "Charlevoix the Beautiful" its name. The village has become the center for the arts complete with galleries and shops. The spring offers Petoskey Stone and other fossil collectors hours of treasure hunting along its many sandy beaches. Don't forget to visit Petoskey's unique shops in the historic Gaslight District. Harbor Springs' scenic beauty compares to few and includes the very scenic 31 mile route to Cross Village through the Tunnel of Trees. Harbor Springs also features several interesting shops where you'll want to take time to browse. We can't overlook Boyne's high-peaked hills, that provide the scene for some of lower Michigan's finest downhill skiing.

Some outstanding restaurants in the area include *The Rowe Inn* (Ellsworth), *Tapawingo* (on St. Clair Lake) and *Pete and Mickey's* at the *Edgewater* (Charlevoix). For other good fixin's in Charlevoix, try homestyle cooking at *Darlene's*, dine on the lake at *Round Table Restaurant* or, for a Friday night fish-fry, tasty hamburgers, pasties, or Mexican there's the *Lumberjack Saloon*.

BAY VIEW

THE GINGERBREAD HOUSE   (231) 347-3538
MARY GRULER   BED & BREAKFAST
Pastel hues, white wicker and floral gardens provide a romantic setting for this 1881 renovated Victorian cottage situated in the heart of Bay View, a National Historic Landmark. All rooms with view of Little Traverse Bay, private entrances and baths, A/C. Deluxe continental breakfast. No smoking/pets. Open mid-May-October. 4 rooms.
Nightly $115-$175

BOYNE CITY/BOYNE MOUNTAIN

DEER LAKE BED & BREAKFAST   **(231) 582-9039**
SHIRLEY & GLENN PIEPENBURG   BED & BREAKFAST

★ EDITOR'S CHOICE ★

Contemporary waterfront B&B on Deer lake in quiet country setting. An all season resort area near Boyne Mountain. Features five rooms with private baths, individual heat and A/C. Enjoy full breakfast by candlelight on china and crystal. Personalized jewelry class available.

Nightly $95-$115

Editor's Note: Beautiful setting. Impressively designed interior with gracious hosts. You won't be disappointed. See our review in this edition.

HARBORAGE CONDOMINIUMS   **(231) 582-2000 • (888) 285-2111**
RICK SMITH (HARBORAGE PROPERTY RENTALS)   CONDOS
Two and 3 bedroom condos close to Lake Charlevoix and near a full-service marina. Completely equipped and beautifully decorated.

Weekly $1,700-$2,000 (prices exclude holidays)

R & H CHALET   **(734) 676-1405 • EMAIL: brichards@trenton-mi.com**
BARB   PRIVATE CHALET
Beautiful three bedroom, two full bath chalet, located on Deer Lake at Boyne Mountain in Northern Michigan. All conveniences of home. Fireplace, equipped kitchen, CATV, VCR. 120' lake frontage with beach and dock. Weekly rentals during summer, weekend rentals during ski season. Open year around. No pets.

Weekly $1,000   Nightly $200

Editor's Note: Cozy chalet, comfortably styled and competitively priced. See our review in this edition.

SCHADE COTTAGE   **(734) 675-2452 • (734) 675-2873**
CHRIS SCHADE   PRIVATE CONDO
Spacious, 3-level condo overlooks Lake Charlevoix. Furnished (with linens), sleeps 6. Features king/queen beds, full kitchen, microwave, dishwasher, 4 baths, fireplace, sauna, private beach and dock, balcony, patio, CATV, VCR, washer/dryer. Minimum 1 week. $775 non-refundable deposit per week. No pets. References.

Weekly $1,550 ($75 cleaning fee)

THE LANDINGS   **(800) 968-5115 • (231) 547-1222**
VACATION PROPERTY RENTAL AND MGT. CO.   CONDO RESORT
Two bedroom/2 bath condos on the shores of Lake Charlevoix in the heart of northwest Michigan's recreational playground. Sandy beach, heated pool, boat slips. Only minutes from Boyne Country Championship Golf. An excellent rental value, located in Boyne City. Call early for best availability.

Weekly $1,800

NANCY SERRA

(810) 625-8705
PRIVATE CHALET

★ EDITOR'S CHOICE ★

In prime golf area. Overlooks Lake Charlevoix. Only steps to beach. Conveniently located 2 blocks from marina. Chalet features 3 bedrooms (4 twin, 1 full, 1 queen). All amenities including CATV, BBQ, washer/dryer and linens. Weekly rentals. $250 deposit. No pets. Rental season May-October.

Weekly $750

Editor's Note: Lovely chalet with contemporary Indian motif ... very appealing. Spacious lot with view of lake somewhat obstructed by homes. Good price for the area.

WATER STREET INN

(800) 456-4313
MAIN RENTAL OFFICE INN/
CONDOS

On beautiful Lake Charlevoix, 27 suites with lake views feature living room/ dining area, separate bedroom, kitchenettes, gas fireplaces, whirlpool bath, CATV, king size beds. Boating, shopping, fishing or just relaxing, the Inn offers the finest available options just minutes from ski hills, snowmobile trains, sledding, ice skating and more.

Weekly $1,200   Nightly $75-$200

Editor's Note: Good location and well decorated rooms make this a nice choice.

WOLVERINE/DILWORTH INN
MAIN RENTAL OFFICE

(800) 748-0160 • (231) 582-7388
INN

Built in 1912, the Historic Wolervine Dilworth Inn has 24 rooms with A/C, private baths, suites (multi-rooms), phone and CATV. Inn offers continental breakfast and banquet facilities for weddings and special events. Open year around.

Nightly $129

CHARLEVOIX

AARON'S WINDY HILL GUEST LODGE   (231) 547-6100 • (231) 547-2804
BED & BREAKFAST

Victorian home with a huge riverstone porch. Homemade buffet-style breakfast. Eight spacious rooms have private bath (some with A/C). Two rooms accommodate up to 5. One block north of drawbridge, one block east of Lake
Michigan. Children welcome. Open May - Oct.

Nightly $75-$140

THE BLUFFS   (734) 663-8056
LAURA MCREYNOLDS   PRIVATE LOG CABIN

Charming 1920's log cabin on Lake Michigan with fieldstone fireplace,
beamed ceilings, sunroom with gorgeous sunset views, antiques and cozy
cabin furniture. Full kitchen, washer-dryer, fenced yard and private beach. 2
bedrooms plus sleeping loft (sleeps 6). Open year around. No smoking/pets.

Weekly $1,400 (June-August; off-season rates avail. Sept.-May)

BOULDER PARK COTTAGES   (847) 256-5767 • (231) 547-6480
JOAN CHODAK   PRIVATE COTTAGES

2 charming stone cot-
tages (1 and 3 bed-room)
are located in Earl
Young's Boulder Park
on 2 acres of land in a
park-like setting. Only
800 ft. to Lake Michi-
gan. Includes: bed lin-
ens, dishwashers, mi-
cro-waves, phones,
VCR, CATV and fire-
places. Outdoor furnish-
ings, camp-fire, flowers
abound. 50% deposit. Pets allowed.

Weekly $980 (1 bedroom); $1,400 (3 bedroom) Off-season rates available

*Editor's Note: Part of Charlevoix's history. These 2 cottages are built in the style
of Earl Young's boulder homes and are located on a quiet side street.*

THE BRIDGE STREET INN
(231) 547-6606
BED & BREAKFAST

Built in 1895, this Colonial Revival home retains the charm of yesteryear. Relax on its sweeping porch with view of Lake Michigan or in the bright living room. Seven guest rooms - floral rugs on wooden floors, antique furnishings, plush beds. Breakfast/coffee served on the porch.

Nightly $90-$145 (May to October)

CHARLEVOIX COUNTRY INN
(231) 547-5134
BED & BREAKFAST

Visitors will feel welcomed as they enter this 1896 country decor inn. Relax and get acquainted in the common room, balcony or porch while watching boats and Lake Michigan sunsets. 8 bedrooms/2 suites, all with private baths. Continental breakfast buffet. Late afternoon beverage, wine and cheese social.

Nightly $90-$145

HIDDEN VALLEY RESORT
(231) 547-4580 (Leave Message)
COTTAGE RESORT

Quiet, unspoiled resort on 620 ft. of Nowland Lake with natural shoreline. Each cottage has been renovated to retain knotty pine charm and modern conveniences. 1 bedroom (sleeps 4 with pullout), private bath, equipped kitchen, TV, screened porch. Sandy beach, excellent fishing lake.

Weekly $700-$900 (call for 3-4 night rates)

SUE HUMMEL
(248) 855-3300 • (248) 363-3885
PRIVATE CONDOS

Lakefront condos sleep 2-8+ with 1-2 baths, A/C, fireplace, 2 person Jacuzzi and CATV. Designer furnished. Includes linens and towels. Within walking distance to Charlevoix, marinas, beach. Heated pool. Lots of skiing within 1/2 hours. Available year around. 50% deposit.

Weekly $400-$1,200   Nightly $100-$200 (summer rates)

LARRY KISH
(517) 349-5474 (HOME) • (517) 482-7058 (WORK)
PRIVATE HOME

Lake Charlevoix home features 4 bedrooms/2 baths, 128 ft. water frontage, 600 sq. ft. deck, dock, raft, 5 sliding glass doors and lots of windows. Dishwasher, washer/dryer, TV/VCR and stereo. Vaulted ceiling. Fabulous view. Available year around.

	Sept.-June	July/Aug.	Xmas/New Years
Weekly	$1,900	$2,600	$2,600

LAKEFRONT LOG LODGE   **(231) 536-2851**
SHARON & AL FROST   PRIVATE HOMES
These 2 spacious, 7 bedroom vacation homes with serene setting offers a spectacular view of Lake Charlevoix. Features 7 full baths, large modern kitchens, CATV, fireplaces, docks, campfire area and swing sets, 3 decks and 200 ft. of sandy beach. Large Jacuzzis. Sleeps up to 28—great for 3 or 4 families. Only 50 ft. from Lake Charlevoix and 5 minutes from town. Great swimming and fishing. Near Boyne Mountain. Available year around. 50% deposit. No pets. *Website: www.greatrentals.com/mi/2211.html*
Weekly $4,000-$6,000 per home (off-season rates available)

POINTES NORTH INN   **(231) 547-0055**
CONDO RESORT
1-2 bedroom suites with lofts and full or partial kitchens. Indoor/outdoor pool. CATV, A/C, VCR and Jacuzzi whirlpools in all units. Located in downtown Charlevoix. Pets allowed - call for information. Corporate, off-season rates available.
Nightly $240-$325 (2-night min.)

EASTPORT

EDEN SHORES   **(231) 264-9604**
MARILYN & CHARLES WILMOT   PRIVATE COTTAGE
Eastport cottage sits in a secluded wooded area. Quiet, clean. Bright sunroom with lots of windows. 5 minute walk to Lake Michigan beach. Recently re-done — new carpeting, tile, walls, bathroom. Full kitchen. Linens provided. No pets/smoking.
Weekly $450

ELLSWORTH

THE HOUSE ON THE HILL B&B   **(231) 588-6304**
CINDY & TOM TOMALKA   EMAIL: innkeeper@thehouseonthehill.com
BED & BREAKFAST

★ EDITOR'S CHOICE ★

This ultimate hostess overlooks peaceful St. Clair Lake. 53 acres with on-property activities including hiking, canoeing and kayaking. Walking distance to gourmet restaurants Tapawingo and Rowe Inn. Evening social hour. Full breakfast. Seven rooms/private bath - king or queen bed. Winter packages. Open all year.
Nightly $135-$150

Editor's Note: Picturesque B&B with beautifully designed rooms. An excellent choice for the area. Highly recommended.

HARBOR SPRINGS

KIMBERLY COUNTRY ESTATE   **(231) 526-7646**
RONN & BILLIE SERNA   **BED & BREAKFAST**

This colonial plantation style B & B welcomes its guests with a lovely veranda and terrace overlooking the swimming pool and Wequetonsing Golf Course. On several secluded acres. Features 6 exquisitely decorated rooms, some with fireplace, sitting area and Jacuzzi. 4 min. to Boyne Highlands or Nubs Nob.

Nightly $155-$275

HAMLET VILLAGE   **(231) 526-2754 • (800) 678-2341**
C/O LAND MASTERS   **HOME/CONDO RESORT**

★ EDITOR'S CHOICE ★

Contemporary country styling located in the secluded, rolling hills of Harbor Springs. Slope side condos features ski-in/ski-out access to Nubs Nob. Condos offer 1-4 bedroom + loft. Homes/chalets (between Boyne Highlands and Nubs Nob) vary in size. A few miles from beaches/marinas/golf. Prices vary based on season and size of accommodation. Full range of pricing options available.

Weekend Pkgs: Condos: $300-$1,260 (Add'l. nights with weekend $127-$314); Homes: $300-$1,030 (Add'l. nights with weekend $113-$265)

Editor's Note: Scenic locations and well maintained properties make Hamlet Village accommodations a good choice. You Nubs Nob fans will love their condo's ski-in/out privileges.

THE VERANDA BED & BREAKFAST   **(231) 526-0202**
    BED & BREAKFAST

Delightful B&B is as warm and inviting as a Norman Rockwell painting. Guests are treated to a full gourmet breakfast in the morning, and wine with appetizers in the evening. Convenient to shops, restaurants, tennis courts, and beaches. Open year around. 6 rooms. *Website: www.harborspringsveranda.com*

Nightly $125-$295

TROUT CREEK CONDOMINIUM RESORT (800) 748-0245 • (231) 526-2148
CONDO RESORT

★ EDITOR'S CHOICE ★

Family resort with beautifully furnished units (accommodate 2-12), full kitchens and fireplaces. 2 outdoor pools, spas, fitness center, indoor pool, tennis courts, trout ponds, nature trails. Nearby skiing with on-site cross-country trails. Nearby golf, beaches. Children's programs during summer. Romantic packages available. Sorry, no pets.

Nightly $90-$451

Editor's Note: Contemporary, comfortable setting with plenty to do for couples or families.

HOUSE ON THE HILL (231) 539-8909
ZULSKI BROTHERS PRIVATE VACATION HOME

★ EDITOR'S CHOICE ★

New home situated on 400 secluded acres. Fully furnished, three bedroom getaway. Close (1/2 hour and less) to golf, skiing, beaches, shopping and dining. Access to groomed snowmobile trails. Scenic views, wildlife and miles of hiking trails. Satellite TV. No pets/smoking.

Weekly $800

Editor's Note: Spacious, well-designed and abundantly comfortable home resting on secluded, scenic grounds overlooking woods and walking trails. Highly recommended. See our review this edition.

LITTLE TRAVERSE BAY

HOLIDAY ACCOMMODATIONS (800) 968-4353 • (231) 348-2765
CONDOS/COTTAGES/CHALETS

Your *Upnorth Connection* - Over 100 quality rental properties for all seasons in the Little Traverse Bay area. Studio to 6 bedroom homes, cottages and condominiums for groups of 2 to 14. *Website: www.upnorth.com*

Weekly $750-$3000 (June-Aug.); $375-$1,200 (Off-season)

ODEN

WINDJAMMER MARINA   **(231) 347-6103**
                                                        HOUSEBOATS

On Crooked Lake, the 40 ft. Royal Capri sleeps 8 includes head with hot water, shower, refrigerator with freezer, gas stove/oven, dishes and utensils. The 28 ft. Riviera Cruiser sleeps 4 and has stove, ice box, porta potty, hand pump water system, dishes and utensils. Deposit required. Rates do not include gas. No linens.

Weekly $1,500 (40 ft.); $750 (28 ft.)

PETOSKEY

EL RANCHO ALANSON   **(586) 777-6808 • EMAIL: donapp@ameritech.net**
LOT 42   **RV (RECREATIONAL VEHICLE)**

Located 10 minutes from Petoskey. Three bedroom Park Model RV, 12'x35'. Completely carpeted and furnished, ceiling fans, satellite TV, VCR. Full size bath/kitchen. 80 acre resort grounds feature swimming pool, tennis/basketball courts, shuffleboard, horseshoes. Waterfront and skiing nearby. Open year round. No pets/smoking.

Weekly $400   Nightly $65

BARBARA OR MARTHA   **(303) 499-4089 • EMAIL: martymoyers@attbi.com**
MOYERS   **PRIVATE COTTAGE**

Walloon Lake frontage. Located on 6 acres of scenic, mature forest, this 2,304 sq. ft. home features 4 bed-rooms, 2 baths (can sleep 10 people), full kitchen with dishwasher and microwave, plus mini-kitchen on the lower level. TV/VCR, phone, free-standing fireplace. Lounge deck looks down towards the trees and lake. Child's swing set. On 200 sq. ft. of shoreline. Firepit, sandy beach for children to play. Large dock to sunbath, moor boats. Lake bottom sandy at end of dock. No weeds, gradual slope, swimming rafts. No pets, smoking, linens.

Weekly $2,300 (late June-Aug.) Off-season rates & shorter says in the fall.

WILDWOOD ON WALLOON
(231) 582-9616
MAIN OFFICE - RESERVATIONS
CONDO RESORT

Lovely townhouse community near the borders of Walloon Lake. Enjoy 3 professionally designed holes of golf and two carefully sited tennis courts private beach. Contemporary units vary in design and sleep 6-12, up to 5 bedrooms, 2 bath with fully equipped kitchens. Amenities frequently include fireplace, TV/VCR. No pets.

Weekly (summer) $1,500-$1,900

Editor's Note: On well groomed grounds surrounded by trees, the units we visited varied in decor but maintained a very comfortable, contemporary theme.

TRAVERSE CITY & SURROUNDING AREAS

INCLUDES: ACME • ARBUTUS LAKE • BELLAIRE • BENZONIA • BEULAH • CEDAR • EAST BAY • ELK LAKE/ELK RAPIDS • FRANKFORT • GLEN ARBOR • GRAND TRAVERSE BAY • HONOR • INTERLOCHEN • KALKASKA • LAKE LEELANAU • LAKE SKEGEMOG • LELAND • LONG LAKE • NORTH PORT • OLD MISSION PENINSULA • PLATTE LAKE/PLATTE RIVER • SILVER LAKE • SPIDER LAKE • SUTTONS BAY • THOMPSONVILLE • TORCH LAKE • WEST BAY

From beautiful sunsets and lazy days on a sandy beach to the rush of downhill skiing—**Traverse City** and the surrounding areas have a variety of fun and exciting activities in a setting of blue water, rolling hills, and natural beauty. Dining, shopping, entertainment, and even gambling will fill your days and nights.

One of the City's biggest events is the annual Cherry Festival, held the week of July 4th. Thousands of people come to the area to enjoy parades, concerts, fireworks, air shows, Native American pow-wows and crafts along with other family activities. If you're interested in coming by, we highly recommend you plan well in advance for this very popular event.

Enchanting **Interlochen** is a wonderful place to visit throughout the year. You'll want to stroll along its cool waters, scented pines and natural grounds. Here you'll find the internationally known Interlochen Center for the Arts and the Interlochen Fine Arts Camp. Here gifted young artists (ages 8-18) develop their creative talents with concentrated studies in their specialized areas of theatre, painting, sculpturing, music and more. In addition to over 750 student performances yearly, the Interlochen Center for the Arts also hosts a variety of nationally known music and recording artists. From classical and folk to jazz, blues and pop, the diversity of music continues to attract area residents and visitors from across the world. For performance and ticket information, call (231) 276-6230.

Want to try something a little *lifting*? Get a really scenic view of the Traverse City area from a hot-air balloon. You'll be awed by views of **Elk and Torch**

Lakes, East and West Grand Traverse Bay, Manitou and Fox islands, to name a few. Contact the area Chamber of Commerce (see Chamber section of this book) for further information.

The 70,000 acre Sleeping Bear Sand Dunes National Lakeshore is another must see while visiting the area. Drive south along M-22 through the charming communities of **Leland** and **Glen Arbor**. The Pierce Stocking Scenic Drive (closed in mid-November) is a relaxing and enjoyable car tour. Of course, hiking the dunes in the park has become a fun challenge for youngsters of all ages. And, if you still have energy after getting to the top, take a short walk across the sand to a wonderful overlook of Lake Michigan.

The **Leelanau Peninsula** and **Old Mission Peninsula** are known for their beautiful scenery. They're also known as *wine country*. Winery tours and tasting have become a popular day time diversion for many. Check out our "Michigan Wineries" section for further information.

Feeling like Lady Luck is on your side today? Then put on that lucky hat and head out to one of two area casinos. The Leelanau Sands Casino is 20 miles north of Traverse City near **Suttons Bay**; and the Turtle Creek Casino is four miles east of **Acme** in Williamsburg. Our Michigan "Casinos" chapter provides phone numbers and addresses of casinos in this area and throughout Michigan.

Take a ride on the Malabar, a two-masted schooner. Then drop by The Music House north of Traverse on US-31 (Acme) to enjoy a unique museum where history, education and entertainment combine.

Just about time to eat? There are many popular restaurants in the area. Just a few: *Poppycock's* (on Front Street in downtown Traverse City) is known for inventive dinner entrees, fresh pastas and unique salads (we personally recommend their Front Street Salad). Others include *Hattie's Grill* or *Boone's Prime Time Pub* (Suttons Bay); *Trillium* (Grand Traverse Resort); *Boone's Long Lake Inn; Sweitzer's by the Bay* (Traverse City); *Scott's Harbor Grill* (M-22 on Sleeping Bear Bay Beach); *LeBear* (M-22 in Glen Arbor); *Bluebird* (Leland); or *Stubbs* (Northport). *Windows* (on West Bay Shore Drive, north of Traverse City), though pricey, has developed a reputation for preparing some of the area's finest cuisine. *Spencer Creek Fine Dining* in the **Torch Lake** area (also higher priced) prepares creative and diverse fare with a very distinctive Italian flavor and, being on Torch Lake, the view is wonderful.

For tasty and inexpensive "eats" give *Art's Tavern* a try (**Glen Arbor**) for breakfast, lunch or dinner. Their special 1/3 pound ground chuck burger with bacon, blue cheese along with homemade chili (not too spicy) is quite good. For good pizzas and burgers in a country-styled family restaurant, try *Peegeos Restaurant* in the **Spider Lake** area. *Mabel's* (in Traverse City, on Front Street) is known for freshly prepared baked goods and traditional homemade meals. For a fun 50's decor atmosphere and to re-discover the taste of good old-fashioned hamburgers, *Don's Drive-In* is definitely a dandy choice.

We can't forget the *Grand Traverse Dinner Train* for a truly unique dining experience. You'll enjoy a four-course lunch or five-course gourmet dinner while touring the scenic Boardman River Valley area. For additional information on the dinner train, call (231) 933-3768.

ACME

GRAND TRAVERSE RESORT AND SPA

(800) 748-0303 • (231) 938-2100
CONDO RESORT

★ EDITOR'S CHOICE ★

Luxury condos — some with wet bars, whirlpool baths and fireplaces. Casual to fine dining in a variety of restaurants. Enjoy shopping galleries, indoor-outdoor tennis, weight room, indoor-outdoor pools and aerobic studio. Children's center. Groomed x-country ski trails and 54 holes of championship golf including *The Bear* and *The Wolverine*.

Call for Rates

Editor's Note: Premier resort. Excellent accommodations with abundant amenities.

ARBUTUS LAKE

MAC'S LANDING RESORT

(231) 947-6895
COTTAGE RESORT

14 cottages (1-3 bedrooms, sleeps 2-8) on 700 ft. of beautiful lakefront property. Scenic setting and sandy beach. Features docks, great swimming, raft, boats and motors, campfire pits, playground, volleyball and horseshoes. Bring linens. Open June-Sept. Pets allowed.

Weekly $350-$790

PINEVIEW RESORT

(231) 947-6792
COTTAGE RESORT

12 cottages on the lake (some fireplaces), 2-3 bedrooms (sleeps 5-8). Fire pit on beach, lounge deck and dock on lake. Enjoy volleyball, shuffleboard, horseshoes and playground area. Boats, motors, pedal boats and pontoons available for rent.

Weekly $680-$898 (Off-season rates available)

SHADY CREST RESORT

(231) 947-9855 • EMAIL: shady@traverse.net
COTTAGE RESORT

Eight very clean and comfortably furnished cottages. 1-3 bedrooms that sleep 4-10. Kitchens with all the extras, bath with shower. Cable with TV's in some cottages, ceiling fans. Linens and towels are not provided. Deck overlooking lake and beach area. Playground and laundry. Boat included with cottage, kayak and paddle boat available. Dock space available. Motor and pontoon rental, bait and pop available. Open all year. Pets welcome.

Weekly $400-$625 (Summer) Nightly & off-season rates available)

Editor's Note: Friendly owners making a real effort at updating this older resort. Simple but very clean cottages.

SHOESTRING RESORT **(231) 946-9227** • EMAIL: info@shoestringresort.com

COTTAGE RESORT

19 cottages. 1-3 bedrooms cottages and 2 bedroom mobiles. An extended stay facility. A place more home than a hotel. Clean and well equipped with air conditioning, nicely furnished including linens, full kitchens or kitchenettes, CATV with 27" TV and complimentary coffee. Remote with amenities of the city and nature easily reached. 8 miles south of Traverse City. Open all year. *Website: www.shoestringresort.com*

Weekly $245-$500

BELLAIRE

GRAND VICTORIAN **B&B INN**   **(800) 336-3860** • EMAIL: info@grandvictorian.com
STEVE AND GLENDA SHAFFER   BED & BREAKFAST

1895 Victorian mansion built by lumber barons. On National Register. Inn features antiques, 3 fireplaces, etched glass and wicker-filled porch/balconies overlooking park. Elegant breakfast. Close to golf and skiing. 4 rooms w/private baths. No smoking.

Nightly $115-$135

SHANTY CREEK RESORT   **(231) 533-8621** • **(800) 678-4111**
ROOM/CHALET/CONDO RESORT

Four season resort on the lake. 3 championship golf courses including *The Legend* by Arnold Palmer. 41 downhill slopes, 31 km of x-country trails. Tennis, mountain biking, health club, beach club and indoor/outdoor pools. Fine dining, live entertainment. 600 rooms, condos and chalets some with full to partial kitchens, fireplaces, Jacuzzis. Great swimming. No pets.

Golf Get-a-way Packages   (starting at) $59 (per person/per night)
Ski Season Packages   (starting at) $72 (per person/per night)

RICHARD & JO-ANN SOCHA   **(734) 663-3766**
PRIVATE CHALET

This 3 bedroom, 2 bath chalet sleeps 7 and offers a secluded setting. Fully furnished, TV/VCR, fireplace (wood provided), dishes, linen and maid service. Near the top of Schuss Mountain, it offers ski-in/ski-out. A mecca for golfers, swimming pools in village. No pets/smoking. Open June-August.

Weekly $850

CLARE TAYLOR (AT SHANTY CREEK RESORT)　　　　**(517) 394-4162**
PRIVATE CHALET

On a secluded lot in the wooded, rolling hills of Schuss Village. Lodging features 3 bedrooms/2 full baths, fully equipped kitchen with microwave, ski storage area, electric heat, CATV with VCR, telephone. Linens provided. Use of hot tub, pool and sauna at Schuss Village Lodge. Available year around.

Weekly　　　$500　　　　　　Nightly　　　$150-$250

BENZONIA

CRYSTAL-RENTALS, INC.　**(800) 221-0928** • **EMAIL:** vacation@crystal-rentals.com
PRIVATE HOMES/COTTAGES

Seasonal and year round homes and cottages in Benzie County. Waterfront properties on Crystal Lake, Lake Michigan, Platte Lake, Long Lake, Bear Lake, Betsie River and Platte River. Visit our Website for pictures, occupancy and prices. *Website: www.crystal-rentals.com*

Weekly　　　$800-$2,800 (Daily rates available)

HANMER'S RIVERSIDE RESORT　　　**RES: (800) 252-4286** • **(231) 882-7783**
JOYCE & JOE WITTBRODT　　　　　　　　　　　　　　COTTAGE RESORT

Eleven very clean, modern cottages (accommodates 2-12 people) overlooking the beautiful Betsie River. Indoor pool, spa, canoe/kayak rentals. Open year around. Close to summer activities, winter skiing at Crystal Mountain, snowmobile trails. Fall salmon and spring steelhead fishing. *Website: www.hanmers.com*

Weekly　　　$470-$910　　　　Nightly　　$70-$130

BEULAH

NORTHERN RENTALS MGT.   **(888) 326-2352 • EMAIL: gold@coslink.net**
PRIVATE HOMES/CONDOS/COTTAGES

For your "get-away" in beautiful Northern Michigan, we offer beachside cottages, secluded riverside retreats, and spacious homes located at Crystal Mountain Resort. Enjoy skiing, golf, miles of sandy beaches and much more...all in your backyard while visiting scenic Benzie County.

Weekly $995-$2,595

CEDAR

WINGED FOOT CONDO (AT SUGAR LOAF RESORT)   **(616) 846-3978**
JEANNE & JERRY SHERMAN   **PRIVATE CONDO**

Modern, contemporary, 2 bedroom (sleeps 7) condo on 18th fairway at Sugar Loaf Resort. Fireplace, full kitchen, TV, linens, pools. Overlooks golf course, ski hills (Palmer Course on premises). Lake Michigan beach 1 mile, Leland 6 miles, Traverse City 22 miles. Other nearby activities: Horseback riding, casino, boating. No pets. Open year around.

Nightly $150

EAST BAY

THE BEACH CONDOMINIUMS   **(231) 938-2228**
CONDO RESORT

These 30 luxury condos on Grand Traverse Bay feature private sun decks (sleeps 4), whirlpool baths, complete kitchen and 27" stereo CATV. Beautiful sandy beach, outdoor heated pool and hot tub plus daily housekeeping. Adjacent boat launch and close to championship golf. AAA discount, daily rentals, getaway and ski packages.

Nightly $89-$299

NORTH SHORE INN   **(800) 968-2365 • EMAIL: nshinn@pentel.net**
CONDO RESORT

Charming New England style condominium hotel. 26 luxury 1-2 bedroom beachfront units with full kitchens. Nightly, weekly, reduced off-season rates. Spectacular views of East Bay from front decks and balconies. 200' sandy beach, outdoor heated pool. Near golfing, skiing and casino.

Nightly $159-$239 (prime season); $59-$189 (off-season)

Editor's Note: Well maintained, attractively decorated. All rooms offer waterfront views. Very nice beach area.

TRAVERSE BAY INN **(231) 938-2646**
CONDO RESORT

All units are furnished with equipped kitchens including microwaves, A/C, CATV. Some rooms with whirlpool tub and fireplace. Pool, hot tub, gas grills and complementary bicycles. Swimming beach nearby. Pets O.K. Major credit cards accepted. *Website: www.traversebayinn.com*

Weekly $175-$1,175   Nightly $39-$199

Editor's Note: Clean, contemporary, well maintained units. Sizes vary significantly.

ELK LAKE/ELK RAPIDS

CEDARS END ON ELK LAKE **(231) 322-6286 • (972) 442-0008**
DEAN & SHARON GINTHER **Email: Dean_Ginther@tamu-commerce.edu**
PRIVATE HOME

Spacious 3 bedroom, 2 bath home on 450 ft. of private east Elk Lake frontage. Furnished, dishwasher, microwave, cookware, 2 fireplaces, dock with boat mooring. 50 acres of woodland attached. Excellent swimming, hiking, biking, boating and fishing. No linens. No pets.

Weekly $1,800 (off-season $1,000)

ELK RAPIDS BEACH RESORT **(800) 748-0049**
CONDO RESORT

Luxury condos overlooking Grand Traverse Bay, just minutes from Traverse City. Heated pool (in the summer), in room Jacuzzi and full size kitchen. No pets. Call about our free night during the fall color season. *Website: www.elkrapidsbeachresort.com*

Weekly $1,295 (dbl. occ., summer)   Call for Off-Season Rates

Editor's Note: Small condominium resort. Attractive units sit across a quiet section of road with direct access to private, fabulous sandy beach.

WATER'S EDGE RESORT **(231) 264-8340**
COTTAGE/EFFICIENCY/MOTEL RESORT

Come to the "water's edge" of beautiful Elk Lake ... where your family is treated like ours! For your comfort and enjoyment, we offer cottages, units with full kitchens, motel-type accommodations. Also sandy beach/children's play area, two docks, rowboats, a paddleboat, picnic tables, gas grills. Bring linens. No pets.

Weekly $525-$800

WANDAWOOD RESORT & RETREAT CENTER **(231) 264-8122**
COTTAGE/DUPLEX RESORT

On Elk Lake, 17 cottages with lakefront and orchard settings. Each varies in size from small 1 bedroom cottage to duplex and 5 bedroom homes. Full kitchen/bath facilities. Nine beach areas with docks plus 2 swimming rafts. Boats, canoes and paddle boards available. Area for field sports and a paperback book library for those quiet times. Open Memorial Day to mid-November.

Weekly $380-$1,165

WHISPERING PINES   **(616) 329-1937**
JERRY MCKIMMY   **PRIVATE HOME**
Three bedroom lakefront ranch, walkout lower level on the west side of Elk Lake (100 ft). Features C/A, washer/dryer, microwave, dishwasher, CATV/VCR. Linens provided. Boat lift. Sleeps up to 10 people. No smoking/pets.
Call for Rates

WHITE BIRCH LODGE   **(231) 264-8271 • EMAIL: WBLodge@aol.com**
       CONDO/LODGE RESORT

CONDOS ★ EDITOR'S CHOICE ★

Year around resort on Elk Lake. Packages offer 3 meals a day plus water-skiing, wind surfing, sailing, tennis, children's programs and more. Accommodations range from simple lodge rooms to deluxe condominiums. Children 2-12 half price. Call for brochure. *Website: www.whitebirchlodge.org*
Weekly $595-$1,065 (per person)
Editor's Note: A fun family resort. Beautiful grounds and plenty of activities for all ages. We recommend their lovely condominiums as your lodging of choice.

FRANKFORT

THE HUMMINGBIRD   **(314) 965-4598 • EMAIL: gerriemich@aol.com**
       PRIVATE COTTAGE
Three bedroom/2 bath cottage located on two lakes (one lake is a conservancy). Equipped kitchen, attic and ceiling fans, washer/dryer, patio. Linens included. 400 ft. from water, sandy beach, fishing boat, trolling motors, canoe, paddle boat, lounge chairs. No pets/smoking. Open summer-Labor Day
Weekly $825-$1,050

LAKEVIEW LOFT   **(231) 352-5566 • EMAIL: bayer@benziecounty.com**
RICHARD & BILLIE BAYER   **PRIVATE UPSTAIRS COTTAGE**
Close to Lake Michigan, Crystal Lakes and Plattes. Private setting with deck and views of Lake Michigan and woods. Full kitchen with microwave. Linens included. Two twin beds, full kitchen, living room, private bath with tub, shower, CATV/VCR. Available year around.
Nightly $75 (call for weekly rates)

GLEN ARBOR

THE HOMESTEAD   (231) 334-5000
MAIN OFFICE RENTALS   CONDO/HOME RESORT

★ EDITOR'S CHOICE ★

A resort on Lake Michigan surrounded by the Sleeping Bear Dunes. Restaurants, shops, golf, tennis, pools, x-country and downhill skiing, meeting centers, four small hotels, vacation homes and condominiums. Open May-Oct; Christmas week and winter weekends.

Nightly $96-$561 (Weekly rates/package plans available)

Editor's Note: Secluded location in a scenic setting... a favorite of ours for years.

WHITE GULL INN   (231) 334-4486 • EMAIL: gullinglen@aol.com
BILL & DOTTI THOMPSON   BED & BREAKFAST

Older 2-story home on a lovely wooded lot in Glen Arbor. Nestled between Sleeping Bear Sand Dunes and the lake shore of Sleeping Bear Bay. Walking distance to shops, restaurants, tennis courts, hiking trails. Short drive to golf courses and Glen Lakes. 5 rooms. Major credit cards accepted.

Nightly $85-$125

GRAND TRAVERSE BAY

TRAVERSE BAY CASINO RESORT -   (800) 634-6113 • (231) 946-5262
THE BEACH   MOTEL/CONDO RESORT

All season resort located on 700 ft. of sandy beach on the East Arm of Grand Traverse Bay. Most units face the water with double or queen size beds and refrigerator. Some include kitchen, microwave, whirlpool tubs, wetbar, and /or patios/balconies, CATV. Sleeps 2-6 people. No pets.

Nightly $100-$600

HONOR • PLATTE LAKE • PLATTE RIVER

AMERICAN RESORT #14   **(734) 461-3374** • **EMAIL: hockeydad39@aol.com**
ROBERT & TAMMY WENCEL   **PRIVATE CABIN**
Two bedroom, one bath cabin on Little Platte Lake. Fully equipped kitchen, TV. Boat and dock included. Minutes from Lake Michigan, Sleeping Bear Dunes, Crystal Mountain, several golf courses, museums, lighthouses and many other family attractions. Open March-November. Pets allowed.
Weekly $350   Nightly $60

PLATTE LAKE RESORT I   **(231) 325-6723**
                                                      COTTAGE RESORT
On beautiful Big Platte Lake, these 1-3 bedroom cottages are completely furnished and carpeted with kitchenettes. All include dishes, CATV, picnic tables and grills. Fishermen, hunters and golfers welcome. Open April-November. Daily and weekly rentals. No pets.
Weekly $550-$875 (plus tax)

RIVERSIDE   **(231) 325-2121** • **Email: bjweau-wh@centurytel.net**
                                                    PRIVATE COTTAGE
ALL SEASON FUN!! Fish, swim, canoe, hike, ski, sightsee, relax, enjoy ... BE 'UP NORTH'. Two-story home located on the beautiful Platte River in Honor, Michigan. 30 miles from Traverse City; 10 minutes from Lake Michigan and the National Lakeshore. 4 bedroom, 2 bath, full kitchen, CATV, VCR, deck, picnic table. Sleeps 6 adults/2 children. Dock. Non-smoking. No pets. Available all year.
Weekly $360   Nightly $70-$90

INTERLOCHEN

ELLIS LAKE RESORT   **(231) 276-9502**
KEITH & JOAN ATTWOOD   **LOG CABIN RESORT**
Log cabins and rooms on the lake. Retreat-like atmosphere. Kitchen facilities, some with Franklin fire-stoves. Includes private outdoor hot tub, boats, canoes, more. Linens included. Open year around. X-C skiing in winter. Resort featured in *Midwest Living Magazine*. Pets allowed. *Website: www.ellislakeresort.com*
Weekly $530-$800   Nightly $58-$125

JUDY'S PLACE   (231) 263-5634 • (248) 626-2464
                                           PRIVATE LOG HOME

★ EDITOR'S CHOICE ★

Log ranch-style home, built in 1992 on 1.12 wooded acres with sandy beach area on small, clean spring-fed lake. 5 miles to Interlochen, 20 miles SW of Traverse City. 4 bedrooms, 3 full baths, 2 air mattresses available. Full kitchen, stacked, full-size washer/dryer, A/C, ceiling fans. Well behaved pets O.K. with additional $25

charge. Prefer non-smokers. Photos available. Open year around. Everything provided except food, clothing and guaranteed good weather!

Weekly * $1,525   Nightly *$250   3-Nite Pkg.   * $680   (* and up)

Editor's Note: Quality home—packed with features and ambiance. Excellent location. Highly recommended.

MARY MUELLER & MARK PAYNE   (231) 276-6756
                                                      PRIVATE CABIN

Cozy cabin on 2-1/2 wooded acres with 125 ft. Green Lake frontage. One bedroom with additional set of bunk beds. Sleeps 2-4. Fully equipped kitchen with microwave. Provide your own linens/towels. Large wood deck. Private dock and 10 ft. rowboat included. Open May-Sept. No smoking.

Weekly $450

WHITE PINE RETREAT   **(810) 752-1451 • EMAIL: jands@tir.com**
RUDY & VERTA ODZIANA   PRIVATE LOG HOME

★ EDITOR'S CHOICE ★

Spacious ranch-styled log home close to Interlochen with Green Lake access. Four bedrooms (sleeps 8), 2 baths, ceiling fans, equipped kitchen, TV/VCR/Cable/ Stereo, washer/dryer. Towels/linens provided. Covered front porch, rear deck with hot tub, BBQ, picnic table. No smoking/pets. Winter rates available. *Website: www.tir.com/~jands/whitepine.htm*

Weekly $1,500   Nightly $250

Editor's Note: Spacious, well designed, contemporary and very comfortable log home located on quiet, wooded grounds. A short walk to water's edge. Highly recommended.

KALKASKA

MANISTEE LAKE CABIN   **(248) 478-7365**
KATHY STACEY   PRIVATE LOG CABIN

Cozy 2 bedroom cabin on Manistee Lake in Kalkaska. Full kitchen, TV/ VCR. Centrally located between Traverse City and Grayling. Great family getaway! Bring linens. Sandy beach, excellent fishing, hunting, boat launch, water skiing and golf. Open spring through fall. No pets/smoking.

Weekly $675

LAKE LEELANAU

JOLLI LODGE   **(888) 256-9291**
    COTTAGE/APT./LODGE RESORT

This homey retreat offers a great view of Lake Michigan from their 5 cottages, 11 apartments and 6 lodge rooms. Apartments (1-3 bedrooms) are newer. Cottages and lodge simply furnished but clean. Several steps down leads to pebbled beach. Tennis, rowboat, kayaking, volleyball and shuffleboard. Open year around. Major credit cards.

Weekly $750-$1,300

WEST WIND RESORT   **(231) 946-9457**
COTTAGE RESORT

Eleven cottages, 2 to 4 bedrooms (sleeps 4-10) some with fireplaces. Facilities have children's playground, hot tub. Paddle boards, kayaks and canoe rentals. Protected harbor. Open year around. No pets.

Weekly $975-$2,150 (Call for special off-season rates)

LAKE SKEGEMOG

JOHN KING   **(248) 349-4716 • EMAIL: jking1@peoplepc.com**
PRIVATE HOME

Luxury lakefront home on 200 ft. of sandy beach near Traverse City. 4 bedrooms, 2 baths, equipped kitchen, fireplace. Spacious deck overlooking Lake Skegemog which is part of Elk-Torch chain of 5 lakes. Rowboat. No smoking/pets. *Website: http://free.hostdepartment.com/jking1*

Weekly $1,500-$2,500

LELAND

MANITOU MANOR   **(231) 256-7712**
BED & BREAKFAST

Beautifully restored 1900 farmhouse surrounded by cherry orchards and woods. King and queen size beds, private baths, on the main floor in the wing of the home. Huge parlor with fieldstone fireplace and TV. Full breakfast. Near sand dunes, bike trails, beaches, golf, x-country and downhill skiing. Non-smoking. No pets. Open all year. 5 rooms.

Nightly $95-$140

LONG LAKE

RON JONES OR FRED JONES   **(231) 946-5119 • (586) 286-1582**
PRIVATE COTTAGE

Two bedrooms with queen beds, CATV and full kitchen with microwave. Private beach, dock, 12 ft. aluminum boat, gas BBQ grill, picnic table, lawn furniture. Bring linens. Located 6 miles from Traverse City. Available year around. Pets allowed.

Weekly $750 (includes sales tax)

LINDEN LEA ON LONG LAKE **(231) 943-9182 • EMAIL: lindenlea@aol.com**
BED & BREAKFAST

★ EDITOR'S CHOICE ★

"Enchanting spot on a crystal-clear lake...reminiscent of on Golden Pond," Fodor's B&B Guide. Lakeside bedrooms with window seats. Relax by the fire, listen for the loons. Peaceful sandy beach with row boat, paddle boat. Private baths. Full breakfast. Central A/C. 2 rooms. *Website: www.lindenleabb.com*

Nightly $95-$120

Editor's Note: Peaceful, picturesque surroundings and charming hosts make Linden Lea a very nice choice.

NORTHPORT

LAPETITE MAISON SUR L'EAU **(616) 336-8010 • (231) 386-5462**
& WYNDEROK ON THE BAY **PRIVATE HOMES**

2 furnished, private lodgings on Northport Bay easily accessible for water sports,

hiking, bicycling, walking, one mile from Village. No pets/smoking permitted.

LaPetite: Intimate, charming, attractively furnished 1 bedroom home features large picture window overlooking lawn with birch trees onto Northport Bay (Grand Traverse Bay). Fireplace, fully equipped

kitchen, ceramic tiled bathroom and carpeting. Secluded, ideal for honeymooners or small family. Weekly $625

Wynderok: 3 bedroom/1 bath, 1920's nostalgia cottage comfortably furnished with wicker and chintz. Interior balcony overlooks stone fireplace. Located on quiet, private and wooded lot - 166 ft. bay frontage. Beautiful views from 3 screened porches and 2nd balcony onto Grand Traverse bay. Weekly $975-$1,500

Editor's Note: Both properties well maintained. Wyndenrock decorated with a true 1920's ambiance ... particularly appealing for those who enjoy nostalgia.

OLD MISSION PENINSULA

BOWERS HARBOR BED & BREAKFAST   **(231) 223-7869**
BED & BREAKFAST

1870 fully remodeled country farmhouse with private sandy beach is located in the Old Mission Peninsula. Open year around. Enjoy a gourmet breakfast in the dining room overlooking the Harbor. 3 rooms w/private baths. *Website: www.pentel.net/~verbanic*

Nightly $120-$150

CHÂTEAU CHANTAL BED & BREAKFAST   **(800) 969-4009 • (231) 223-4110**
BED & BREAKFAST

★ EDITOR'S CHOICE ★

Old World charm in this fully operational vineyard, winery and B&B. Set on a scenic hill in Old Mission Peninsula, this grand estate features an opulent wine tasting room and 3 delightful guest rooms (includes 2 suites) with private baths. Handicap accessible. Full breakfast.

Nightly $135-$165 (in-season)

Editor's Note: Grand estate with a spectacular view of Old Mission Peninsula. You'll enjoy their "Jazz at Sunset" program. The inn is currently expanding, and anticipates adding 8 new guest rooms (11 total rooms) by the end of 2003.

SILVER LAKE

GERALD NIEZGODA   **(231) 943-9630**
PRIVATE COTTAGE

Furnished cottage on Silver Lake, 80 ft. private frontage, 2 bedrooms (sleeps 4-6), sandy beach, swimming, fishing, sailing, skiing, outstanding view. 4 miles to Traverse City. Includes fireplace, CATV, VCR, microwave, boat and dock. Bring towels. Open all year. No pets/smoking.

Weekly $735 (Based on occupancy of 4)

SILVER LAKE COTTAGE   **(231) 943-8506**
RAYMOND PADDOCK & JILL HINDS   **PRIVATE COTTAGE**

Fully furnished 3 bedroom cottage accommodates 8 people and features full kitchen, fireplace, stereo, TV, grill and 2 decks. Also features dock, swim raft, canoe and rowboat. Open June-Sept. Pets allowed.

Weekly $700 (plus 6% Use Tax)

SPIDER LAKE

HAROLD'S RESORT   **(231) 946-5219 • EMAIL: info@haroldsresort.com**
ROLF & KATHY SCHLIESS   **COTTAGE RESORT**

★ EDITOR'S CHOICE ★

Seven log cabins sit on a private peninsula overlooking beautiful Spider Lake with a terrific, safe and sandy beach. Open all year. Nightly and weekend rates available. Most have beautiful lake views from screened porches. Private bath, equipped kitchens, carpet and ceiling fans. No pets. *Website: www.haroldsresort.com*

Weekly (Summer) $395 (2 people); $800-$900 (2 bedroom cabins/4-6 people)

Editor's Note: Friendly, cozy, picturesque resort with an excellent beach. Cottages kept in very nice condition.

L' DA RU LAKESIDE RESORT, INC.   (231) 946-8999
COTTAGE RESORT

Built in 1923, this lodge was once the hideout for Al Capone. 455 ft. lake frontage. 17 cottages with eating/cooking utensils, coffee maker, toaster and 20" CATV's. Linens and bedding provided. Boats included — motors available. Good swimming beach. Towels extra. Open year around. No pets.

Weekly $950-$1,225   Nightly $65-$150 (off season)

Editor's Note: Great beach, private location with traditional cottages.

JACK & ROSEMARY MILLER   (231) 947-6352
PRIVATE COTTAGE

Attractive lakefront log cottage on Spider Lake. Offers knotty pine interior, 2 bedrooms (with linens), fireplace, electric heat, TV and complete kitchen including microwave. This quiet, quaint hide-away is furnished with antiques, oak dining set, china cabinet, brass bed and marble top dresser. 13 miles from Traverse City. No pets.

Weekly $450   (May-Oct.)

MOONLIGHT BAY RESORT   (800) 253-2853 • (231) 946-5967
ROGER & NANCY HENDRICKSON   COTTAGE RESORT

7 cottages on wooded setting with direct Spider Lake frontage. 1-3 bedrooms. Fully equipped kitchens, CATV, ceiling fans, most cottages with fireplace or woodburning stoves. Rowboats, canoes, pedal boat included. Motor and pontoon boat rental available. Open year around. No pets. *Website: www.moonlightbayresort.com*

Weekly $520-$980

Editor's Note: Traditional cottages. Good beach area.

RED RANCH   **(231) 946-3909**
HAROLD MYERS   **PRIVATE COTTAGE**

Three bedrooms, ranch-style cottage with kitchen, dining area, living room with fireplace, enclosed porch facing the lake, 2 car attached garage. Located in a quiet, private area. Includes bedding, towels, microwave, washer, dryer, CATV, rowboat and dock. Good fishing/swimming. $150 deposit.

Weekly $675 (Seasonal rates)

WILKINS LANDING **II**   **(231) 946-5219**
ROLF & KATHY SCHLIESS   EMAIL: info@haroldsresort.com
                                        PRIVATE COTTAGE

★ EDITOR'S CHOICE ★

An all glass front overlooks a quiet bay of Spider Lake with a large deck on the front. Fieldstone fireplace, full kitchen, TV/VCP, dock, paddleboat and pontoon boat. Near snowmobile, x-country ski trails and Fall Color Tours. Available all year. Pets with extra security deposit. *Website: www.haroldsresort.com*

Weekly (Summer) $1,200 (4-6 people)

Editor's Note: Airy, spacious home, open windows and great deck to view the lake. Pontoon boat takes you to nice swimming area.

WILKINS LANDING **III**   **(231) 946-5219**
ROLF & KATHY SCHLIESS   EMAIL: info@haroldsresort.com
                                        PRIVATE COTTAGE

★ EDITOR'S CHOICE ★

Quiet, private & secluded! Surrounded by private forest. A path through the woods takes you to the waterfront and dock, rowboat and pontoon boat. A screened porch, deck, fireplace, whirlpool tub and queen-size log bed make this a great getaway retreat! TV/VCP. Open year around. No pets. *Website: www.haroldsresort.com*

Weekly $1,100 (4-6 people)

Editor's Note: Very appealing cedar log home with fresh, open design. Lovely wooded setting.

SUTTONS BAY

INN AT BLACK STAR FARMS
CARYN ANDERSON

(231) 271-4970, EXT. 150
EMAIL: innkeeper@blackstarfarms.com
BED & BREAKFAST

★ EDITOR'S CHOICE ★

160-acre year-round destination on the Leelanau Wine Trail combines B&B Inn, winery/distillery, creamery and equestrian center. Eight luxurious guestrooms with private baths. Sauna. Sumptuous gourmet breakfasts. Evening hospitality hour. Hiking and ski trails. On-site tasking room. Boarding for guest's horses. Smoke-free.

Nightly $125-$310

Editor's Note: Impressive rooms in an elegant setting. Winery and equestrian center add a distinctive touch.

THE COUNTRY HOUSE

(231) 271-4478 • (231) 943-9070
PRIVATE HOME

Fully furnished house in Suttons Bay offers A/C and 2 bedrooms (sleeps up to 6). It is centrally located to Lake Michigan and Lake Leelanau. No pets/ smoking, please.

Weekly $650 (June-Aug.)   Daily $125

FIG LEAF BED AND BREAKFAST
JHAKI FREEMAN

(231) 271-3995
BED & BREAKFAST

Bring your camera! One-of-a-kind B&B features charming artistic embellishments throughout, and a 12 ft. natural waterfall. Waterfront park across the street. In Storybook Village of Suttons Bay. Classy and quaint shops, cafes within 2 blocks. Festive breakfasts! Casino, wineries, golf, skiing. Private and shared baths. Visa/MC.

Nightly $80-$145

STRAWBERRY HILL HOUSE AND CABIN
CINDY CURLEY

(314) 726-5266
EMAIL: cindylagc@aol.com
PRIVATE LOG HOUSE/CABIN

Vintage north woods ambiance. Log house on peaceful bluff/shoreline, sleeps up to 6. Log cabin sleeps 2-3. Panoramic orchard and bay views, sand beach. Stone fireplace, antiques, screened porch. Beauty, comfort, and privacy. Furnished except linens. Non-smoking. No pets. Open May-November.

Weekly $1,000-$1,800 (House) ; $600-$900 (Cabin)

Editor's Note: Main home built in 1948, authentic log-style. Mix of older furnishings and family heirlooms. Small, 1-room cabin, simply furnished with basic amenities. Quiet, scenic setting.

THOMPSONVILLE

CRYSTAL MOUNTAIN RESORT   (800) 968-7686 • (231) 378-2000
MAIN OFFICE RENTALS   CONDO/HOME/HOTEL RESORT
Family-owned, year-round resort featuring 36 holes of championship golf, 34 downhill slopes, 40km of cross-country trails, dining, indoor and outdoor pool, fitness center and IACC approved conference facilities. Home to Michigan Legacy Art Park. 28 miles SW of Traverse City on M-115. *Website: www.crystalmountain.com*

Call for Rates

TORCH LAKE

WAS-WAH-GO-NING   (248) 644-7288 • (231) 264-5228
JANE BLIZMAN   PRIVATE COTTAGES
Two secluded homes on 800 ft. of Torch Lake amid 25 acres of woods and fields. Each house has fireplace, color TV/VCR, CD, dishwasher, microwave, washer/dryer, dock with lift, picnic table, grill. No pets. *Website: www.torch-lake.com*
Weekly $1,500* (2 bedroom); $2,000 (5 bedroom)

TORCHLIGHT RESORT   (231) 544-8263 • Email: knott@torchlake.com
ROBERT & GLENDA KNOTT   COTTAGE RESORT

★ EDITOR'S CHOICE ★

Seven cottages with 150 ft. frontage on Torch Lake (part of the Chain of Lakes). Features sandy beach, playground, excellent boat harbor, beautiful sunsets. Located between Traverse City and Charlevoix. Near excellent golf courses and fine restaurants. Open May thru October. No pets.
Weekly $575-$1,775 (Off-season rates available)
Editor's Note: Friendly owners, clean, simple cottages in a lovely setting make this one an enjoyable retreat.

TRAVERSE CITY

BROOKSIDE COTTAGES   (231) 276-9581
KEITH & TAMMY ENSMAN   COTTAGE RESORT
In the Traverse City/Interlochen area. 250 ft. lake frontage. 13 cottages vary in size (studio - 3 bedrooms) and sleeps 6. Includes fully equipped kitchens. Heated, in-ground swimming pool, game/recreational room. Motors and pontoon rentals. Open year around. No pets. 50% Deposit.
Weekly $440-$640 (off-season rates available

THE GRAINERY B&B   (231) 946-8325 • EMAIL: THEGRAINERYBB@AOL.COM
RON & JULIE KUCERA   **BED & BREAKFAST**

1892 Country Gentleman's farm on 10 quiet acres. Decorated in country Victorian tradition. A/C, coffee pot, refrigerator, CATV and outdoor hot tub along with 2 golf greens and a pond. Full country breakfast. 5 rooms/private baths (2 rooms feature Jacuzzi and fireplace).

Nightly $75-$139 (in-season); $55-$139 (off-season)

THIS OLE HOUSE   (231) 946-3842 • EMAIL: jthobby1@aol.com
JIM & CONNIE LEGATO   **PRIVATE HOME**

Well maintained older home, 3 bedrooms, (total 5 beds/sleeps 9). Features air conditioning, washer/dryer, CATV, VCR, phone and data jack for your laptop. A fully equipped kitchen and full line of linens provided. Quiet in-town location 2 blocks from the beach and volley ball courts on Grand Traverse Bay. Four blocks from the heart of the city for shopping and eating, leisure walks or bike rides along the bike path. Public lighted tennis courts 1 block. Available year around. No pets. Credit cards accepted. *Website: www.jthobby.com/rentals/index.html*

Weekly: $950 seasonally; Weekends $425 (Winter $600/weekly; $300/weekend)

Editor's Note: Unassuming 1930's home in quiet neighborhood setting. Full ex- terior renovation in 2000. Good price for the area.

NORTH SHORE INN   (800) 968-2365 • EMAIL: nshinn@pentel.net
                                                          CONDO RESORT

Charming New England style condominium hotel. 26 luxury 1-2 bedroom beachfront units with full kitchens. Nightly, weekly, reduced off-season rates. Spectacular views of East Bay from front decks and balconies. 200' sandy beach, outdoor heated pool New golfing, skiing and casino.

Nightly $159-$239 (prime season); $59-$189 (off-season)

Editor's Note: Well maintained, attractively decorated. All rooms with water views. Very nice sandy beach.

RANCH RUDOLF   **(231) 947-9529**
                                               LODGE/BUNKHOUSE RESORT
Packed with activities, the ranch offers restaurant and lounge with fireplace.
Enjoy the hay rides, sleigh rides, river fishing, backpacking, horseshoes, hiking, tennis, swimming pool, badminton, volleyball and a children's playground. Visa and MC accepted.
Nightly $68-$210

SERENITY BAY ACRES   **(231) 946-5219** EMAIL: **info@haroldsresort.com**
ROLF & KATHY SCHLIESS   PRIVATE COTTAGE
Serenity means: 550' of private waterfront, 2 acres of private forest, no neighbors, beautiful lakeviews from all glass front of a chalet-style cottage. Deck with large cedar swing, dock with Pontoon Boat. One queen, 1 full, 4 twin beds. CATV, VCR, fireplace. No smoking/pets. Open all year
Nightly $160-$300   Weekly $1,400

TALL SHIP MALABAR   **(800) 678-0383 • (231) 941-2000**
                                               BED & BREAKFAST
Unique 'floating' B&B. Large traditional sailing vessel offers overnight accommodations with a 2-1/2 hour sunset sail, picnic dinner and hearty breakfast. Join the crew for a special evening on this 105 ft., two-masted topsail schooner. Reservations 1 month in advance. May-Sept.
Nightly $100-$175 (children 8-12 $47.50)

WHISPERING WATERS   **(888) 880-5557 •** EMAIL: **whisper@gtii.com**
BED & BREAKFAST RETREAT   BED & BREAKFAST
                     ★ EDITOR'S CHOICE ★
Enjoy the tranquility of nature at our retreat surrounded by 42 acres of natural woods and streams. Explore hiking trails, relax in the outdoor hot tub, go tubing in the river. Three rooms/two baths plus 1 cabin. Specially crafted interiors highlight nature. Continental plus or full breakfasts. Personal growth workshops, guided nature walks, therapeutic massage available.
Nightly $80-$95 (Rooms); $150 (Cabin) (2 night min.)
Editor's Note: Lovely setting, creatively and tastefully decorated ... very comfortable for those seeking a quiet, back-to-nature retreat.

WINTERWOOD ON THE BAY   **(231) 929-1009**
R. SCHERMERHORN   PRIVATE COTTAGE
Recently built beach house on East Bay. Sleeps 4 (2 bedrooms), bath, fully furnished kitchen, living/dining room with fireplace. Dishwasher, microwave, VCR and cable TV. Linens provided. Deck and private dock. Open year around. No pets/smoking.
Weekly $775

WEST BAY

RONALD MALLEK   **(231) 386-5041 • (954) 384-6363**

PRIVATE COTTAGE

This charming, 1 bedroom (sleeps 3), English country cottage features a private patio, many gardens and sandy beach. Fully furnished with fireplace, linens and equipped kitchen. No pets/smoking.

Weekly $600

KEN   **(231) 947-5948**

PRIVATE COTTAGE

★ EDITOR'S CHOICE ★

One bedroom weekly rental. Large living room, private sandy beach-Grand Traverse Bay. Three blocks to downtown, one block to city tennis courts. Completely furnished, includes TV, kitchen, microwave, fold out couch, canoe, rowboat. New clients, $100 deposit. Available June 15-September 10.

Weekly $800   (June - $700)

Editor's Note: Small, private cottage with all the conveniences. Quiet setting, large windows with spectacular sunsets. This little gem is popular ... book early.

MANISTEE • ONEKAMA

The Cadillac area is an excellent stop for fishing and water sports enthusiasts with its two lakes (Cadillac and Mitchell) within its city limits, and many other lakes not far away. Wild and tame game are abundant at Johnny's Wild Game and Fish Park which also stocks its waters with plenty of trout. In February, come and enjoy the North American Snowmobile Festival.

On the shores of Portage Lake, with access to Lake Michigan, **Onekama** is a summer resort community with a charter-boat fleet, marina, white sandy beaches and lovely parks.

You'll definitely want to stop by to enjoy the lovely, historic Victorian port city of **Manistee**. The entire central business district of this community is listed in the National Register of Historic Places. You'll be delighted by the district's charming Victorian street lamps, museums, and shops. Stroll along the Riverwalk which winds along the Manistee River for more than a mile. Watch the boat traffic, stop at a restaurant, then take off your shoes and walk in the smooth sand of the beaches along Lake Michigan. The area also offers several challenging golf courses. Of course, you may prefer to take advantage of their charter-boat fishing or river-guide services. In winter, there's plenty of cross-country skiing and snowmobiling trails.

MANISTEE

LAKE SHORE BED & BREAKFAST   (231) 723-7644
WILLA BERENTSEN   BED & BREAKFAST
Enjoy relaxation on the shore of Lake Michigan. Spectacular sunsets, sunrises, freighters and stars. Delicious full breakfasts served at your leisure in our smoke-free new cedar home. Private deck at water's edge. 1 suite with private bath, sitting room.
Nightly $120 (plus tax)

UP NORTH GETAWAY   (248) 668-9925 • (989) 799-2412
Trevor & Dennis Wisnewski   Private Chalet

★ EDITOR'S CHOICE ★

Nestled the Manistee National Forest on all-sports Pine Lake. Newly built, 2 bedroom chalet sleeps 8-10. Includes fireplace, TV, VCR, equipped kitchen with dishwasher, linens, outdoor firepit. Hiking, biking, winter skiing, boating, fishing, golfing, snowmobile and casino in area and more! Open year around. No pets.

Website: www.upnorthgetaway.com.

Weekly $780-$1,050

Weekend $365-$475

Editor's Note: Contemporary home comfortably styled. Breakthtaking lake view from the beautiful great room. Very good value for the area. See our review this edition.

WOODLAND ACRES LAKEHOME   **(708) 460-3113 • Email: jbielecki1@AOL.COM**
JOHN & BRIGID BIELECKI   **PRIVATE CONDO**

★ EDITOR'S CHOICE ★

BRAND NEW LUXURY BEACHFRONT townhouse on the shore of LAKE MICHIGAN with 268' of private sandy beach! Huge, 3 bedroom, 3 bath, 2300 sq. ft. upscale home with living room, dining room, kitchen, master bath with 6 ft. tub, loft-den and cathedral ceiling. The upstairs, full

glass-walled veranda room overlooks the lake. Furnished and decorated to the nines! Enjoy the view and sunsets from your lakefront Jacuzzi on the deck. Stone fireplace, CATV, VCR, stereo, gas grill, washer/dryer. Vacation in style! Close to casino and world class golf. No smoking/pets.

Weekly $1,200-$2,300   Nightly $200-$300

Editor's Note: This luxury, muti-level condo is packed with amenities. Scenic views with excellent Lake Michigan beach frontage. See our review in this edition.

ONEKAMA

LAKE MICHIGAN BEACH CHALET   **(312) 943-7565**
DONNA   **PRIVATE CHALET**

An elegant, 3,500 sq. ft., 3 bedroom/3 bath home on Lake Michigan. This spacious home features fireplaces, fully equipped kitchen, living room/dining room and family room with pool table, 60" CATV, VCR and CD stereo. Lake and sunset viewing deck in addition to wraparound house deck with BBQ. Private setting. Weekly maid service and linens included. No pets.

Weekly $2,100-$3,500   Monthly $9,500

REGION 6

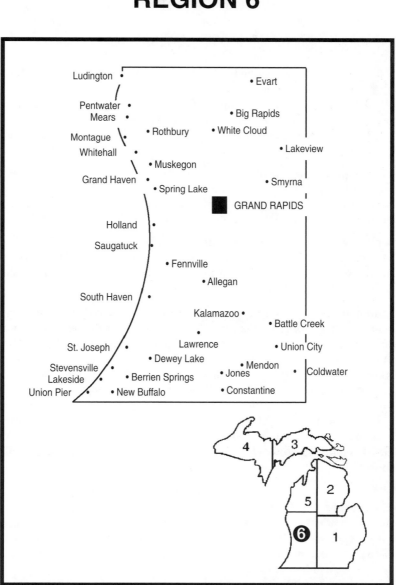

LUDINGTON • GRAND RAPIDS • HOLLAND & SURROUNDING AREAS

INCLUDES: BIG RAPIDS • EVART • GRAND HAVEN • LAKEVIEW • MEARS • MONTAGUE • MUSKEGON • PENTWATER • ROTHBURY • SMYRNA • SPRING LAKE • WHITEHALL

A boardwalk, stretching for 2-1/2 miles from downtown **Grand Haven** to its pier, is bordered by shops, eateries and sandy beaches. For a grand tour, hop on board the Harbor Steamer. For a spectacular sight, see the World's Largest Musical Fountain and visit Michigan's second largest zoo which has 150 species of animals, an aquarium, herpetarium, and more.

Grand Rapids, a unique blend of old and new, the city has many activities to keep you busy! Heritage Hill contains almost 100 historical homes. You'll also want to visit the John Ball Zoological Gardens, Roger B. Chaffe Planetarium, and the Voigt House, a Victorian home built in 1895.

People from all over come to **Holland's** special May event, the Tulip Time Festival; but there is much to see here throughout the year. Dutch Village should not be missed — and don't leave without seeing the Wooden Shoe Factory or Windmill Island.

Ludington's most visited attraction is, Historic White Pine Village, preserves Mason County's history. Visit the Big Sable Point Lighthouse, with daily tours. Enjoy some dune action at beautiful Hamlin Lake or Silver Lake, "home of the world's largest shifting sand dunes". The fall is a particularly breathtaking time. During this season, blue waters of Lake Michigan and white sands of the dunes sharpen the brilliant colors of changing leaves along the shoreline and trails. Bike through 22 miles of nature in Michigan's first linear state park, the Hart-Montage Bicycle Trail State Park. Several notable restaurants in the area include *P.M. Steamers* for a good view of marina activities or *Gibbs Country House* to indulge in their truly sticky, sticky buns and well prepared American cuisine in a family atmosphere.

With miles of sandy Lake Michigan beach, **Muskegon** is the place to book a fishing charter boat, Lake Michigan cruise, or rent a canoe or jet boat at one of many area marinas. You'll enjoy a full day of family fun at Michigan's Adventure Amusement Park & Wild Water Adventure (8 miles north of Muskegon, on U.S. 31). It's one of Michigan's largest amusement parks and features thrill rides, games and live shows for all ages.

Enjoy the New England charm of **Pentwater**, with its cozy cafes and double-decker bus. Stroll through the artisan galleries and little gift shops along Hancock and Second streets. Build a sand castle in the Silver Lake State Park which features a huge sandbox with 450 acres of dunes for off-road vehicles and 750 acres for pedestrians only.

Hungry? Try some of Pentwater's unique restaurants: *Historic Nickerson Inn* for a warm and charming atmosphere (reservations requested); the *Village Pub* for casual pizza, fish sandwiches and evening entertainment of comedy or jazz; the *Antler Bar* known for its special burrito; and *Gull Landing* serves up steak and seafood.

With plenty to do in this great lake playground, you will find the atmosphere relaxed, the people friendly, and the scenery beautiful.

BIG RAPIDS

HILLVIEW RESORT   **(231) 796-5928**
GREG/PATTI BEDUHN   **CABINS & CAMPING RESORT**
Seven cabins, with boats, on Hillview Lake. 1-3 bedrooms, screened porches, kitchens fully equipped. Great fishing, boating, hunting. Sandy beach and swimming area. Boat landing - bring your own boat. RV sites. 7 miles east of Big Rapids. Brochures available.

Call for Rates

EVART

WHITE GABLES B&B   **(231) 734-6940**
TERESE & JIM WHITTEN   **BED & BREAKFAST**
Treat ourself to a great night's rest in "the most expensive home in Osceola County" of 1887. Built during the Michigan Lumber Boom, this historic Queen Anne Victorian is still the "gem" of Evart. Come enjoy the simple pleasures of small town living. The peace and quiet here will melt your cares away. Convenient to mid-Michigan festivals, concerts, hunting, powerchuting, the Pere Marquette rail-to-rail and the Muskegon River. Smoke-free environment. Four guest rooms. Private and shared baths.

Nightly $49-$79; Family Suite $109 (Discounts for stays of 4 or more nights)

GRAND HAVEN

BOYDEN HOUSE INN BED & BREAKFAST   **(616) 846-3538**
                                                    BED & BREAKFAST
1874 Victorian Home. Its eclectic decor represents our varied interests and welcomes guests. Cozy rooms, delightful breakfasts, books, flowers, walks on beaches and boardwalks. Air conditioned rooms feature TV, some with fireplaces, balconies and whirlpool tubs. 7 rooms/private baths.

Nightly $110-$150

KHARDOMAH LODGE
PATTY RASMUSSEN-RAVE & MO RAVE

(616) 842-2990
EMAIL: khardomahlodge@chartermi.net
LODGE/SUITES/COTTAGES

Established 1873. Historic site. Spacious cottage-style facilities located 200 yards from Lake Michigan State Park beach. Nestled in wooded dunes, main lodge has 16 sleeping rooms, partial A/C, sleeps 32+. No TV's or phone in rooms. Great Room has cathedral ceiling, stone fireplace, cable, deck, gas grills and picnic tables. Beautiful private suites offer private entrance, Jacuzzi and fireplace or outdoor hot tub. Sleeps 4-6. Cottage has 3 bedrooms, charming, sleeps 8. Open year around. No smoking/pets. *Website: www.khardomahlodge.com*

Main Lodge (16 BR's), $600-$1,190/Nightly; $4,190-$6,190/Weekly ($50-$68/per room) Suites $125-$185/Nightly; $900-$1,100/Weekly. Cottage $135-$150/Nightly; $890-$1,090/Weekly (Week stays in-season. Minimum weekends)

HARBOURFRONT CONDOMINIUM
LEE HASLICK

(616) 846-5545
PRIVATE CONDO

Prime Grand Haven location only steps from beach, downtown, musical fountain, fireworks, shipping channel, boardwalk. Newer efficiency condo furnished with stove, microwave, refrigerator, CATV, laundry in-room. Sleeps 4. Situated in historic Story and Clark Piano Factory. No pets/smoking. Open year around.

Weekly $620 (summer)   Nightly $80 (off-season)

GRAND RAPIDS

CHICAGO POINT RESORT
DONALD STRAYER

(517) 321-4562
COTTAGE RESORT

Between Kalamazoo and Grand Rapids, on the southeast side of Gun Lake. Al Capone was said to have paid a visit here. Features 2-4 bedroom cottages, furnished and equipped (provide your own blankets, sheets and towels), private beach, fishing docks, picnic area. Rowboats, canoes, paddle boat and motors available. No pets.

Weekly $600-$1,100

HOLLAND

BONNIE'S PARSONAGE 1908 B&B
BONNIE MCVOY-VERWYS

(616) 396-1316
BED & BREAKFAST

Enjoy our lovely, historic B&B. Situated in a beautiful neighborhood near downtown and Hope College. AAA approved. Featured in *Fodor's Best Upper Great Lakes*. Saugatuck resort 12 miles. Two rooms/private baths, third with shared bath. Full breakfasts served in formal dining room. Two nights minimum July/August/Holidays.

Nightly $100-$135

Editor's Note: Quaint B&B. Bonnie pays attention to decorating her antique-filled rooms. You'll be amazed at the detail used to create the right ambiance.

DUTCH COLONIAL INN B&B
PAT & BOB ELENBAAS

(616) 396-3664
BED & BREAKFAST

EDITOR'S CHOICE

1928 inn features elegant decor, 1930 furnishings and heirlooms. All rooms with tiled private baths, some with whirlpool tub for 2. Honeymoon suites for that "Special Getaway", fireplaces. Close to shopping, Hope College, bike paths, x-country ski trails and beaches. A/C. 4 rooms. Full breakfast. Corporate rates. *Website: www.dutchcolonialinn.com*

Nightly $110-$160

Editor's Note: Very welcoming innkeepers and lovely styling make this delightful inn a real treat. See our review, this edition.

EDGEWOOD BEACH
GERALYN PLAKMEYER

(734) 692-3941
PRIVATE COTTAGE

Located just north of Holland, in Beach Front Association. Home has 2 bedrooms, 1 bath, fully furnished, equipped kitchen, fireplace, central heat and CATV. 150 ft. back from Lake Michigan, stairway to long sandy beach complete with sunsets and fire pit. Provide your own linens. Available June-Sept. No pets.

Weekly $500

THE OLD HOLLAND INN
DAVE PLAGGEMARS

(616) 396-6601
BED & BREAKFAST

Nationally registered B&B features 10 ft. ceiling, brass fixtures, stained glass windows and a lovely brass-inlaid fireplace. Antiques, fresh flowers decorate each air conditioned room. Enjoy special house-blend coffee, fresh muffins, fruit and cheese plates each morning.

Nightly $40-$75

ROSEWOOD POINTE RESORT**(616) 396-1502**
BRENT**Email: brent@rosewoodpointe.com**
COTTAGE/HOME RESORT
Located in Holland. Four large, waterfront cottages and three homes ... including an 8 bedroom retreat house (sleeps 30). Resort features private, groomed beach, boat docks, fishing and beach volleyball. Great place for family reunions. No pets. Smoke-free. Open year around. *Website: www.rosewoodpointe.com*
Weekly$1,400 - $4,200

Editor's Note: Great beach. Comfortable accommodations in a cluster. Really nice for small groups or family reunions. See our review in this edition.

SUMMER PLACE RESORT PROPERTIES**(616) 399-3577**
BOB JOHNSONEMAIL: bob@summerplaceresort.com
PRIVATE COTTAGES/HOMES
Furnished resort homes and cottages for your vacation comfort. Located along Lake Macatawa 1/2 mile from Lake Michigan. All homes are upscale, super clean with all the conveniences of home including A/C, ceiling fans, fireplaces, CATV, VCR. No Pets. Smoke free. *Website: www.summerplaceresort.com*
Weekly$585-$2,895

LAKEVIEW

LAKEVIEW COTTAGE(616) 874-9197 • EMAIL: bonewell3@yahoo.com
KELLY & JULIE BONEWELLPRIVATE COTTAGE
Private cottage on all-sports lake. Excellent fishing, lots of wildlife, great swimming, beautiful views. Three bedrooms (sleeps 7), one bath, fully equipped kitchen, TV, VCR, canoe. Provide your own linens. Available May-Sept. No smoking/pets.
Weekly$425 (Friday-Friday rental)

LUDINGTON

BED & BREAKFAST AT LUDINGTON**(231) 843-9768**
GRACE & ROBERT SCHNEIDER**BED & BREAKFAST**
Explore woods, trails, gardens and creek, shade tree canopy, tree-swing, campfires. Widely separated rooms enhance privacy. Popular barnloft ideal for families or honeymooners. Ski, toboggan, snowshoe and relax in Jacuzzi. Homey atmosphere. Big breakfast. Pet friendly. *Website: www.carrinter.net/bedbkfst*
Nightly$45-$75 (and a 20% discount successive nights)

THE INN AT LUDINGTON   (800) 845-9170 • EMAIL: diane@inn-ludington.com
DIANE NEMITZ   BED & BREAKFAST
The charm of the past meets the comfort of today in a picture perfect Queen
Anne Victorian. Relax and feel at home in casual elegance. Breakfast is an
event here, not an afterthought! Bridal suite, fireplaces, CATV, family suite.
Walk to shops, restaurants, beach. *Website: www.inn-ludington.com*
Nightly $90-$110

THE LAMPLIGHTER B & B   (231) 843-9792 • RES. (800) 301-9792
JUDY & HEINZ BERTRAM   BED & BREAKFAST
Victorian Style, European Elegance and American Comfort are the hallmarks of
"The Lamplighter Bed and Breakfast". Your stay in our individually decorated
rooms with queen size beds, private baths, A/C, CATV and phones will be the
most relaxing possible. 2 rooms feature a whirlpool for special occasions. All
rooms as well as the common areas—parlor, living room and dining room— are
decorated with original art and antiques. Full gourmet breakfasts are served
either in our dining room or outdoors in the gazebo. AAA 3 Diamonds *Website:
www.ludington-michigan.com*
Nightly $115-$145
Editor's Note: Charming accommodations and gracious owners.

PARKVIEW COTTAGES   (231) 843-4445
DENNIS & JILL   COTTAGE RESORT
Nestled in a grove of shade trees, 1 block from Lake Michigan. Cottages
sleep 2-6. Each features knotty pine interiors, private bath with ceramic tiled
shower, fully equipped kitchen, gas heat, CATV (with HBO), fieldstone fire-
place (firewood included). Large wood deck with grills and patio furniture.
Across the street from public beach. Open year around.
Nightly $70 (and up)

SCHOENBERGER HOUSE   (231) 843-4435
TAMARA SCHOENBERGER   BED & BREAKFAST

★ EDITOR'S CHOICE ★

This singularly beautiful neoclassical mansion, built by a lumber baron in 1903, has been home to the Schoenberger family for half a century. Included in *Historic Homes of America and Grand Homes of the Midwest*, this elegantly furnished B&B features exquisite woodwork, magnificent chandeliers, 5 fireplaces, music room with 2 grand pianos, an intimate library, the master bedroom suite and four other bedrooms, all with private bath. Just minutes from the Lake Michigan beach, city marina, car ferry and the majestic dunes of Ludington State Park. Smoke-free. Visa/MC.

Nightly $145-$245

Editor's Note: Absolutely beautiful woodworking and attention detail in his impressive home built by one of Ludington's early lumber barons. A real visual treat. See our review, this edition.

TWIN POINTS RESORT   (231) 843-9434
JIM & BARB HUSTED   COTTAGE RESORT

Ten cottages (1-3 bedrooms) rest on 2 wooded bluffs overlooking lovely Hamlet Lake. Walk down to large and sandy swimming beach. Boaters can back their trailers down with ease. Moor your boat in covered docks. Motors and boats available for rent. Cottages are fully furnished and equipped. Most have knotty pine interiors. Close to Ludington State Park.

Call for Rates

WILLOW BY THE LAKE RESORT   (231) 843-2904 • RES. (800) 331-2904
GORDON/DAVID BETCHER & MARTIN LUTZENKIRCHEN   COTTAGE RESORT

Attractive, clean, 1-2 bedroom cottages with equipped kitchens. Guests provide linens/towels. Beautiful view of sand dunes and sunsets from east shore of Hamlin Lake. Sandy beach/play areas for children. Dockage/boat rentals available. Open May-October. No pets. *Website:www.hamlinlake.com/willow*

Weekly $415-$520

MEARS

THE LAKE HOUSE   (313) 886-8996
     PRIVATE COTTAGE

Custom built (1997), 3 bedroom, 2 bath home. One door off of "private" sandy Lake Michigan beach. 1,000 sq. ft. wrap-around and screened porch. 24'x26' great room. 17 ft. vaulted ceiling. Oak floors, outside hot and cold shower, BBQ and more. Open year round.

Weekly $800-$1,200

Editor's Note: Open styling offers plenty of room. Clean and comfortable. Lake Michigan access is just down the road. See our review in this edition.

MONTAGUE

LIFE GUARD ROAD HOME (231) 893-2054 • Email: jeffreyckinney@yahoo.com
JEFF KINNEY   PRIVATE HOUSE

Year around Lake Michigan dune beach house adjacent to White Lake. Near fishing pier and boat dock. 4 bedrooms (10 beds), 2 baths. Moonsets/sunsets. Linens included. Washer/dryer, dishwasher, microwave, fireplace, CATV, telephone, screened/sheltered porch. Close to Michigan Adventureland. No pets. Open year around. *Website: www.angelfire.com/mi4/jeffk*

Weekly $700-$3,000

MUSKEGON

IDLEWILD RETREAT   (616) 842-5716
CAROLYN MILLER   PRIVATE HOME/EFFICIENCY

Beautiful home on Lake Michigan with adjoining efficiency with loft bedroom (sleeps 5/efficiency 4). Both have supplied kitchens, baths, linens, TV, phone and heat. Main cottage has dishwasher, washer, dryer and fireplace. Rented together only. Private beach on Lake Michigan. Available May-Dec. No pets.

Call for Rates

PENTWATER

HISTORIC NICKERSON INN   (231) 869-6731
HARRY & GRETCHEN SHIPARSKI   EMAIL: nickerson@voyager.net
     BED & BREAKFAST

Offering guests exceptional hospitality since 1914. Completely renovated. Thirteen room with private baths and A/C. Three Jacuzzi suites with fireplaces and balconies overlooking Lake Michigan. Two blocks to beach and shopping district. Full breakfast included. Casual fine dining, cocktails. *Virtual tour: www.nickersoninn.com*

Nightly $110-$235 (May 15-Oct); $85-$200 (Off season)

PENTWATER INN BED & BREAKFAST
(231) 869-5909
BED & BREAKFAST

Beautiful 1869 Victorian home located on a quiet village street just a short walk from Lake Michigan sandy beach, shops and restaurants. 5 antique-filled rooms with private baths. A large parlor with CATV. Full gourmet breakfast. Featured in The Bed & Breakfast Cookbook of Great American Inns.

Nightly $75-$125 (weekly discounts)

Editor's Note: Well-established B&B. Tastefully styled. Very nice choice.

THE CANDLEWYCK HOUSE B&B
JOHN & MARY JO NEIDOW
(231) 869-5967
BED & BREAKFAST

★ EDITOR'S CHOICE ★

This 1868 farmhouse style inn offers a unique and comfortable getaway in the historic Lake Michigan port of Pentwater. Six rooms with private baths, A/C, CATV (2 with fireplaces and mini-kitchens). Walk to shops, restaurants and beach. Full country breakfast. Open May-November. *Website: www.candlewyckhouse.com*

Nightly $99-$129

Editor's Note: Cozy, comfortable and very welcoming. Colonial American decor with folk-art crafts add to the ambiance. See our review in this edition.

ROTHBURY

DOUBLE JJ RESORT RANCH
(231) 894-4444 • (800) DOUBLEJJ
HOTEL/CONDO RESORT

★ EDITOR'S CHOICE ★

Open year-round. Enjoy horseback riding, championship golf, swimming, waterslide, snow tubing, dog sledding, children's program, dinner theatre and more. Room vary from bunkhouse to hotel rooms, log cabins and luxury condos. All inclusive packages available with meals and activities. *Website: www.doublejj.com*

Nightly   Standard Hotel: $69-$149; Condos: $99-$389

Editor's Note: Excellent horseback riding, top-rated golf course, beautiful grounds and friendly ranch hands too...Yee-ha!

SMYRNA

DOUBLE 'R' RANCH RESORT
(616) 794-0520
CHALET/BUNK HOUSE/MOTEL RESORT

Lets go tubing on the Flat River! Great fishing too — pike and small mouth bass. Volleyball, horseback riding, golf, canoeing, hay rides. Each chalet has electric stove, refrigerator and all dishes. Chalets rent by week or day. For overnight stays, try the rustic western atmosphere of the Bunk House Motel. Call for Rates

SPRING LAKE

MILL POINT CONDO #101   **(517) 783-3310 • EMAIL: scsoper@dmci.net**
SHIRLEY SOPER   **PRIVATE CONDO**
One bedroom waterfront condo at bridge into Grand Haven, Juncture Spring Lake and Grand River (Lake Michigan 3 miles). Sleeps 4. A/C, CATV, VCR, completely furnished, washer/dryer. Linens included. Patio, carport. Light, airy throughout. Handicapped accessible. Indoor/outdoor pool. River boardwalk bordering marina. Open year around. No pets.
Weekly: $850

SEASCAPE BED & BREAKFAST   **(616) 842-8409**
SUSAN MEYER   **BED & BREAKFAST**
On a private Lake Michigan beach. Enjoy the "country living" ambiance of this nautical lakeshore home. Full breakfast served in gathering room (with fieldstone fireplace) or sun deck with panoramic view of Grand Haven Harbor. Stroll or x-country ski on dune land nature trails. 4 rooms.
Nightly $90-$175

WATERFRONT CONDO   **(616) 846-1541**
LARRY & JOYCE GOLDMAN   **PRIVATE CONDO**
Waterfront condo adjacent to the new Holiday Inn. Rental includes use of indoor/outdoor pool and exercise room. Completely furnished, CATV, VCR, dishwasher, microwave, washer/dryer, A/C. Two bedrooms/2 baths. Children welcome. Sorry, no pets. 5 minutes to Grand Haven.
Weekly $1,200; 4 Nights $700; 3 Nights $600

WHITEHALL

MICHILINDA BEACH LODGE   **(231) 893-1895**
                                                     COTTAGES/LODGE ROOMS
Modified American Plan resort with weekly activities and plenty to do. Well groomed grounds on scenic location. Cottages and lodge rooms offer private baths, most with sitting areas (no kitchens). Many rooms with lake views. Price includes breakfast/lunch. 49 rooms. Open May to early October. No pets.
Weekly $950-$1,500 (assumes 2 people)

Editor's Note: Well groomed, picturesque resort with plenty to keep families and couples busy. Rooms comfortable and clean.

Scenic Drive Home **(231) 893-2054** • Email: jeffreyckinney@yahoo.com
Jeff Kinney **Private House**
25 yards/35 stairs to 100+ ft. of private Lake Michigan sandy, shallow beach. Year around home with 2 fireplaces, 4 bedrooms (10 beds) and 2 baths. A/C, cable, sheltered/screened porch, open deck. Washer/dryer, dishwasher. Linens included. No pets. Near Michigan Adventureland. Open year around. *Website: www.angelfire.com/mi4/jeffk*
Weekly $700-$3,000

White Swan Inn **Toll Free: (888) 948-7926** • Email: info@whiteswaninn.com
Cathy & Ron Russell **Bed & Breakfast**
1880's Queen Anne home with screened porch. Gracious hospitality in a relaxing setting. Spacious rooms, mix of antiques and wicker furniture. Whirlpool suite. Walk to shops, restaurants, marinas. Near Hart-Montague Bike Trail. Gift shop on premises. Open year 'round. Delicious breakfast. Seasonal packages. *Website: www.whiteswaninn.com*
Nightly $95-$155
Editor's Note: Cozy B&B offering guests a welcoming atmosphere.

SAUGATUCK • KALAMAZOO • UNION PIER & SURROUNDING AREAS

Includes: Battle Creek • Berrien Springs • Coldwater • Constantine • Dewey Lake • Jones • Lawrence • Mendon • New Buffalo • St. Joseph • South Haven • Stevensville • Union City

Battle Creek, home of the cereal pioneers W. K. Kellogg and C. W. Post, has given this city the name of "Cereal Capital of the World". It is also the site of Fort Custer National Cemetery and the International Hot-Air Balloon Championship which last for 8 days in June.

Kalamazoo — how very diverse. Whatever you wish to do, or see, is here. Visit Victorian homes and quaint inns, tour museums and enjoy their community theaters. Stroll through their historic district. For additional galleries and antique shops stop at Lakeside.

Explore the village of **Saugatuck**. This enchanting, historical town earned its title as "The Art Coast of Michigan" with unique art galleries, shops and festivals. Stop at the city's 75-year-old drug store that makes the best hand-creamed sodas and shakes in the world. For a little fun and adventure, tour the dunes or take a dune ride. Cruise up the Kalamazoo River in the historic *Queen of Saugatuck*, a 67 foot-long stern-wheel riverboat. The water may make you thirsty, so head over to the Tabor Hill Wine Port and refresh yourself.

A visit to Saugatuck wouldn't be complete without a day at Oval Beach. Many travel magazines have recognized Saugatuck's main beach as one of the best in the world. In fact, MTV ranked it in the "Top 5" U.S. beaches.

South Haven not only prides itself as the "Blueberry Capital of the World" it is also one of our major yachting and sport fishing ports. Explore the many parks and go hang gliding in the Warren Dunes State Park just south of **St. Joseph**. In the fall, harvest festivals and color tours are popular. May brings the Blossom Time Festival, celebrated for over 80 years. In mid-July the Venetian Festival turns the lakefront park and boulevard into a giant midway. You don't want to miss this one.

Getting hungry yet? Try out *Jenny's* on Lakeshore Road (between New Buffalo and Union Pier). Creatively prepared food and homey atmosphere featuring Great Lakes Indian art and high-beamed ceiling with skylights make this a worthwhile stop! Also, *Schu's Grill & Bar* on Lake Boulevard (St. Joseph) prepares excellent meals — their Blackout Cake is a wonderful treat. We understand the *North Beach Inn* serve's up very memorable blueberry pancakes or waffles. For casual dining on the water, give *Three Pelican's* (South Haven) a try.

BATTLE CREEK

GREENCREST MANOR   (269) 962-8633
TOM & KATHY VAN DAFF   BED & BREAKFAST
Grand French Normandy mansion on St. Mary's Lake is constructed of sandstone, slate and copper. Formal gardens include fountains and cut stone urns. A/C. Private baths. 8 rooms. Featured in "Country Inns Magazine" as Inn of the Month and Top 12 Inns of North America of 1992. *Website: www.greencrestmanor.com*
Nightly $95-$235

BERRIEN SPRINGS

PENNELLWOOD RESORT   (269) 473-2511
DAVID & JAMIE SPACEY   COTTAGE RESORT
One price includes everything—meals, lodging, recreation and entertainment. 40 cottages have 2 and 3 bedrooms. Bring beach towels, life jackets and tennis racquets. Enjoy fishing, pontoon rides, volleyball, softball, shuffleboard, square dancing. 2 heated outdoor pools. Reservations require deposit. No pets. *Website: www.pannelwoodresort.com*
Weekly $450 (per adult - children less)

COLDWATER

CHICAGO PIKE INN   **(517) 279-8744**
REBECCA SCHULTZ   **BED & BREAKFAST**
Turn of the Century reformed Colonial Mansion adorned with antiques from the Victorian era. 6 guest rooms in main house, two with whirlpools in Carriage House, all with private baths. Formal dining room, library, and reception room feature sweeping cherry staircase and parquet floors. Full country breakfast and refreshments.
Nightly $100-$195

CONSTANTINE

INN AT CONSTANTINE   **(269) 435-3325 • (800) 435-5365**
JAN MARSHALL   **EMAIL: jan@innatconstantine.com**
     BED & BREAKFAST
Located in Historical Village near antique centers. Inn features antique fireplace mantels, European antiques, in-ground pool. Rooms offers private bath (2 with Jacuzzi) and fireplaces. Full breakfast. Near Amish Shipshewana, Indiana. Canoeing, carriage rides, fishing on St. Joseph River/lakes. 5 rooms/ private bath. *Website: www.innatconstantine.com*
Nightly $85-$165

DEWEY LAKE

SHADY SHORES RESORT   **(269) 424-5251**
     COTTAGE RESORT
On Dewey Lake, 30 miles east of Benton Harbor. Furnished and equipped housekeeping cottages have electric ranges, refrigerators, heat, private bath, blankets and cooking/eating utensils. Includes boats, bicycles, playground, badminton, shuffleboard, croquet and tennis. Safe swimming on sandy beach.
Weekly $400-$600

JONES

SANCTUARY AT WILDWOOD (800) 249-5910 • EMAIL: info@sanctuaryatwildwood.com
DICK & DOLLY BUERKLE   BED & BREAKFAST/COTTAGES

EDITOR'S CHOICE

Lodge and cottages rest on more than 90 acres of woods and meadows. The Sanctuary provides security for 2 herds of whitetail deer as well as many waterfowl that visit the pond. Nature is emphasized throughout the lodge. Private decks/balconies. Each room or cottage with private baths, fireplace, Jacuzzi and refrigerator. Jeniaire kitchenette available. Heated pool. Special romantic, canoe or golf packages. Deluxe breakfasts served. Conference room available. *Website: www.sanctuaryatwildwood.com*

Nightly $159-$219 (2 night minimum. Weekday rates Sun.-Thurs.)

Editor's Note: Lovely setting, beautiful rooms, a true "Sanctuary"...highly recommended.

KALAMAZOO

HALL HOUSE   (269) 343-2500 • (888) 761-2525
SCOTT & TERRI FOX   BED & BREAKFAST

"Experience the Difference". Premier lodging in National Historic District. Guests enjoy the exceptional craftsmanship, polished mahogany and cozy fireplaces of this 1923 Georgian Revival City Inn. Six large guest rooms offer private bath, CATV, VCR, in-room phone, and A/C. Romantic Jacuzzi suite. Smoke free.

Website: www.hallhouse.com
Nightly $79-$155

LAWRENCE

OAK COVE RESORT

(269) 674-8228 • (630) 983-8025
HISTORIC LODGE/COTTAGE/HOME RESORT

Modified American Plan resort...sumptuous breakfasts and dinners served daily. Historic property nestled on 16 beautiful wooded acres with 500' of sandy beach on sparkling Lake Cora. Units recently updated and include A/C, microwaves, refrigerators. Linens provided. Enjoy the heated pool, bicycles, paths in the woods, rowboats, canoes and paddleboats. 18 holes of FREE GOLF, daily. Other activities include shuffleboard, badminton, horseshoes, volleyball and gameroom. Nearby antique shops, flea markets, wineries, horseback riding, go carts, movies and bowling. *Website: www.oakcove.com*

*Weekly $880 (lodge)   *$980 (cottages/homes)

*Per couple, children's rates vary

Editor's Note: This traditional cottage resort offers a beautiful lake view, friendly owners, great food and plenty to do.

MENDON

MENDON COUNTRY INN

GEFF & CHERYL CLARKE

(269) 496-8132 • EMAIL: vasame@aol.com
BED & BREAKFAST

Overlooking St. Joseph River, this romantic country inn has antique filled guest rooms with private baths. Free canoeing, bicycles built for two, fifteen acres of woods and water. Restaurant and Amish Tour guide. Featured in Country Living and Country Home magazines. 9 Jacuzzi suites w/fireplace. 18 rooms.

Nightly $79-$169

Editor's Note: Charming historic inn. For those seeking contemporary styling, the Creekside Lodge rooms (in the back of the lot) make for one romantic stay.

NEW BUFFALO

SANS SOUCI EURO INN & RESORT   (269) 756-3141
ANGELIKA SIEWERT   EMAIL: sans-souci@worldnet.att.net
                                   SUITES/HOME/COTTAGE RESORT

This gated nature retreat offers 50 acres of towering trees, groomed landscapes, and a myriad of wildlife on a shimmering, secluded lake. Tendering
vacation homes, getaway suites, and lakeside cottages, all with whirlpool
baths and wood burning fireplaces. *Website: www.sans-souci.com*

Nightly $160-$220/bedroom (Call for off-season and weekly rates)

SAUGATUCK

BEACHWAY RESORT &   (269) 857-4321 • EMAIL: info@beachwayresort.com
    BAYSIDE INN   SUITES/PRIVATE COTTAGES & HOMES, B&B

Located on the banks of the Kalamazoo River, Beachway Resort is next to
the award-winning Oval Beach. It includes luxury units with a diverse range
of amenities. Outdoor pool. Their B&B, once a boathouse, is a charming
home located on the water in downtown Saugatuck. Private decks and baths.

Nightly $70-$450

BEECHWOOD MANOR B&B AND COTTAGES   (269) 857-1587
JAMES & SHERRON LEMONS   BED & BREAKFAST/COTTAGES

The historic inn of Beechwood Manor. Privately owned and fully restored.
Built for a diplomat in the 1870's, on National Register. Private baths. Additional features include boat slips, tandem bikes, off-street parking. Private
cottages are also available.

B&B Nightly $125-$150   Cottages Weekly $995 (and up)

*Editor's Note: B&B maintains that Old-world ambiance. Located on a residential
side street..*

BRIAR-CLIFFE   **(269) 857-7041** • EMAIL: **briarcliffe@macatawa.com**
DAVID & SHIRLEY WITT   **GUEST SUITES**

★ EDITOR'S CHOICE ★

Luxury suites on a scenic bluff overlooking the sandy shores of Lake Michigan. Comfortable sitting room with fire-place, TV/VCR. 5 acres of woods. Queen sized canopy beds. Ceramic bath with Jacuzzi for two. Refrigerator, microwave. Stairway to private sandy beach.

Website: www.lakemichiganbnb.com

Nightly $150-$200

Editor's Note: Classic styling combined with antique-filled rooms and a very quiet setting make this a nice place for that special getaway.

GOSHORN LAKE FAMILY RESORT   **(800) 541-4210** • **(269) 857-4808**
RIC GILLETTE   **COTTAGE RESORT**

★ EDITOR'S CHOICE ★

22 housekeeping cottages, some with wood burning fireplaces. All with A/C, equipped kitchens, picnic tables and BBQ grill. Sandy, private swimming beach, volleyball, horseshoes, basketball, fire pit area and rowboats. Near Saugatuck, Lake Michigan beaches and golf. Pets allowed in some units.

Website:www.usagetaways.com/saugatuck/goshornlake

Weekly $750-$1,200

Editor's Note: Refreshing changes and expansions! We recommend the newest cottages, which are well designed with contemporary comforts. Spacious grounds with small but sandy beach area.

MASON HOUSE (847) 498-2938 • EMAIL: patkresq@msn.com
PATRICIA ROTCHFORD PRIVATE COTTAGE

★ EDITOR'S CHOICE ★

Beautifully landscaped, upscale 4-Seasons home in quiet residential area, 1/4 block to town and Lake Michigan. Newer home sleeps 8-10. Two baths, dining room, living room, laundry room, full kitchen with extras such as dishwasher, popcorn popper, cappuccino maker. Two bedrooms,

sofa sleeper and blow-up bed. Florida room with sleeper, deck with grill and sink, two sitting garden rooms, fenced yard, shared inground pool, fuel fireplace, central A/C and heat. Towels/linens included. TV, VCR, telephone/computer hook up. Open year round.

Ask about pet policy.

Weekly $750* and up Weekends from $345* (*off-season rates)

Editor' Note: Immaculate home, delightfully styled and very comfortable. Located on a quiet side street. See our review in this edition.

PARK HOUSE B&B & COTTAGES (800) 321-4535 • (269) 857-4535
LYNDA & JOE PETTY BED & BREAKFAST & COTTAGES

★ EDITOR'S CHOICE ★

On National Historic Register. Saugatuck's oldest residence (1857) hosted Susan B. Anthony. Eight rooms, queen beds, private baths. Four cottages with equipped kitchens, TV/VCR. All include A/C. Two luxury suites, two cottages offer jet tubs, fireplaces. Close to town, beach, ski trails. *Website: www.parkhouseinn.com*

Nightly $95-$225

Editor's Note: Inviting ambiance retains the style of its period with the added comforts today's guests appreciate. Lovely choice for the area.

THE KINGSLEY HOUSE   **(269) 561-6425** • EMAIL: **garyking@accn.org**
GARY & KARI KING   BED & BREAKFAST
In Fennville, minutes from Saugatuck, 1886 elegant Queen Anne Victorian B&B. Featured in Innsider Magazine, rated as a "Top Fifty Inn" in America by Inn Times. AAA approved. Near Holland/Saugatuck. Private baths, whirlpool/bath. Special getaway suite. Beautiful surroundings, family antiques. Homemade breakfast. A/C. 8 rooms.
Nightly $85-$175
Editor's Note: Well appointed rooms and welcoming proprietors...very nice.

THE KIRBY HOUSE   **(800) 521-6473** • EMAIL: **info@kirbyhouse.com**
RAY RIKER & JIM GOWRAN   BED & BREAKFAST
The most popular bed and breakfast in the Saugatuck/Douglas area. Furnished with antiques. Private baths, air conditioning and fireplace rooms available. Pool, Jacuzzi and bicycles. Full gourmet breakfast buffet. Close to shopping and lake Michigan. Reservations imperative. Major credit cards accepted.
Website: www.kirbyhouse.com
Nightly $100-$175

WICKWOOD COUNTRY INN   **(269) 857-1465**
JULEE ROSSO-MILLER & BILL MILLER   BED & BREAKFAST
★ EDITOR'S CHOICE ★
A charming European-style Inn located in the beautiful Victorian Village of Saugatuck on the Eastern Shores of Lake Michigan. Owner Julee Rosso-Miller, serves up breakfast and hors d'oeuvres daily using recipes from her four best selling cookbooks. "The Silver Palate", "The Silver Palate Good Times", "The New Basics" and "Great Good Foods". 11 rooms with private baths.
Nightly $145-$325
Editor's Note: In the heart of Saugatuck. Beautifully decorated rooms. Just a short walk to shops, restaurants and more.

ST. JOSEPH

THE SAND CASTLES   **(800) 972-0080** • EMAIL:**info@sandcastlecottages.com**
    COTTAGE RESORT
Located halfway between South Haven and St. Joseph. 11 housekeeping cottages (sleep 2 to 8). Kitchenette or full kitchen. Ceiling fans, A/C, and heat. Larger units have separate bedrooms and living/dining/kitchen areas. Cable w/HBO hookups (bring your own TV). No pets. 4 blocks to Lake Michigan beaches. *Website: www.sandcastlescottages.com.*
Weekly $350-$800
Editor's Note: Traditional cottages with well maintained interiors and some nice extras like ceiling fans and A/C. Sizes range significantly.

South Cliff Inn Bed & Breakfast
Bill Swisher

(269) 983-4881
Bed & Breakfast

Overlooking Lake Michigan, traditional brick home has luxurious accommodations and relaxed atmosphere. Tastefully decorated rooms with traditional and antique furnishings. The private beach is just steps away. Continental breakfast. Room with whirlpool tub /fireplace available. A/C. Seven rooms.

Website: www.southcliffinn.com
Nightly $85-$195 (Seasonal)

SOUTH HAVEN

Arundel House—An English B&B
Pat & Tom Zapal

(269) 637-4790
Bed & Breakfast

Turn-of-the-century, fully restored resort home. Registered with the Michigan Historical Society. Rooms decorated with antiques and maintained in English tradition. Continental buffet breakfast and afternoon tea. Walking distance to beach, restaurants, shops, marinas.

Nightly $70-$125

Editor's Note: Quaint B&B in the English tradition.

A Country Place Bed & Breakfast & Cottage
John & Cindy Malmstrom

(269) 637-5523
Email: acountryplace@cybersol.com
Bed & Breakfast/Cottage

Restored 1860's Greek Revival furnished with American antiques. Five charming guest rooms with private baths feature English country themes. Full breakfast served daily. Cozy cottage features pine interior, full kitchen, king size bed, and 3 single beds in the loft and porch, Franklin fireplace. Lake Michigan beach access 1/2 block from property. Open year around. *Website: csi-net/acountryplace*
B&B Nightly $100-$145   Cottage Weekly $750 (Daily off-season $125)

GREENE'S VACATION HOMES
(269) 639-8383 • (269) 637-6400
PRIVATE COTTAGES

Vacation homes near town and marinas, with public beach access. Linens provided (bring towels). All lodgings have fully equipped kitchens, baths, telephones, CATV, ceiling fans, some with central air. Sleeps 6 or more. Monthly and off-season rates available. *Website: www.greenehomes.com*
Weekly $700 (and up, June, July-Aug.)

LAST RESORT B&B INN
(269) 637-8943
BED & BREAKFAST/COTTAGE

Built in 1883 as South Haven's first resort inn. Most rooms with view of Lake Michigan or harbor. Penthouse suites provide best views and feature Jacuzzi. A/C. Open April-Oct. 14 rooms/private baths. Also available, cottage for two with view of the harbor. *Website: www.lastresortinn.com*
Nightly $80 (and up)

LOKNATH-CHANDERVARMA, HARBOR'S UNIT #32
(269) 344-3012
PRIVATE CONDO

2 bedroom/2 bath condo (sleeps 7). Elegantly furnished, large master bedroom. A/C, CATV, equipped kitchen, microwave, dishwasher. Panoramic view, private beach, pool, laundry, garage. Provide your own towel and linens. Minimum 7 day stay. Available all year. No pets.
Weekly $1,100 (May-Sept.)

MICHI-MONA-MAC LAKESHORE COTTAGES
(847) 332-1443 • (269) 637-3003
COTTAGE RESORT

Watch spectacular sunsets from the pure, spotless beach. One and 2 bedroom cottages with new kitchens, private baths. Beachside rooms with lovely bay windows and fireplace. Open all year. No pets. Great family vacation or romantic getaway.
Weekly $775 (and up)   Off-Season, Nightly $115 (and up)

Editor's Note: The beach is small but lovely with incline taking you to water's edge. Units are linked together apartment style. Small but well maintained.

NORTH BEACH INN & PIGOZZI'S
(269) 637-6738
INN

1890's Victorian styled B&B overlooks Lake Michigan Beach. All rooms offer private baths. Restaurant, Pigozzi, serves full breakfasts, lunch and dinners. Call for Rates

RIVERBEND RETREAT **(269) 637-3505 •** EMAIL: **riverbnd@accn.org**
PRIVATE COTTAGES

★ EDITOR'S CHOICE ★

Two cozy cedar cottages on beautiful Black River. Enjoy the peacefulness. In-ground heated pool, boat dock, canoes, boat, private hot tub, stone fireplace, central air. Fully equipped for 12 people, including towels and bedding, phone, TV, VCR, dishwasher, laundry. Open year around. Off-season priced for couples or groups. No pets.

Weekly $1,900-$2,100 (in-season, 12 people)

Editors Note: Luxurious vacation homes ... many amenities. Set back from the road on a spacious lot overlooking the Black River. Highly recommended!

THE OAKLAND **773-388-3121**
LYNN & BOB BRUNO PRIVATE HOME

Historic landmark resort built in 1927. Immaculately maintained and fully equipped for 8-10 people. Steps away from South Haven's North Beach providing beautiful views of the harbor, lake and sunset. A/C, CATV, VCR, W/D. No pets/smoking. *Website: www.megsint.net/~kmb/oakland.html*

Weekly $2,100 (June-Sept.); Nightly (off-season) $50 (per person)

THE SEYMOUR HOUSE **(269) 227-3918 •** EMAIL: **seymour@cybersol.com**
FRIEDL SCIMO BED & BREAKFAST/LOG CABIN

Enjoy the unsurpassed beauty of this 1862 Victorian mansion on 11 wooded acres. Picturesque 1-acre pond. Trails through the woods. Minutes to Saugatuck, South Haven, beaches, restaurants, galleries, horseback riding, golf and orchards. 5 rooms/private bath, fireplaces, Jacuzzi.

Guest log cabin. A/C, gourmet breakfasts *Website:www.seymourhouse.com*
Nightly $80-$145

Editor's Note: Scenic backyard, nature trails and a well maintained historic home combine for a relaxing stay.

SLEEPY HOLLOW RESORT
(269) 637-1127
COTTAGE/APARTMENT/DUPLEX RESORT

This 58 years old Art Deco style resort provides the "all in one" family vacation. Six tennis courts, volleyball, Olympic-size pool, children's activities on the resort promises to keep you busy. Cottages and apartments include partial to full kitchens, private baths. Open May 1-Oct. 7.

Weekly $870-$3,440 ($440-$2,380 off-season)

Editor's Note: Lots of activities at this resort have made it popular over the years. Lodgings vary significantly.

SOUTH HAVEN VACATION HOMES   (269) 637-5406 • EMAIL: soukup@i2k.com
PRIVATE HOMES

Vacation homes feature 3 bedrooms/2 baths, large living room, kitchen, dining room, family room. Includes microwave, washer/dryer, CATV. Large yard for family recreation. Walk to Kids' Corner and Lake Michigan.

Weekly $850 (off-season rates available)

SUNSET HAVEN
(269) 639-7140
LYNNE VANLEERDAM
PRIVATE HOMES

Several furnished homes offered for your vacation comfort. Ideally located 1-2 blocks from Lake Michigan, an easy walk to downtown. Amenities include AC, equipped kitchens, CATV, VCR. Available year around. No pets/smoking.

Website: www.sunsethaven.com

Weekly $650 - $1,800 (June-Aug.)   Nightly $125-$225 (Sept.-May)

TANBITHN
888-304-5894
MAC & RAE LEE HOWARD
PRIVATE COTTAGE

Two bedroom (sleeps 5) cottage on North Shore Drive. Features CATV, VCR ceiling fan and room A/C. Linens provided (bring towels). Light and airy interior. Only 1/2 block from beach, 1 block from marina. Fall/winter rates negotiable. No pets.

Weekly $900 (June-Aug.)   Nightly $125 (Sept.-May)

Editor's Note: Small but bright and appealing interior and decor. Sits right off the sidewalk ... fun for people watching.

THOMPSON HOUSE   (269) 637-6521 • EMAIL: JLT_KT@cybersol.com
JOYCE THOMPSON
PRIVATE HOME

Charming home, sleeps six. One block to South Beach, Riverfront Park. Great garden, umbrella table, wraparound porch and deck. Enjoy all the modern conveniences including CATV, microwave, dishwasher, laundry, central air, electronic air cleaner, a water purifier and whirlpool bathtub. No pets.

Weekly $1,000

Editor's Note: Well maintained home, simply furnished, on a quiet side street. A nice place to be away from the maddening crowds.

VICTORIA RESORT B & B   (800) 473-7376 • (269) 637-6414
BOB & JAN   BED & BREAKFAST/COTTAGE RESORT

Three acre resort located 1-1/2 blocks from Lake Michigan. Close to downtown. Some rooms and cottages feature fireplaces and whirlpool tubs. Outdoor pool, bikes, tennis and basketball courts. Winter packages include: two-night stay, dinner, breakfast in bed, and more. *Website: www.victoriaresort.com*

Cottages, Weekly $1,120 and up

Editor's Note: Comfortable and very clean accommodations for family fun.

YELTON MANOR BED & BREAKFAST   (269) 637-5220
ELAINE HERBERT & ROB KRIPAITIS   EMAIL: elaine@yeltonmanor.com
    BED & BREAKFAST

★ EDITOR'S CHOICE ★

"Top of the crop in luxury B & B's". On the sunset coast of beautiful Lake Michigan. 17 guest rooms with private baths. Some have Jacuzzi, fireplace and private decks. Extravagant honeymoon and anniversary suites. Gourmet hors d'oeuvres, fabulous breakfast and day-long goodies. A true make-yourself-at-home, luxurious geta-way. Take a tour at our *website: www.yeltonmanor.com*

Nightly $90-$220

Editor's Note: A premiere resort for executive retreats. No direct view of the Lake, but still a great way to forget about the...STRESS.

STEVENSVILLE

CHALET ON THE LAKE   (269) 465-6365
    CHALET/CONDO RESORT

51 A-frame duplexes on Lake Michigan, 7 miles south of St. Joseph. Includes 2 bedrooms (sleeps 8) will full kitchen, dining area, living room, CATV. Resort features volleyball, 5 tennis courts, 2 pools and a large private beach. Bring towels. Open year around. No pets.

Weekly $865-$1,200 (plus tax)

UNION CITY

VICTORIAN VILLA INN
RONALD J. GIBSON
(800) 34-VILLA • (517) 741-7383
BED & BREAKFAST
19th Century Italianate inn. Fourth floor tower offers birds-eye view of the town. "Victoria's" restaurant offers 7-course champagne candlelight dinners. Private baths. 7 bed chambers, 3 suites (2 with fireplace, 1 with hot tub). Credit cards. Outdoor smoking.
Nightly $85-$120 (Sun-Thurs); $125-$160 (Fri./Sat, holidays)

UNION PIER

GARDEN GROVE B&B
PAULA & JERRY WELSH
(269) 469-6346 • (800) 613-2872
BED & BREAKFAST
Pamper yourself with comfort and beauty at a vintage 1925 inn. Decorated with colorful flair and botanical style; we bring the garden indoors year-round. Deluxe accommodations. Jacuzzi-whirlpools, fireplaces, balconies, private dining. Everything the discriminating inn guest expects: Charm, romance, hospitality, scrumptious breakfast. Outstanding area: wineries, beaches, shopping.
Nightly $90-$200

THE INN AT UNION PIER
BILL & JOYCE JANN
(269) 469-4700
BED & BREAKFAST
Harbor Country's premier bed & breakfast...just 200 steps from the beach! Choose from 16 spacious guest rooms, most featuring woodburning fireplaces and porches or balconies, 2 Jacuzzi suites. Relax in the outdoor hot tub and sauna. Gourmet breakfast and complimentary refreshments. Bicycles. Corporate retreats. *Website: www.innatunionpier.com*
Nightly $150-$225
Editor's Note: Large B&B with comfortable rooms, uniquely styled. Located on quiet side street.

RIVER'S EDGE BED & BREAKFAST **(269) 469-6860**
KEITH & PRUDENCE EMAIL: sindelarkp@earthlink.com
BED & BREAKFAST

On 30 acres of wooded trails and orchards, bordering a half mile of the Galien River, you'll find peaceful River's Edge. Eight large rooms all feature double size jacuzzis, fireplaces, TV/VCR/CAB, ceiling fans, and unique beds styled by artisan Andy Brown. Bikes, cross-country skis, and canoe available to guests, and only one block to Michigan's beaches. A full hot breakfast is served every morning. *Website: wwwriversedgebandb.com.*

Nightly $99-240 (in-season)

Editor's Note: Plenty of land with the home featuring a distinct contemporary, country flavor. Very nice retreat.

PINE GARTH INN **(269) 469-1642 • (888) 390-0909**
NESSA & DENISE BED & BREAKFAST/COTTAGES/HOME

★ EDITOR'S CHOICE ★

Beautiful lakefront estate and guest houses located on 200 ft. of private sugar sand Lake Michigan beach. B&B has 7 rooms, spectacular lake views, queen beds, private baths and VCR. Guest houses are charming with 2 bedrooms, full kitchens, fireplaces, hot tubs, grills, private decks and some screened porches. Carriage House is romantic and the Villa House is 4,000 sq. ft. of heaven with beautiful lake views, screened porches, unbelievable kitchen; perfect for families or adult getaways. Open year around. *Website: www.pinegarth.com*

Nightly $155-$210 (Rooms)*; $250-$280 (Cottages)*

* Call for off-season rates and Villa House rates.

Editor's Note: Lovely B&B with beautiful lake view. Well-styled cottages are located on the quiet street behind . Excellent sandy beach accessed down stairway.

Michigan Wineries & Casinos—Map

$ = Casinos   🍷 = Wineries

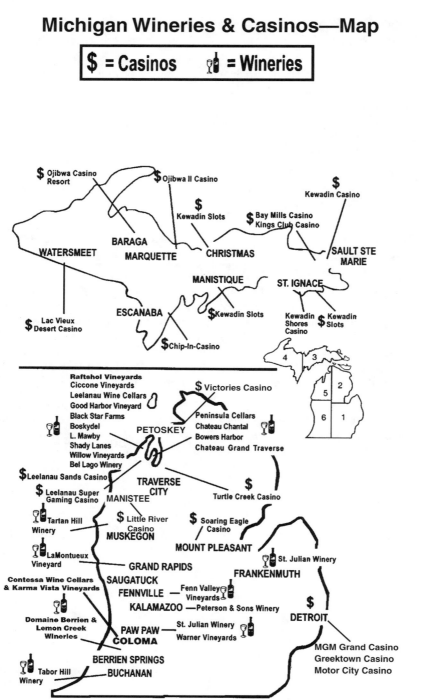

Michigan Wineries

Nestled along Michigan's shorelines in some of our state's most scenic areas, wineries are flourishing. Boasting a unique collection of wines, our winemakers continue to receive national and international recognition.

An enjoyable part of any Michigan experience is a leisurely drive through beautiful wine country. Visit our tasting rooms and see why Michigan wines have gained international attention.

Of course, be responsible, We want you to have a *safe* and *enjoyable* Michigan vacation.

REGION 1

FRANKENMUTH, MONROE & PARMA

St. Julian Winery

989-652-3281
Monroe: 734-242-9409
Parma: 989-531-3786

One of Michigan's oldest and largest wineries. Family-owned and operated since 1921.

REGION 5

CEDAR

Bel Lago Winery

6530 S. Lakeshore Dr.
231-228-4800

Produces wines taken from grapes grown in family-owned vineyards. Provides Pino Grigio, Chardonnay, Pino Noir and a variety of sparkling wines. Tasting room treats visitors to a panoramic view of Lake Leelanau.

LAKE LEELANAU

Boskydel Vineyards

2881 S. Lake Leelanau Dr.
231-256-7272

Small winery preparing limited but very nice dry and semi-sweet table wines ... presented in a unique tasting room. We understand during Christmas you can also pickup your holiday tree here.

Good Harbor Vineyards

34 S. Manitou Trail
231-256-7165

Excellent wines come from this 50-acre, well-tended vineyard. Known for Chardonnay, Pinot Gris, Riesling, Pinot Noir, Seyval and champagne.

OLD MISSION PENINSULA

Chateau Chantal

15900 Rue de Vin
231-223-4110

Operating B&B and vineyard. Impressive, Old World-styled winery. Known for Chardonnay, Pinot Gris, Pinot Noir, Merlot, Riesling and Gewurztraminer, Ice Wine and champagne. Several award winning specialties. Incredible views of East and West Grand Traverse Bays.

Chateau Grand Traverse

12239 Center Road
231-223-7355
Williamsburg: 231-938-2291
Traverse City: 231-941-4146
Large wine-making facility grows and produces award-winning, premium varietal wines. Estate-grown. Excellent Riesling, Pinot Noir, Merlot, Cabernet Franc and Ice Wine. Also a variety of area specialties like Spiced Cherry Wine, Cranberry Riesling, to name a view. Overlooks Grand Traverse Bay.

Peninsula Cellars

18250 Mission Road
231-223-4050 • 231-223-4310
Using the finest grapes in the area, wines are estate bottled with limited production. Specialties include Chardonnay, Dry Riesling, Raftshol Red and a variety of dessert wines.

OMENA

Leelanau Wine Cellars

12683 E. Tatch Road
231-386-5201
Very nice selection of dry to semi-sweet wines ... barrel-fermented, aged Chardonnays and Reislings. Also produces a variety of seasonal and fruit wines. Tours available.

SUTTONS BAY

Black Star Farms

10844 E. Revold Rd.
231-271-4884
South of Sutton's Bay. State-of-the art wine producing facility. European vinifera varieties. Lovely estate with trails winding through woodlands and orchards. Elegant, fully operational B&B. Impressive equestrian center also operated on the estate.

Chateau de Leelanau

5048 Wouth West Bay Shore
231-271-8888
One of the Leelanau Peninsula's newest wineries. Noted for being Michigan's first winery owned by women. Specializes in still and sparkling wine made from Chardonnary, Gewurztraminer and Cabernet Franc.

Ciconni Vineyards

10343 East Hilltop Road
231-271-5551
Operated by Silvo (father of rock star, Madonna) and his wife, Joan. Noted for dry Gewurz-traminer along with Cabernet Franc, Pino Noir, Chardonnary, Pino Grigio and rose de Cabernet. New tasting room.

L. Mawby Vineyards

4519 S. Elm Valley
231-271-3522
Original vines date to 1973. Limited but pure winemaking production ... barrel-fermented made with simple machinery. Specializing in white table wines and methode champenoise sparkling wines. Most wines taken from estate.

Raftshol Vineyards

1865 North West Bay Shore Dr.
231-271-5650
Opened November 1999. Specializing in Bordeau varietal reds, including Merlot and Cabernet Sauvignon and white wines, including Chardonnay.

Shady Lane Cellars

9580 Shady Lane
231-947-8865
On historic 100-acre farm Maintains more than 10,000 vines. Gold medal award winners producing excellent methode champenoise sparkling wines along with Pinot Noir, Riesling and Chardonnay. New tasting facility.

Willow Vineyards

10702 East Hilltop Rd.
231-929-4542

Est.1992. Panoramic views of West Traverse Bay enhance the ambiance of this vineyard. Producer of premium Chardonnay, Pinot Noir and Pino Gris all estate or regionally grown.

TRAVERSE CITY
Bowers Harbor Vineyards

2896 Bowers Harbor Road
231-223-7615

Small but delightful winery offering a beautiful overlook of Bowers Harbor. Chardonnay, Riesling and sparking wines plus specialty fruit wines.

Peninsula Cellars

11480 Center Road (M-37)
Winery: 231-223-4050
Tasting Room: 231-933-9797

Family operated. Wines are estate bottled using the area's finest fruit. Known for Chardonnary, Dry Riesling, Raftshal Red, Apple, White Cherry and Jubilee dessert wines.

St. Julian Winery

(Main winery in Paw Paw)
Traverse City: 231-933-6120

REGION 6

BERRIEN SPRINGS
Lemon Creek Winery

533 E. Lemon Creek Road
269-471-1321

Producer of the first commercial, entirely Michigan-grown Cabernet Sauvignon. 11 white/9 red wines. Home winemakers can purchase picked grapes or grape juice.

Domaine Berrien Cellars

398 E. Lemon Creed Road
269-473-WINE (9463)

Opened in 2001. All wines made from grapes grown on their vineyard. Nice selection of red and white wines. Tasting room and tours available.

BUCHANAN
Tabor Hill Winery

185 Mt. Tabor Road
800-283-3363
Bridgman: 269-857-6566
Saugatuck: 269-857-4859

Numerous award-winning wines, sparkling wines and non-alcoholic juices. Gift shop. Fine meals served in rustic dining room overlooking the vineyards. Their 'Classic Demi-Sec' is the only Michigan wine served at the President's table in the White House.

COLOMA
Contessa Wine Cellars

3235 Friday Road
269-468-5534

Newly opened, just off Exit 39 on I-94. Beautiful facillity with exceptional wines. Tasting room and tours from 12-5.

Karma Vista Vineyards

6991 Ryno Road
269-468-WINE (9463)

Also off Exit 39 on I-94. Premium wines include Carbernet Franc, Riesling and Chardonney.

FENNVILLE
Fenn Valley Vineyards

6130 122nd Avenue
269-561-2396

Known for estate-bottled Reislings, Champagnes, Pinot Gris and barrel-aged red wines. Barrel fermented white made from a new variety of Chardonel. Winners of numerous awards and honors.

KALAMAZOO

Peterson & Sons Winery

9375 East P. Avenue
269-626-9755
Producer of wines without use of chemicals or preservatives. Over 30 variety of Michigan-grown fruits and grapes.

PAW PAW

St. Julian Winery

716 S. Kalamazoo
616-657-5568 • 800-732-6002
Union Pier: 269-469-3150
Michigan's oldest and largest winery (since 1921). Producer of over 40 wines. Fine dining also available at the Apollo Restaurant.

Warner Vineyards

706 S. Kalamazoo
269-657-3165
Family-operated for over 30 years. Located in an historical structure built in 1898. Produces a variety of sparkling, table and dessert wines. Self guided tours.

Michigan Casinos

Oh, Lady Luck you done me wrong, but I keep coming back for more.

REGION 1

DETROIT

Greektown Casino
555 E. Lafayette Blvd.
888-771-4386

MGM Grand Detroit
1300 John C. Lodge Service Dr.
313-393-7777 or 877-888-2121

MotorCity Casino
2901 Grand River Ave.
877-777-6711

REGION 2

MT. PLEASANT

Soaring Eagle Casino
6800 Soaring Eagle Blvd.
888-7EAGLE7 or 989-775-7777

REGION 3

BRIMLEY

Bay Mills Resort & Casino
11386 W. Lake Shore
888-422-9645 or 877-229-6455

Kings Club Casino
12140 W. Lake Shore
906-248-3241

CHRISTMAS

Kewadin Slots
105 Candy Cane Lane
906-387-5475

HESSEL

Kewadin Slots
Three Mile Road at M-134
906-484-2767

MANISTIQUE

Kewadin Slots
Route 1
906-341-5510

ST. IGNACE

Kewadin Shores Casinos
3039 Mackinac Trail
906-643-7071

SAULT STE. MARIE

Kewadin Casino
2186 Shunk Road
906-632-0530

REGION 4

BARAGA

Ojibwa Casino Resort
797 Michigan
906-353-6333

ESCANABA

Chip-In-Casino
W399 Highway 2 & 41
906-466-2941
800-682-6040

MARQUETTE

Ojibwa II Casino
105 Acre Trail
906-249-4200

WATERSMEET

Lac Vieux Desert Casino
N5384 US 45
906-358-4227

REGION 5

MANISTEE

Little River Casino
2700 Orchard Highway
(Corner of US 23 & M22)
231-723-1535 or 888-568-2244

PETOSKEY

Victories Casino & Entertainment
1967 US 131 South
231-439-6100 or 877-4-GAMING

SUTTONS BAY

Leelanau Sands Casino
2521 NW Bayshore Drive
231-271-4104
800-922-2946

Leelanau Super Gaming
    Palace
2649 NW Bayshore Drive
231-271-6852
800-922-2946

WILLIAMSBURG

Turtle Creek Casino
7741 M-72, E
231-267-9574
888-777-8946

MICHIGAN FALL COLOR TOURS

Our Faavorite Fall Color Tours

BEST COLOR VIEWING TIMES

Mid-September to Early October

What fall time experience is complete without a leisurely stroll or relaxing drive among the vivid colors of Michigan's beautiful landscapes?

Late September to Mid-October

Early to Mid-October

Mid to Late October

EAST LOWER PENINSULA (Region 1 & 2):

- *The River Road, National Scenic Byway.* The tour begins three miles south of Oscoda on River Road Scenic Byway. Follow this scenic, 22 mile road which runs along the bluffs above the Au Sable River. This drive offers panoramic views of the river, its forested banks and islands. You'll find outstanding fall colors and the Lumberman's Monument (only 20 minutes west of Oscoda on River Road Scenic Byway) which offers a wonderful overlook. Then, just 1-1/2 miles west of the Monument's Visitors Center, is the *Eagles' Nest Overlook* which has been the home to families of eagles for over 10 years. The overlook also offers a photographer's dream view of Cook Pond and the river valley.

- *AuSable River Vista. Listed as a National Forest Scenic Overlook*, this beautiful vista has breathtaking, vibrant colors in the fall and offers a 20-mile stretch of the AuSable River Valley and Alcona Pond. To begin this tour, go north on M-65 and turn west on F-30 in Glennie. Continue three miles to AuSable Road and turn right. This vista is about four miles north of AuSable Road. Enjoy the view.

- *Irish Hills Tower.* The lovely hills make this area a choice spot for any driving tour. The variety of trees found here create a beautiful bouquet of fall colors. The Tower (one mile west of US 12 and M-124) offers an excellent, panoramic view of northern Lenawee County.

UPPER PENINSULA (Regions 3 & 4):

The truth is, just about anywhere in the Upper Peninsula is a perfect spot for fall touring. Just taking a quiet side road may bring you to one of the UP's many scenic views or majestic waterfalls highlighted by brilliant fall colors.

If you're not into impromptu exploration, however, here are a few "planned" routes that offer plenty of great scenery with a wonderful blend of autumn colors.

- *Porcupine Mountain National Park & Lake of the Clouds Scenic Overlook* (approx. 170 miles). You can enjoy the colors from your car but will need to do a little hiking if you want to truly experience panoramic views of fall's beauty on this trip. One such view is the Lake of the Clouds Scenic Overlook. It's a 1/4 mile hike up a rather steep hill. However, this is a view you don't want to miss. At the top you'll find yourself perched high above the lake. You'll be awed by the spectacular view of the Porcupine Mountains, filled with vivid colors of green, gold and red, reflecting off the still waters of the lake. From Baraga, take 41 north to Chassell, west to Painesdale. Take 26 north to the Highway 38 intersection and go west to Ontonagon. Take 64 west to Silver City and the Porcupine Mountains State Park. You'll return to Baraga on Highway 38.

• **Seney National Wildlife Refuse & Tahquamenon Falls** (approx. 88 miles). Again, the beauty here is only enhanced by the vivid colors of autumn. From Grand Marais, go South on 77 to Seney National Refuge where you'll want to explore nature at its finest. Then continue east on 28 to Newberry, north on 123 to Paradise (gateway to the Whitefish Point Lighthouse, Whitefish Point Bird Observatory, and Tahquamenon Falls). To return, follow 123 to 28 and go west, back to 77.

NORTHWEST LOWER PENINSULA (Region 5)

• **Old Mission Peninsula** (38 miles): Combine stops at roadside fruit stands, charming restaurants and shops with this relaxing fall color tour. This is a delightful trip through the peninsula which divides Grand Traverse Bay into East and West Arms. Take M-37 (Center Road) north from Traverse City's Garfield Road. Stay right where M-37 and Peninsula Drive fork, continue north to the tip of the peninsula. Backtrack on M-37. Turn right on Peninsula Drive, along the West Bay shore to Traverse City.

• **Leelanau Peninsula** (approx. 93 miles): Touring through Michigan's "little finger" has been a popular fall experience for generations. It's an easy and beautiful tour which takes you along shorelines, through quaint villages including Suttons Bay, Omena and Northport with homey restaurants and shops. Feeling lucky? Stop by the casino. Then, on to the tip of the little finger. Tour the Grand Traverse Lighthouse, the view is outstanding.

More brilliant colors can be seen as you continue along the western coast through Leland, Glen Arbor and Sleeping Bear Dune where you'll find spectacular colors along the 7-mile Pierce Stocking Scenic Drive. You'll want to checkout the Dune Climb for a little *exercise* before your return trip. To take this tour, follow M-22, from Traverse City, along the coast to Northport (to get to the "little finger" take M-201 to C-629). M-22 continues south from Northport through Leland into Glen Arbor, then M-109 brings you to the Pierce Stocking Scenic Drive at the Sleeping Bear Dune National Lakeshore. M-109 will meet up with M-22 and M-72 for your return to Traverse City.

• *Interlochen/Benzie County* (approx. 98 miles): Let the sounds of nature mingle with the sounds of music from the Interlochen Center for the Arts. This premiere music education center is open all year and features well-known professional entertainers as well as student performances. On natural grounds, the Center offers inviting pathways through the trees and natural shrubbery which will surround you in the brilliant colors of fall. Then onto your exploration of Benzie County where you'll find fine art and craft galleries and plenty of small town ambiance.

Follow US-31/M-37 south from Traverse City to the M-37 and US-31 intersection. Turn right on US-31, then left on M-137 to C-70, and right in the town of Karlin, then right on County Line Road. This will take you through Thompsonville. Take a right on M-115 and travel to Benzonia and Beulah to loop back onto US-31 south. A left turn at Chum's Corners will return you to Traverse City.

• *Tunnel of Trees* (50-110 miles, depending on tour route): This is a wonderful drive at any time of the year, but it's really impressive during the fall. We should note this drive is a bit trickier than the others because there are no road shoulders. The driver will have to stay focused on the road.
From the Harbor Springs, go north along M-119. We recommend exploring the Thorn Swift Nature Preserve on lower Shore Drive. Pass Cross Village and continue a few more miles to the stop sign, turn left following Lake Shore Drive to Lakeview Road. At Sturgeon Bay explore the dunes and beach. Continue on Lakeview which changes to Gill Road.

From here you can take two different routes, depending on your time and interest. The shorter tour will take 1.25 hours with the longer taking 2.5 hours. The shorter one is as follows: Take Gill Road for 3 miles toward Bliss and the Pleasantville Road (C-81) junction. Continue on Pleasantville Road back to M-119 and take a right to return to Harbor Spring.

Here's the long tour: Gill Road to Cecil Bay Road (5 miles). Go left and continue to the road's end, then right on Wilderness Park Drive (if you want to visit the Park, take a left). Continue north passing Colonial Fort Michilimackinaw and pass under I-75 at the base of the Mackinaw Bridge. You'll begin the Cheboygan County Scenic Route on US-23 and continue south along US-23 into Cheboygan. Take a right at the M-27 junction. Continue on M-27 passed Mullett and Burt Lakes which will take you through Indian River to the junction of M-68. Turn right to Alanson and then left on US-31 to Petoskey. Head north on M-119 which will take you back to Harbor Springs.

SOUTHWEST LOWER PENINSULA (Region 6):

• *Lakeshore Drive from Grand Haven to Holland* (approx. 22 miles): This beautiful drive on Lakeshore is a photographer's paradise. Stop at Kirk Park and Tunnel Park to enjoy the crisp air as you take in the surrounding brilliance of autumn at its best. This drive is a simple one—just start in Grand Haven and go south on Lakeshore Drive.

• *Grand River Basin* (approx. 40 miles): Scenic bayous and brilliant colors combine to make this tour a fun experience. To begin, start in Grand Haven (Robbins Road) and go east to Mercury Drive (continue east). You'll pass a few Grand River bayous and will want to stop and enjoy the colorful Riverside Park. When you leave, turn south on 104th Avenue and go to Osborn Street. Stay east on Osborn (it turns into Warner Street, so don't be surprised when the name changes). Then turn north on 66th Avenue and cross the bridge at Eastmanville. Travel west on Leonard Road back to Spring Lake.

• *P.J. Hoffmaster State Park to Muskegon* (approx. 20 miles). Here's another nice tour we recommend because of the dunes and nature center along the way. Just go west on Pantaluna Road to Lake Harbor Road. P.J. Hoffmaster State is where we highly recommend you explore the dunes area and the Gillette Nature Center. Then head north on Lake Harbor Road to Muskegon.

TRAVEL MICHIGAN (Main Office)
888-78-GREAT

Offices Listed Alphabetically by City

Allegan Co. Tourist & Recreation Council
269-686-9088 • 888-4-ALLEGAN
113 Chestnut St., Allegan, MI 49010

Alpena Convention & Visitors Bureau
989-354-4181 • 800-425-7362
235 W. Chisholm, Alpena, MI 49707

Ann Arbor Convention & Visitors Bur.
734-995-7281 • 800-888-9487
120 W. Huron Street
Ann Arbor, MI 48104

Au Gres Area Travelers & Visitors Bureau
517-876-8131
PO Box 586, Au Gres, MI 48703

Baraga County Tourism
906-524-7444
755 E Broad St., L'Anse, MI 49946

Greater Battle Creek/Calhoun County Visitor & Convention Bureau
269-962-2240
34 W Jackson Street, Suite 4-B
Battle Creek, MI 49017

Bay Area Convention & Visitors Bureau
989-893-1222 • 888-229-8696
901 Saginaw St., Bay City, MI 48708

Blue Water Area Con. & Visitors Bur.
810-987-8687 • 800-852-4242
520 Thomas Edison Parkway
Port Huron, MI 48060

Boyne County Conv. & Visitors Bureau
800-845-2828 • 231-348-2755
401 E Mitchell St.
Petoskey, MI 49770

Branch County Tourism Bureau
517-278-5617 • 800-968-9333
20 Division St., Coldwater, MI 49036

Bridgeport Tourist Commission
989-777-0673
6191 Sheridan Rd.
Saginaw, MI 48601

Cadillac Area Visitors Bureau
231-775-0657 • 800-225-2537
222 Lake St., Cadillac, MI 49601

Charlevoix Area Con. & Visitors Bur.
231-547-2101 • 800-367-8557
408 Bridge St., Charlevoix, MI 49720

Cheboygan Area Tourist Bureau
231-627-7183 • 800-968-3302
847 S. Main St., Cheboygan, MI 49721

Clare County Con. & Visitors Bureau
989-386-6400
PO Box 226, Clare, MI 48617

Delta County Tourism & Conv. Bureau
906-786-2192
230 Ludington St.
Escanaba, MI 49829

Metro Detroit Convention & Visitors Bur.
313-259-7583 • 800-DETROIT
211 W. Fort St., Detroit, MI 48226

Flint Area Con. & Visitors Bureau
800-25-FLINT
519 S. Saginaw, Flint, MI 48502

Tourism Assoc. of Dickinson County
906-774-2945 • 800-236-2447
600 S. Stephenson
Iron Mountain, MI 49801

Drummond Island Tourism Assoc.
906-493-5245 • 800-737-8666
PO Box 200
Drummond Island, MI 49726

Elk Co. Visitors Bureau
989-742-4732
2780 M-32, Hillman, MI 49746

Flint Area Con. & Visitors Bureau
810-232-8900 • 800-253-5468
519 S. Saginaw St., Flint, MI 48502

Four Flags Tourism Council
616-684-7444
321 E. Main St., Niles, MI 49120

Frankenmuth Con. & Visitors Bureau
989-652-6106 • 800-386-8696
635 S. Main St. Frankenmuth, MI 48734

Garland Area Conv. & Visitors Bureau
989-469-4200
HCR-1 Box 364M, County Rd. 489
Lewiston, MI 49756

Gaylord Area Conv. & Tourism Bureau
989-732-6333 • 800-345-8621
101 W. Main St., Gaylord, MI 49735

Gogebic Area Visitors & Conv. Bureau
906-932-4850
137 E. Cloverland Dr.
Ironwood, MI 49938

Grand Haven-Spring Lake Visitors Bur.
616-842-0379 • 800-303-4092
1 S. Harbor Dr.,
Grand Haven, MI 49417

Grand Rapids/Kent County Convention & Visitors Bureau
616-459-8287 • 800-678-9859
140 Monroe Center NW, #300
Grand Rapids, MI 49503

Grayling Area Visitors Council
989-348-2921 • 800-937-8837
213 N. James St., Grayling, MI 49738

Harbor Country Lodging Assoc.
269-469-0097 • 800-362-7251
3 W. Buffalo, New Buffalo, MI 49117

Holland Area Conv. & Visitors Bureau
616-394-0000 • 800-506-1299
100 E. Eight Street, #120
Holland, MI 49423

Houghton Lake Area Tourist & Convention Bureau
989-422-2822 • 800-676-5330
4621 West Houghton Lake Drive
Houghton Lake, MI 48329

Huron County Visitors Bureau
989-269-6431 • 800-358-4862
250 E Huron Avenue, #303
Bad Axe, MI 48413

Iron County Tourism Council
906-265-3822
50 E. Genesee St., Iron River, MI 49935

Ironwood Tourism Council
100 E. Aurora St., Ironwood, MI 49938

Jackson Convention & Tourist Bureau
517-764-4440 • 800-245-5282
6007 Ann Arbor Rd., Jackson, MI 49201

Kalamazoo County Convention & Visitors Bureau
269-381-4003 • 800-222-6363
346 W. Michigan Avenue
Kalamazoo, MI 49007

Keweenaw Tourism Council
906-482-2388 • 800-338-7982
326 Shelden Ave.
Houghton, MI 49931

Lake Michigan Convention & Visitor Bur.
269-925-6100
185 E. Main St.
Benton Harbor, MI 49023

Greater Lansing Convention & Visitors Bur.
517-377-1401 • 800 648-6630 x401
1223 Turner, Suite 200
Lansing, MI 48906

Lenawee Co. Conf. & Visitors Bureau
517-263-7747
738 S. Main St., Adrian, MI 49921

Les Cheneaux Islands Area Tourist Assoc.
906-484-3935
PO Box 422, Cedarville, MI 49719

Livingston County Visitors Bur.
517-548-1795
207 N. Michigan, Howell, MI 48844

Ludington Area Con. & Visitors Bur.
231-845-0324 • 800-542-4600
5827 W. US-10, Ludington, MI 49431

Mackinac Island Visitors Bureau
906-847-1000 • 888-MAC-ISLE
PO Box 1951
Mackinac Island, MI 49757

Mackinaw Area Tourist Bureau
231-436-5664 • 800-666-0160
708 S. Huron, Mackinaw City, MI 49701

Manistee Area Visitors & Convention Bur.
231-723-7975 • 888-584-9860
PO Box 13, Manistee, MI 49660

Manistique Area Tourist Council
906-341-6954
315 Range, Manistique, MI 49854

Manistique Lakes Area Tourism Bur.
906-586-9486
PO Box 411, Curtis, MI 49820

Marquette Co. Conv. & Visitor Bureau
906-228-7749 • 800-544-4321
2552 W. US-41, #300
Marquette, MI 49855

Mecosta Co. Convention & Visitor Bur.
231-796-7640 • 800-833-6697
246 N. State St., Big Rapids, MI 49307

Midland Co. Convention & Visitors Bur.
989-839-9901 • 888-464-3526
300 Rodd Street, #101
Midland, MI 48640

Mt. Pleasant Area Con. & Visitors Bur.
989-772-4433 • 800-772-4433
114 E. Broadway
Mount Pleasant, MI 48858

Munising Visitors Bureau
906-387-3536
422 E. Munising Avenue
Munising, MI 49862

Muskegon Co. Convention & Visitors Bur.
231-722-3751
610 Western Avenue
Muskegon, MI 49440

Newberry Area Tourism Assoc.
906-293-5562
PO Box 308, Newberry, MI 49868

Novi Convention & Visitors Bureau
248-349-7940
43700 Expo Center Drive, #100
Novi, MI 48375

Oceana County Tourism Bureau
231-873-3982 • 800-874-3092
100 State Street, PO Box 168
Hart, MI 49420

Oscoda Area Convention & Visitors Bur.
989-739-7322 • 800-235-4625
4440 N-US 23, Oscoda, MI 48750

Paradise Area Tourism Council
906-492-3310
PO Box 64, Paradise, MI 49768

Petoskey-Harbor Springs-Boyne Country Visitors Bureau
231-348-2755 • 800-845-2828
401 E. Mitchell St.
Petoskey, MI 49770

River County Tourism Council
800-447-2821
150 N. Main St., Sturgis, MI 49091

Rogers City Travelers & Visitors Bur.
989-734-4777
540 W. Third St.
Rogers City, MI 49779

Saginaw Co. Convention & Visitors Bur.
989-752-7164 • 800-444-9979
One Tuscola Street, #101
Saginaw, MI 48607

St Ignace Area Tourist Association
906-643-6950 • 800-338-6660
506 N. State St., St Ignace, MI 49781

Sanilac County Tourist Council
810-648-2732 • 800-651-8687
37 Austin St., Sandusky, MI 48471

Saugatuck-Douglass Convention & Visitors Bureau
269-857-1701
PO Box 28, Saugatuck, MI 49453

Sault Convention & Visitors Bureau
906-632-3301
2581 I-75 Business Spur
Sault Ste Marie, MI 49783

Shiawassee County Convention and Visitors Bureau
989-723-5149
215 N. Water St., Owosso, MI 48867

Sleeping Bear Dunes Visitors Bureau
231-334-2000
PO Box 517, Glen Arbor, MI 49636

South Haven Conv. & Visitors Bureau
269-637-5252 • 800-764-2836
415 Phoenix St.
South Haven, MI 49090

Southwestern Mich. Tourist Council
269-925-6301
2300 Pipestone Rd.
Benton Harbor, MI 49022

Tawas Bay Tourist & Convention Bur.
989-362-8643 • 800-558-2927
402 E. Lake St., Tawas City, MI 48764

Traverse City Con. & Visitors Bureau
800-TRAVERS
101 W. Grandview Parkway
Traverse City, MI 49684

Tuscola County Tourism Office
989-673-2849
157 N. State St., Caro, MI 48723

Upper Peninsula Travel & Recreation Association
906-774-5480 • 800-562-7134
PO Box 400
Iron Mountain, MI 49801

West Branch-Ogemaw Co. Travel Bur.
989-345-2821 • 800-755-9091
422 W. Houghton Avenue
West Branch, MI 48661

West Michigan Tourist Association
616-456-8557 • 800-442-2084
1253 Front Avenue, NW
Grand Rapids, MI 49504

Western Upper Peninsula Convention & Visitor Bureau
906-932-4850
137 E. Cloverland Drive
Ironwood, MI 49938

White Lake Area Con. & Visitors Bur.
231-893-4585
124 W. Hanson
Whitehall, MI 49461

Ypsilanti Con. & Visitors Bureau
734-483-4444
301 W. Michigan Avenue, Suite 101
Ypsilanti, MI 48197

The sun it setting. It's time to return to daily living.
But you'll remember the excitement, the challenge,
the peace and serenity of green forests,
rolling hills, crystal waters and snow white valleys.
And you'll dream of the things yet to come.

For you are the dreamer, and I am your dream maker ...
the vacation land for all seasons.

Michigan

Until We Meet Again ...
Your Friends at the Michigan Vacation Guide

by: C. Rydel

INDEX